John Stuart Mill – Thought and Influence

More than 200 years after his birth, and 150 years after the publication of his most famous essay *On Liberty*, John Stuart Mill remains one of the towering intellectual figures of the Western tradition. This book combines an up-to-date assessment of the philosophical legacy of Mill's arguments, his complex version of liberalism and his account of the relationship between character and ethical and political commitment. Bringing together key international scholars, including Martha Nussbaum and Peter Singer, this book combines the latest insights of Mill scholarship with a long-term appraisal of the ways in which Mill's work has been received and interpreted from the time of his death in 1873 to today.

The book offers compelling insights into Mill's posthumous fate and reputation; his youthful political and intellectual activism; his views on the formation of character; the development of his thought on logic; his differences from his father and Bentham; his astonishingly prescient, environmentally sensitive and 'green' thought; his relation to virtue ethics; his conception of higher pleasures and its relation to his understanding of justice; his feminist thought and its place in contemporary debates and feminist discourses; his defence of free speech and its fundamental significance for his liberalism; and his continued contemporary relevance on a number of major issues.

This book will be of interest to students and scholars of politics, political theory, philosophy, history, English, psychology, and also cultural studies, empire studies, nationalism and ethnicity studies.

Georgios Varouxakis is Reader in History of Political Thought at Queen Mary, University of London, UK. He is the author of *Mill on Nationality* (also published by Routledge) and *Victorian Political Thought on France and the French* and the co-editor of *Utilitarianism and Empire*.

Paul Kelly is Professor of Political Theory and Head of the Department of Government, London School of Economics and Political Science, UK. His publications include (as author) *Locke's Second Treatise of Government; Liberalism*; and (as editor) *Political Thinkers*, second edition.

Routledge Innovations in Political Theory

A Radical Green Political Theory
Alan Carter

Rational Woman
A feminist critique of dualism
Raia Prokhovnik

Rethinking State Theory
Mark J. Smith

Gramsci and Contemporary Politics
Beyond pessimism of the intellect
Anne Showstack Sassoon

Post-Ecologist Politics
Social theory and the abdication of
the ecologist paradigm
Ingolfur Blühdorn

Ecological Relations
Susan Board

**The Political Theory of Global
Citizenship**
April Carter

Democracy and National Pluralism
Edited by Ferran Requejo

Civil Society and Democratic Theory
Alternative voices
Gideon Baker

**Ethics and Politics in Contemporary
Theory**
Between critical theory and post-marxism
Mark Devenney

Citizenship and Identity
Towards a new republic
John Schwarzmantel

Multiculturalism, Identity and Rights
Edited by Bruce Haddock and Peter Sutch

Political Theory of Global Justice
A cosmopolitan case for the
World State
Luis Cabrera

**Democracy, Nationalism and
Multiculturalism**
*Edited by Ramón Maiz and Ferrán
Requejo*

Political Reconciliation
Andrew Schaap

**National Cultural Autonomy and
Its Contemporary Critics**
Edited by Ephraim Nimni

**Power and Politics in Poststructuralist
Thought**
New theories of the political
Saul Newman

Capabilities Equality
Basic issues and problems
Edited by Alexander Kaufman

Morality and Nationalism
Catherine Frost

Principles and Political Order
The challenge of diversity
*Edited by Bruce Haddock, Peri Roberts
and Peter Sutch*

**European Integration and the
Nationalities Question**
*Edited by John McGarry and Michael
Keating*

**Deliberation, Social Choice and
Absolutist Democracy**
David van Mill

Sexual Justice / Cultural Justice
Critical perspectives in political theory and
practice
*Edited by Barbara Arneil, Monique
Deveaux, Rita Dhamoon and Avigail
Eisenberg*

**The International Political Thought of
Carl Schmitt**
Terror, liberal war and the crisis
of global order
*Edited by Louiza Odysseos and Fabio
Petito*

In Defense of Human Rights
A non-religious grounding in a
pluralistic world
Ari Kohen

**Logics of Critical Explanation in Social
and Political Theory**
Jason Glynos and David Howarth

Political Constructivism
Peri Roberts

The New Politics of Masculinity
Men, power and resistance
Fidelma Ashe

Citizens and the State
Attitudes in Western Europe and
East and Southeast Asia
Takashi Inoguchi and Jean Blondel

Political Language and Metaphor
Interpreting *and* changing the world
Edited by Terrell Carver and Jernej Pikalo

Political Pluralism and the State
Beyond sovereignty
Marcel Wissenburg

Political Evil in a Global Age
Hannah Arendt and international theory
Patrick Hayden

Gramsci and Global Politics
Hegemony and resistance
Mark McNally and John Schwarzmantel

Democracy and Pluralism
The political thought of William E.
Connolly
Edited by Alan Finlayson

Multiculturalism and Moral Conflict
*Edited by Maria Dimova-Cookson
and Peter Stirk*

**John Stuart Mill – Thought and
Influence**
The saint of rationalism
*Edited by Georgios Varouxakis
and Paul Kelly*

John Stuart Mill – Thought and Influence

The saint of rationalism

Edited by Georgios Varouxakis and Paul Kelly

Routledge
Taylor & Francis Group

LONDON AND NEW YORK

First published 2010
by Routledge
2 Park Square, Milton Park, Abingdon, Oxon, OX14 4RN

Simultaneously published in the USA and Canada
by Routledge
270 Madison Avenue, New York, NY 10016

Routledge is an imprint of the Taylor & Francis Group, an informa business

© 2010 Georgios Varouxakis and Paul Kelly for selection and editorial matter;
individual contributors their contribution

Typeset in by Times New Roman by GreenGate Publishing Services, Tonbridge, Kent

Printed and bound in Great Britain by the MPG books Group in the UK

British Library Cataloguing in Publication Data
A catalogue record for this book is available from the British Library

Library of Congress Cataloging-in-Publication Data
John Stuart Mill, thought and influence : the saint of rationalism / edited by
Georgios Varouxakis and Paul Kelly.
p. cm. -- (Routledge innovations in political theory ; 36)
Includes bibliographical references and index.
1. Mill, John Stuart, 1806-1873. 2. Political science--Philosophy. I. Varouxakis,
Georgios, 1966- II. Kelly, P. J. (Paul Joseph)
JC223.M66J648 2010
320.092--dc22

ISBN 13: 978-0-415-55518-0 (hbk)
ISBN 10: 0-415-55518-3 (hbk)

ISBN 13: 978-0-203-85558-4 (ebk)
ISBN 10: 0-203-85558-2 (ebk)

Contents

Contributors   ix

Acknowledgements   x

**1 John Stuart Mill's thought and legacy: A timely
   reappraisal**   1
GEORGIOS VAROUXAKIS AND PAUL KELLY

**2 The primacy of the political and the problem of cultural
   authority in an age of transition**   19
BRUCE KINZER

**3 Competing theories of character formation: James vs.
   John Stuart Mill**   35
TERENCE BALL

**4 Wild natural beauty and the religion of humanity:
   Mill's 'green' credentials**   57
DONALD WINCH

5 Parallel lives in logic: The Benthams and the Mills   67
FREDERICK ROSEN

6 John Stuart Mill and virtue ethics   84
WENDY DONNER

7 Justice as higher pleasure   99
JONATHAN RILEY

8 Mill's feminism: Liberal, radical and queer   130
MARTHA NUSSBAUM

viii   *Contents*

9   Liberalism as free thought   146

JOHN SKORUPSKI

10   Mill's relevance today: A personal view   159

PETER SINGER

Index   173

Contributors

Terence Ball is Professor in the Department of Political Science at Arizona State University.

Wendy Donner is Professor of Philosophy in the Department of Philosophy, Carleton University, Ottawa.

Paul Kelly is Professor of Political Theory and Head of Department in the Department of Government at the London School of Economics and Political Science (LSE).

Bruce Kinzer is Professor of History in the Department of History, Kenyon College, Ohio.

Martha Nussbaum is Ernst Freund Distinguished Service Professor of Law and Ethics at the University of Chicago.

Jonathan Riley is Professor of Philosophy at Tulane University and a faculty member of the Murphy Institute of Political Economy, Tulane University.

Frederick Rosen is Emeritus Professor of the History of Political Thought at University College London (in the Bentham Project, of which he was Director for many years, and in the Department of History).

Peter Singer is the Ira W. DeCamp Professor of Bioethics at the University Center for Human Values, Princeton University and Laureate Professor at the Centre for Applied Philosophy and Public Ethics (CAPPE), University of Melbourne.

John Skorupski is Professor of Moral Philosophy in the School of Philosophical, Anthropological and Film Studies at the University of St Andrews.

Georgios Varouxakis is Reader in History of Political Thought in the Department of History at Queen Mary, University of London.

Donald Winch is Emeritus Professor of Intellectual History at the University of Sussex (Centre for Intellectual History).

Acknowledgements

The editors would like to thank the authors of the articles in this volume for their contributions, support and patience. Georgios Varouxakis would also like to thank very gratefully Professor Philip Schofield of University College London who co-organized with him *The John Stuart Mill Bicentennial Conference 1806–2006* at UCL in April 2006, at which earlier versions of the papers published in this volume were delivered as keynote lectures. Georgios would also like to thank Roger Crisp, Ross Harrison, Paul Kelly, Fred Rosen and J. B. Schneewind for their generous advice and support during the preparation of the Conference, as well as Kate Barber for her invaluable help. Like all books on J. S. Mill published in the last three decades, this book would not have been possible without the monumental scholarly contribution of the late John M. Robson and his colleagues at the University of Toronto's Mill Project for their edition of *The Collected Works of John Stuart Mill*. The editors would like to acknowledge the British Academy for its generous support of *The John Stuart Mill Bicentennial Conference* through an award from the Worldwide Congress Grants scheme. Finally, the editors would like to express their gratitude to the staff at Routledge for their faith in this project and for their patience and hard work in bringing it to completion.

Georgios Varouxakis and Paul Kelly
London, September 2009

1 John Stuart Mill's thought and legacy

A timely reappraisal

Georgios Varouxakis and Paul Kelly

John Stuart Mill was born more than two centuries ago, in 1806. He distinguished himself in many overlapping roles as a philosopher, political thinker, political economist, journalist, intellectual and politician. It is difficult to exaggerate Mill's significance and influence. He was not merely an astonishingly versatile thinker who made major contributions to many areas of philosophy. He was also a 'public moralist' *par excellence*, a committed thinker who, by the last two to three decades of his life, obtained a rare ascendancy over his contemporaries as well as over thinkers and students of subsequent generations. As befits this fundamentally cosmopolitan thinker, his reputation and influence reached far beyond his native country. His major works (as well as some less well known) found translators in several languages very soon after their publication in English. With a moral earnestness that is bound to surprise people in our more cynical times, Mill made strenuous efforts, on behalf of a variety of causes, 'either as theorist or as practical man, to effect the greatest amount of good compatible with his opportunities'.[1] Two centuries after his birth, and more than thirteen decades after his death, he is still strikingly relevant every time issues of liberty, its concrete meaning and limits, individuality, diversity, freedom of thought and speech, the unequal treatment and social conditioning of women, the best form of democracy, political representation, and a great number of other political and philosophical questions are raised and debated.

Although the bicentennial of John Stuart Mill's birth in 2006 provided a further opportunity to consider his contributions to ethics and social and political philosophy, his stature and importance to contemporary discussions and debates hardly needs such an invitation as this collection of essays by important philosophers and Mill scholars will amply attest. The essays brought together in this volume, which originated as keynote lectures at a bicentennial conference held in London in the spring of 2006, range over a number of important issues that are often obscured from traditional treatments of Mill's contribution to moral or political philosophy narrowly conceived.[2] In particular the essays consider both the development of Mill's intellectual biography as well as his impact on the ideas of a number of the most prominent authors of essays in this collection, offering a timely opportunity to reflect on Mill's continuing significance. By way of introduction to these essays we would like to set a context for the broad range of issues discussed by the respective contributors, by examining the reception of Mill's social and political philosophy since his death in 1873. This introductory essay is divided into three main parts. The first two sections examine the development and fortunes of Millian liberalism in the domestic context of British ethical and political theory and then in relation to international political theory. The third and final part of this introductory essay will provide a brief overview of the individual contributions to this volume. Mill's work is so wide-ranging that it is difficult to encapsulate in a single volume, yet he remains a crucially important figure and source for how we understand the current intellectual and political climate.

1. Millian political liberalism from 1873 to the present

By the time of his death in 1873, Mill's reputation had already been partly dented by his resolute support of radical issues and causes such as female emancipation. Though still a towering figure of mid-Victorian intellectual life, it soon seemed as if his time had passed. The immediate circumstances of his death were soon overshadowed by the consequences of a mean-spirited obituary in *The Times* by Abraham Hayward. Hayward resurrected the story of an incident early in Mill's life when he had been detained by the authorities for passing on contraceptive advice. The initial allusions in *The Times* obituary to '… the Malthusian principle', were soon clarified in a brief pamphlet, as involving the spread of contraceptive advice amongst maid-servants.[3] This incident and the ensuing controversy was to discourage any more popular acknowledgement of the passing of the 'Saint of Rationalism',[4] but it also reinforced the view that Mill was a marginal figure to the main development of liberal politics in the rest of the century and out of line with the spirit of the age of mid-to late-Victorian England. This event in Mill's biography is particularly illuminating because the underlying issue of sexual morality, public harm and individual responsibility was an inspiration for the rediscovery of the relevance of Millian Liberalism in the twentieth century, by such figures as H. L. A. Hart.[5] Yet this was not merely a further indication of Mill's advanced progressive ideas being ahead of his time; it also coincided with an eclipse of Mill's social and political theory that was only to be fully recovered in the late twentieth century. The political and moral philosopher of liberalism who cast such a long shadow over contemporary moral and political debate, at least in the English world, was soon overshadowed by developments in moral and political theory that challenged Mill's contributions.

Mill's untimely moral and social opinions cut against the grain of conventional Victorian *mores* as indeed did the outward expression of his private life. The acknowledgement and defence of the need for this kind of non-conformity was at the heart of *On Liberty*. But his advanced opinions on the place of private non-conformity in public life also alienated him from the subsequent development of later nineteenth-century social and political philosophy. The response of authoritarian utilitarians such as James Fitzjames Stephen illustrated how the radical utilitarian tradition had no necessary connection with radical liberalism, whatever Bentham or John Stuart Mill might have believed.[6] Stephen's attack on Mill, which has continued to be rehearsed by subsequent commentators, such as Cowling and Devlin, and in a more modest form by Joseph Hamburger, all reflect an ambiguity in the development of nineteenth- and twentieth-century liberalism, between its 'moralistic' and its political manifestations.[7] Mill's utilitarian liberalism set an agenda for much contemporary liberal theory with its focus on the legitimate limits of state action. His ethical theory provided an account of the foundation of ethical judgements and a decision procedure for personal and political moral action. Yet for many critics at the time and since, Mill's political theory appeared to lack any clear sense of the fundamental problem of politics, namely the nature and status of political power and authority. Although *Considerations on Representative Government* does appear to offer a conception of the state, its underlying approach to the state and government is designed to reinforce the fundamentally ethical perspective of Mill's liberalism as set out in *On Liberty*. For Mill, as indeed for the earlier utilitarians such as Bentham, the problem of the state was not a theoretical problem at all, but rather a matter of fact. The identity and nature of political power was given by historical experience and the task for the political philosopher or legislator was to reform and rationalise that existing set of institutions along utilitarian lines. Utilitarianism, therefore, conceived of all political problems as essentially ethical problems about the nature and distribution of individual human welfare. As such it had no necessary connection to any particular state form or set of institutions. Although, Mill's utilitiarian liberalism was to be continued in a more modest form in the late nineteenth century by Henry Sidgwick, it was precisely this lack of a clear conception of the problem of politics that partly marginalised his political liberalism for the subsequent seven decades. The absence of a distinct conception of the claims of politics had its roots in the conception of the state that utilitarians and their intuitionist and Coleridgean opponents held. For both perspectives, the problem was what to do with the state rather than with challenges to the state as such. Mill was certainly aware of problems of state building and the claims of nationalism, as will be discussed in the next section, but he lacked any sense of the radical pluralism of the British state of the sort that was to preoccupy British politics for the subsequent sixty years and to dominate British political theory in the early twentieth century. The Idealist, realist liberal and pluralist reactions to the inherent pluralism of the British state with the challenges of home rule, nationalist secession and class politics all put the state at issue in a way that seemed far more urgent than concerns over the liberals' attack on paternalism.[8] Mill's moralistic liberalism appeared redundant to the main political debates of British politics and society, or at best highly marginal, a fact that increased in significance in light of the political upheavals of war and depression.

In the intervening period between his death and the subsequent rediscovery of Millian Liberalism in the 1950s, the two main components of his theory, namely his utilitarianism and his liberalism, came apart in the minds of many moral and political philosophers, with the consequence that Mill was considerably underrated as a major philosopher within a short period following his death. The history of utilitarianism following Mill's death, in the examples of Jevons and Edgeworth, suggested a return to Bentham as opposed to Mill, as the problems of providing a metric for utility shaped debates: their approach was to be replaced in turn by the marginalist revolution in economics which transformed debates about welfare and its role in understanding individual behaviour and regulating the boundaries of government action. Not only was there a turn away from Millian concerns about limiting government action and distinguishing between higher and lower pleasures but, more importantly, there was a professionalisation of the social sciences with the development of modern Economics which started to undermine the unified ethical theory that sustained Mill's liberalism. Mill's status as the author of the dominant textbook introduction to economics was lost as he was replaced in that role by Alfred Marshall. This professionalisation was also manifested in the development of philosophy as a discipline in the early twentieth century. As economists settled technical questions about welfare, distribution and exchange, philosophers turned to the question of what was the status of their activity. Meanwhile, sociology and anthropology seemed to provide the substantive materials that Mill had hoped to develop in his naturalistic 'ethology'. As a consequence, Philosophy responded to these challenges by turning to an analytical and under-labourer conception of itself, where it focused on logic and language, with a view to removing conceptual confusion rather than with developing substantive knowledge. G. E. Moore's *Principia Ethica*, which was to be one of the foundation texts of this new approach to philosophy, was especially critical of Mill's naturalistic conception of ethics. Although primarily concerned with displacing the dominance of Henry Sidgwick, Moore's assault on naturalism was to leave a perception of Mill's utilitarianism as a naïve and simplistic muddle.[9]

In the field of political philosophy, the fortunes of Mill's liberalism were no better. Spencer's positivist sociology gave rise to a much more radically libertarian conception of liberalism which reinforced the classical liberals' concern with limiting the power of the state, rather than Mill's concern with the threat of democracy and mass opinion. At the same time, Mill's progressive liberal ideals were taken up and developed by T. H. Green amongst the British Idealists. For Green and his successors, the task was to save liberalism from the threat of utilitarianism, which had no necessary tendency to sustain a liberal ethical order, and to challenge the reductivist positivism of Spencer's libertarianism. Under the influence of Idealists such as Green, the spirit of the age seemed to be turning more towards the successors of Coleridge than to the successors of Bentham. As Mill's liberalism had continued to offer a synthesis of both perspectives he was clearly caught in the middle, and as he offered little by way of additional support to either position, his significance waned amongst those who considered themselves as advanced liberals. Throughout the early twentieth century, New Liberalism, with its activist conception of the state, drew far more from the Coleridgean or intuitionist sources of Idealism than from Mill. He remained a figure to honour, amongst the likes of L. T. Hobhouse, but his ideas were characterised as those of a bygone age. Later in the twentieth century, following the liberal reaction to Keynesianism and the rise of the welfare state, Mill seemed to offer an insufficiently robust defence of classical liberalism. For Friedrich Hayek and classical liberals inspired by him, Mill became a figure of deep suspicion. This is perhaps most curious in the case of Hayek who, whilst regarding Mill as a liberal apostate, was also important in encouraging a number of scholarly initiatives that contributed to the subsequent late-twentieth-century reappraisal of Mill's ideas. Echoing the views of some late-nineteenth-century critics, Mill's modest defence of socialism, and his distinction between questions of production which were purely a matter for the market mechanism, and questions of distribution which could be an ethical or political matter, was seen as a form of apostasy from true liberalism that was leading to the modern activist welfare state, which for Hayek was but a step on the road to serfdom.

Given this rather pessimistic account of the fortunes of Millian liberalism in the first seventy years following his death, it might seem rather curious that he has the significance that this volume attributes to him. Yet there has undoubtedly been a resurgence of interest in Mill's liberalism. The best way to explain this is not simply to focus on the developments within moral philosophy that have contributed to a more sensitive hearing to Mill's ideas, but to look at the political context in which this reappraisal has taken place.

If the absence of a proper theory of the state or a conception of the political was one of the reasons for the partial eclipse of Mill's liberalism in the late nineteenth and early twentieth century, it was precisely the absence of a theory of the state that suited Mill's contribution to political theory from the 1950s to the present. Where the nature of the state and the identity and site of political action is the crucial issue Mill's liberal moralism was seen as having little to offer. However, in the context of a settled consensus on the nature of the liberal democratic state with fixed borders, the issues of the proper use of state power by the people against each other re-emerge as fundamental political issues. The broad social context that led to the resurgence of interest in Mill and in his conception of the nature and purpose of political theory is the stabilisation of the liberal democratic state and its vindication following the Second World War. When that is coupled with the Cold-War international order with its coercive settlement of European state borders under the competing Soviet and western blocks, the scope for a theoretical engagement with politics shifted from what Karl Popper characterised as the utopian to piecemeal social engineering. It is precisely in this context that the moralisation of the political takes place and it is this which encouraged a reappraisal of the value of Mill's ideas and his peculiar conception of liberalism.

The story of the re-emergence of Millian liberalism, therefore, connects with the emergence of liberal moralism as the dominant style of political philosophy in the mid-to-late twentieth century. A number of eminent scholars are responsible for the shaping of British political theory in the post-Second-World-War period, but perhaps the most important in terms of his impact on the development of interest in Mill and themes from Millian liberalism is H. L. A. Hart. Hart's own work in political philosophy, as opposed to jurisprudence where he develops Bentham's ideas (which – on matters of jurisprudence – were largely shared by

Mill), focused on the tension between the claims of utilitarianism as a principle guiding policy-making and a defence of a liberal stance on private morality and its public regulation. Mill's liberalism was concerned with defending a much more coherent synthesis of these two dimensions than Hart could ever accept, but that broad agenda was passed on through his teaching and influence onto a whole generation of scholars who subsequently made Mill the direct object of their interest, such as Alan Ryan, David Lyons or C. L. Ten, or who took this Millian style and agenda into their own political theory, for example, Brian Barry. Hart's rediscovery and defence of a modest Millian liberalism was also to feature in his public defence of the Wolfenden Committee's *Report on Homosexual Offenses and Prostitution* of 1959, which became the focus of an extended debate with Patrick Devlin, who took on the role of J. F. Stephen to Hart's Mill. This association between Mill scholarship and the liberal transformation of British public life became a significant theme of Maurice Cowling's critical volume on Mill, and a similar argument condemning Millian liberalism in American public life was made by Gertrude Himmelfarb.[10]

The fortunes of Mill's liberalism in Britain have been closely tied to the political context of moral and social philosophy since his death in 1873. It is worth noting that precisely the kind of issue that Hayward used to denigrate Mill's memory in the *Times* obituary was also what gave his liberalism a peculiar resonance in contemporary politics. It is the possibility of using his conception of liberalism as a template for theorising a practical public philosophy that makes Mill so resonant now, as opposed to his ability to answer some perennial question about the nature of political community or political power. In this respect, Mill's political liberalism is more flexible and less prone to the kinds of critiques that have been raised against contractualist and deontological liberalisms, such as that of John Rawls' *A Theory of Justice*. As Stefan Collini has argued, whatever claim to attention Mill has on us today or in the future 'it will be on account of the continued vitality of political theory calling itself "liberal".'[11] Mill's liberalism is not the only candidate liberal theory, but its value and potential claim to superiority over its rivals is precisely the tendency to 'moralism' that earlier appeared to marginalise Mill from scholarly debates in political philosophy. 'Moralism' itself is not a category mistake that arises from the failure to see the significance of true political questions, rather it is a political response to problems of public life that arise in distinct but not peculiarly special circumstances. These circumstances held for much of the mid-nineteenth century and continue to hold, at least for the foreseeable future, in the early twenty-first century, despite the claims of multiculturalists and globalisation theorists. It is precisely in those circumstances that Mill's comprehensive vision can still attract both scholarly and practical attention. That said, these circumstance are peculiar to domestically stable political communities such as contemporary liberal democracies: whether and how Mill's political liberalism holds beyond the confines of a domestic political community has become a concern of many scholars as they turn their attention to Mill's contribution to the international or global domain.[12]

2. Mill, liberalism and the international order

For decades during the latter part of the twentieth century the ever-increasing Mill scholarship focused on various aspects of Mill's philosophy, economic thought and political theory in a domestic context. As far as this latter is concerned, the books *On Liberty* and *Considerations on Representative Government* proved the most popular works for analysis, accompanied by some shorter articles. But at least since the late 1990s much attention has turned to Mill's thought on international relations, nationality and empire. This tendency is related to the more general increased interest in what is now called 'international political thought'.[13] Meanwhile, an ever- increasing number of articles and essays are being written still today which claim that Mill's thought on international politics has been ignored or neglected, in general or by at least some related academic discipline. Such claims today are ill-timed by around a decade. A time was, before the recent explosion of interest in 'international political theory', when there was indeed very little commentary on Mill's thought on international relations. It speaks volumes that the late Martin Wight even confused him with his father.[14] The nineteenth century more generally had, it has correctly been said, 'largely ... dropped out of view'.[15] J. S. Mill was more or less absent from most general studies of political thought on international relations until the late 1990s.[16] Precious few works noted some of his pronouncements briefly and his views on international relations were the main focus of no more than one (rather unsatisfactory) article written in 1961.[17]

This has changed in the last decade or so. There is an ever-growing literature on one or other aspect of Mill's thought on international politics.[18] He now has a place in anthologies of political thought on international relations or international ethics.[19] These days the younger Mill is accorded the status of one of the 'leading international thinkers', who are set apart by 'the fact that their thought retains its intellectual force long after it was written down and the events that provoked it have faded into history'.[20] Differently put, in the last few years Mill has been 'canonised' in the emerging canon of 'international political theory' (as he had long been part of the canon of the history of political and economic thought).[21] This is how Michael Walzer assessed Mill's relevance to contemporary debates on international relations quite recently: '[W]henever we need to argue about whether it is right or wrong, just or unjust, to send an army across a border, it is useful to return to Mill's "few words" [on non-intervention] ... He is our contemporary. Indeed, I argue that he speaks directly to current U.S. debates about foreign policy and international society.'[22]

But the picture of past neglect and current belated recognition or rehabilitation can be exaggerated. Mill never completely lost his place as an iconic liberal figure, once it was established by the 1860s.[23] What has been said above should not obscure the fact that Mill was always something of a major authority for liberals on all sorts of issues, and that international politics was not an exception. The early-twentieth-century liberal internationalist Gilbert Murray referred to Mill as his 'special saint and prophet'.[24] And this is what another major early-twentieth-century liberal internationalist (and indeed the first Professor of International Relations), Alfred Zimmern, wrote, during the Great War:

> I pass now to deal with an objection which must have been in some people's minds when I drew a distinction between Statehood and Nationality … States and nations ought, they will say, to be coterminous … And they will invoke the authority of John Stuart Mill, whose words on the subject in his book on 'Representative Government', have passed almost unchallenged for two generations as the pure milk of Liberal doctrine. 'It is', says Mill, 'in general a necessary condition of free institutions that the boundaries of governments should coincide with those of nationalities.'[25]

Zimmern went on to criticise what he took to be Mill's position on the matter, but that is not the point here. What is of interest is that he was adamant that by attacking Mill's position, he was attacking liberal orthodoxy on the subject. Examples could be multiplied. Thus, when all is said and done, the increased interest of the last decade or so in Mill's theorising on international politics, nationality and related topics is not exactly a 'fashion'. It is just that, comparatively increased interest, not unrelated to the rise and rise of 'international political theory' as a sub-discipline.

It may be otherwise with the explosion in the production of works dealing with Mill's attitude towards imperialism and the British Empire in the last decade.[26] Mill is seen as the iconic liberal and criticisms of his attitudes are very often used as generic indictments of a whole tradition called 'liberalism' which is more often referred to than defined. Many such attempts to attack 'liberalism' without always defining it are laden with misconstructions.[27] No less fraught with difficulties is the particular line of attack on Mill's thought. The commentary on these issues that has emerged in the last few years spans a great gamut of works, from books or articles of serious scholarship and analytical reflection to writings displaying quite lousy scholarly standards and lazy thinking. Some of the 'post-colonial' criticisms of Mill have raised important issues regarding the degree of ignorance, prejudice and Euro-centrism displayed by many of his statements, or the way in which different cultures and historical periods were hastily and mistakenly lumped together in much of what Mill wrote. But some of them have also indulged in strikingly anachronistic mis-readings of Mill's statements, to the extent (for example) that several academics have presented Mill as a kind of arch-racist – an accusation that is egregiously unfair and misplaced, directed against the man who was, on the contrary, the leader of the anti-racist camp in his time and was seen as such by his contemporaries.[28] Furthermore, it is the very indulgence in the 'blame game' that is marring the discussion. And, as always, one extreme feeds another, so the excesses of *some* post-colonial critics have led to the slow emergence of a body of work that might be in danger of underestimating the problems with Mill's attitude towards the extra-European world.[29] Only serious and thorough historical scholarship and contextualisation of what Mill wrote as well as did (as an activist) can offer an accurate picture. The definitive study of Mill on empire and imperialism has yet to be written.

Besides his pronouncements on the British Empire, the other most commented upon of Mill's contributions to international political thought is his article 'A Few Words on Non-Intervention', published near the end of that tumultuous year, 1859.[30] One of the main reasons why Mill's 'A Few Words' has gradually become part of the 'canon' is the (favourable) attention paid to it by Michael Walzer in his seminal book *Just and Unjust Wars* (1977). Walzer was right in stressing the importance of Mill's refusal to allow what is now called 'regime change' because of Mill's belief in what Walzer called the 'self-help' argument.[31] In other words, Walzer was right to draw attention to Mill's insistence that foreigners should not interfere with the internal struggles for liberty in a country because a free government supported by foreign bayonets was a contradiction in terms and would not last. By the same token Mill insisted that, when, however, that balance was already being interfered with by foreigners supporting the 'wrong side' (the anti-liberal forces within the country), then liberal powers had a right and indeed an obligation to intervene (whenever they could prudently do so) in order to restore the internal balance. This was the argument for counter-intervention to enforce non-intervention that Mill had already supported as of 1831.

For Mill had discussed the subject of foreign intervention elsewhere as well, at various stages of his life. It has been argued that Mill began analysing arguments on the justifiableness or otherwise of intervention in foreign disputes quite early on, in 1830–31, as a result of his close attention to (and reporting of) the political debates in France during the early years of the July Monarchy. In the course of a few months (between December 1830 and April 1831) he seems to have adopted and defended in his journalistic writings the position on intervention propounded by some of the leaders of the French 'left' of the time, the opposition to Louis Philippe's monarchy (the *parti du mouvement*). They were arguing that counter-intervention to restore the balance of internal forces in a country where the despotic European Powers had already intervened was not a violation of the 'principle of non-intervention' but rather a stricter and more correct interpretation of it.[32] Mill repeated this argument in various formulations in an article he co-authored in 1837, in the oft-quoted article 'A Few Words on Non-Intervention' of 1859, as well as in a number of expositions of his principles in his electoral campaign of sorts for the Westminster election in 1865.[33]

However, there is an important work where Mill went further than the principle outlined so far – a difference that has escaped later commentators' attention.[34] In his 'Vindication of the French Revolution of February 1848' (1849), he went beyond defending counter-intervention.[35] To all intents and purposes, in 1849 Mill asserted the right of liberal powers 'to assist struggling liberalism' wherever possible, without reference to whether or not any of the 'despotic' powers had already intervened. It is clear from both his *Autobiography* and his correspondence that Mill was emboldened to say, in the immediate aftermath of the Revolutions of 1848, things that he feared would have been too radical to state publicly earlier.[36] There is no gainsaying a noticeable degree of radical and indeed revolutionary exuberance in what Mill wrote about international affairs in the 'Vindication'. But he did not repeat those statements and positions again. Rather, his arguments in 'A Few Words' ten years later are much closer to what he had written in 1831 and 1837.

The main reason for the difference was Mill's changing attitude towards the principle of 'nationality'. In 1849, though even then not as naïve and unaware of the dangers posed by nationalism as later commentators would have us believe, he certainly offered his support for national liberation as a means to the attainment and better working of free representative government. The argument in question is better known from his (much more careful and qualified) exposition of it in Chapter XVI of his book *Considerations on Representative Government* (1861).[37] However, what has escaped the attention of commentators is that Mill clearly became more and more worried about the implications of nationalist sentiments and increasingly reluctant to afford them any encouragement. This increasing uneasiness about nationalism as well as some other more concrete worries about particular international developments in 1859 led Mill to state the principles he laid down on non-intervention in the careful way he did in 'A Few Words'.

Mill's attitude towards nationality/nationalism, patriotism and cosmopolitanism is another complex question where endless misconceptions have arisen – not least due to the complexity and subtlety of Mill's position, which does not offer itself to anything approaching easy categorisation or pigeonholing. Received wisdom has been that Mill was a staunch supporter of nationalism because he thought representative government was next to impossible in a country composed of different nationalities. This view is based on Mill's statements – or rather, on *some* of Mill's statements – in Chapter 16 of his book *Considerations on Representative Government* (1861). What such narrow readings of Mill on nationality miss is the broader picture though. In Chapter 16 Mill discusses nationality *in its relation to representative government*, not the merits and demerits of nationality in the abstract. The gist of his argument is that, *where the sentiment of nationality exists in any force*, and different nationalities that loath each other live in the same borders, the working of representative government is rendered almost impossible, because of the reasons he gives (the central government playing one nationality against another, the army and the people not seeing themselves as of the same people, etc.). In such cases, Mill wrote, *if and wherever possible* (and he knew it was a very big 'if', as he made clear in the next few pages), representative government had a better chance to succeed if the limits of nationality coincided with those of government – if each nation had its own state and each state was composed of one nationality. He then went on to spend most of the chapter in question explaining why this neat one-nation-one-state model was impossible to implement in many parts of Europe where populations were too intermingled. Moreover, he also stressed that the coexistence and merger through mutual influences and *heterosis* of different ethnic groups within the same people offered major civilisational and moral advantages. Mill was adamant already in 'Vindication' that people's tribal attachment to their ethnic/racial group was 'characteristic of barbarians' and should not be encouraged. But where it was a fact on the ground, and different nationalities had developed such 'barbarous' feelings and hated each other, it could not be wished away and ignored. That is already a picture considerably more complex than what the received wisdom of Mill as a 'nationalist' would have us believe. But it is nothing compared to the picture that emerges if one looks at Mill's statements on nationality, patriotism and cosmopolitanism throughout his life. Such a thorough analysis of Mill's views and pronouncements has yielded results much more complex than the image of Mill as a naïve supporter of nationalism.[38]

3. An overview

Following this introductory chapter, in Chapter 2, Bruce Kinzer argues that J. S. Mill remained a quintessentially political being even during the late 1820s and early 1830s, years when he was engaged in rethinking and revising his Benthamite inheritance, pursuing his programme of internal culture, and striving to enhance his understanding of the complexities attendant upon the search for truth. Throughout these years Mill sustained an allegiance to democratic radicalism, an allegiance that fitted well with his temperamental responsiveness to the pull of political action. Contending that Mill was keen to make his mark in the realms of both speculation and action, the essay demonstrates, chiefly through an analysis of his 1831 series, *The Spirit of the Age*, and his numerous articles on French politics in the early 1830s, that his personal ambition became intricately linked to a growing absorption in the challenges posed by the problem of authority in an age of transition. Moreover, it illuminates the ways in which this ambition produced a striking generational dimension to his assessment of the kind of leadership required in a time of rapid cultural, social and political change, with youth given precedence over age.

In Chapter 3, Terence Ball reconsiders James and John Stuart Mill's contrasting views of the formation of human character. After briefly sketching the elder Mill's decidedly deterministic Owenite view, he takes a closer look at J. S. Mill's proposed 'science' of character formation, which in his *System of Logic* (1843) he called 'ethology'. Although Mill never wrote a treatise on ethology, Ball shows that his major works can be read as case studies in applied ethology. Thus, Mill's *Autobiography* shows how a single individual, viz. himself, was able to reform a partially deformed character. *The Subjection of Women* is about the deformation and possible reformation of the characters of half the human race, viz. women. *Considerations on Representative Government* is concerned with the formation of civic character. And not least, *On Liberty* is concerned with the conditions conducive to the formation of vital and vigorous individual characters.

In Chapter 4, Donald Winch argues that the origins of Mill's environmentalist concerns can be found in his interest in botany and mountain scenery acquired as a fourteen-year-old in the Pyrenees, and nurtured by an interest in Wordsworth's nature poetry that climaxed with a pilgrimage to the Lake District in 1831. The mature economic version of these concerns was embodied in Book IV of the *Principles of Political Economy*, where it took the form of speculations on the benefits of a zero-growth society. This brought together Mill's neo-Malthusianism, his Wordsworthian appreciation of tranquillity in the presence of wild natural beauty, and a diagnosis of the emerging state of Britain's economy. Winch shows that, in advancing the ultimate grounds of an environmentalist ethic, Mill substituted his own altruistic version of the religion of humanity for Christian ideas of reverence towards God's creation.

In Chapter 5, Fred Rosen offers a study in the history of ideas and, particularly, of those related to the history of logic, exploring the relationships between Jeremy Bentham and his nephew, George Bentham, the distinguished botanist, on the one hand, and James and John Stuart Mill on the other, in an attempt to answer several questions. Rosen's first concern is to answer the question, why was J. S. Mill hostile to developments in the use of technical symbols and mathematics in logic which began to develop during his lifetime and which has characterised much of the subsequent development of logic? The second question Rosen pursues is, why did both James and J. S. Mill ignore George Bentham's *Outline of a New System of Logic* and Jeremy Bentham's earlier work in logic, as published in *Chrestomathia* and elsewhere? Then, third, to what extent was Mill's indifference to George Bentham's *Outline* related to his mental crisis of 1826–27? And finally, the fourth question Rosen explores is, did the debate over the quantification of the predicate vindicate some of the work of both Benthams in logic? The chapter thus confronts three puzzles. The first is that Mill's logic was so important and influential but had little influence on the development of modern logic. The second is that while Jeremy Bentham and James Mill were supposedly related as master and disciple, their philosophical writing displays little influence in this respect. Third, although George Bentham and John Stuart Mill began their work in logic in France at the same time, as Rosen shows, this relationship was never developed by either of them and, particularly, never acknowledged by Mill. Rosen suggests that these puzzles might be related, and together they reveal a curious side of J. S. Mill's work and development in logic. Using materials which have received little attention, the essay explores some of the underlying tensions between the Benthams and the Mills concerning the development of their ideas, and particularly the intellectual context for the development of arguably J. S. Mill's most important work, the *System of Logic Ratiocinative and Inductive*.

In Chapter 6, Wendy Donner explores John Stuart Mill's utilitarianism and its connections and indebtedness to virtue ethics. She begins with an examination of the structure of Mill's moral philosophy, as set out primarily in Book VI of the *Logic* and in *Utilitarianism*. In the *Logic* Mill lays out the Art of Life 'in its three departments; Morality, Prudence or Policy, and Aesthetics; the Right, the Expedient, and the Beautiful or Noble'. The distinction between Morality or Duty, on the one hand, and Nobility or Virtue, on the other, plays a crucial role within Mill's theory and yet this distinction is often underplayed or completely neglected. This can lead to some serious misunderstandings of Mill's arguments and commitments. For example, blurring the distinction between Duty and Virtue can lead to mistaken projects in which virtue is turned into a moral duty, even though Mill explicitly rejects the notion that people can be coerced into leading better or more virtuous lives. Similarly, excessive focus upon the rule-centred character of moral duties can obscure the agent or character-centred aspects of the Art of Life and their role in the promotion of happiness and well-being. The chapter analyses Mill's indebtedness to the lineage of virtue ethics and politics and examines a list of elements that are part of the virtue ethics tradition and how they are present in Mill's theory. Virtue ethics enlarges the focus of concern beyond human action and widens its gaze to include concern with and evaluations of intentions, character and how we should live. Mill's theory calls upon many of the tools for training in the virtues that are associated with virtue ethics. Mill's utilitarianism shares with virtue ethics an appreciation of the value of emotional cultivation. Thus notions of emotional sensitivity, attunement and engagement receive his attention. Donner also examines the varieties of human excellences featured in Mill's theory. In scrutinising the kinds of virtues featured in Mill's theory, she argues that many current discussions of Mill's use of human excellences and virtues concentrate almost exclusively on reason and autonomy and individuality. Donner argues that this leaves out half of the equation, for Mill always brings in the importance of the emotions, compassion, and sociability and community. Donner points out that Mill's theory has strong holistic features and is not purely foundational. She argues that he works with models of interconnectedness and balance rather than invoking dualisms and dichotomies. For Donner, Mill's utilitarianism is a comprehensive theory designed to provide the grounding and justification for the numerous practical moral, social and political arts.

In Chapter 7, Jonathan Riley argues that the complex pleasure or enjoyment associated with the moral sentiment of justice is located near the top of the hierarchy of different kinds of pleasures which Mill mentions in connection with his notorious doctrine of the higher pleasures. In his view, the sentiment of justice is a feeling of security that the individual acquires after living in a community where equal claim-rights and correlative duties are distributed and enforced as a matter of course. Moreover, for Mill, one kind of pleasure is said to be higher than another if and only if the one kind is experienced by competent individuals to be infinitely more intense (and thus more valuable) than the other kind. Once these crucial aspects of his peculiar version of hedonistic utilitarianism are clarified, we can see that justice in the sense of general security of equal rights takes lexical priority over all competing social and political considerations within his utilitarian doctrine. Given the nature of the rights he recommends, in particular, the right of complete self-regarding liberty, Riley maintains that Mill's doctrine is properly classified as a coherent and radical liberal utilitarianism or utilitarian liberalism.

In Chapter 8, Martha Nussbaum argues that Mill's feminism is usually understood as the paradigm of 'liberal feminism', which is, in turn, often taken to be a bland doctrine focused on sameness of treatment, with little potential for the radical critique of hierarchies of power or the social deformation of desire. Calling this characterisation into question, Nussbaum holds the arguments of *The Subjection of Women* and related arguments in *On Liberty* up against four major varieties of feminism that are influential today: liberal feminism, radical feminism, 'difference' feminism and 'queer' feminism. She argues that *The Subjection*, while recognisably in the liberal tradition, in its focus on human autonomy and liberty, nonetheless anticipates the major insights of radical feminism, with its shrewd analysis of the power structure of the family and its account of the ways in which power deforms desire. While Mill gives us strong reasons not to buy into Gilligan's 'difference feminism', he does accord positive worth to the cultivation of emotional capacities, thus affirming the most worthwhile conclusion of 'that deeply defective brand of feminism'. Most surprisingly, by focusing on the tyranny of convention and casting doubt on all social norms that inhibit the development of unusual ways of life, Mill anticipates some of the conclusions of 'queer' feminism, the tradition influenced by Foucault's critique of normativity. Nonetheless, according to Nussbaum, in the end Mill stops short in this domain, failing to imagine alternatives to the conventional division of labour within the family. Had he carried his ideas concerning 'experiments in living' into *The Subjection*, it would have been a more completely radical and challenging work than it is. Even as it is, however, Nussbaum argues that it continues to offer a great deal to feminist thought. Indeed, she maintains that it develops a form of liberal feminism that can answer some of the most powerful critiques of liberalism that have been made by feminists in the past few decades. These charges include: (a) the charge that liberalism is excessively individualistic, slighting values of community and care, (b) the charge that liberalism is unable to give an account of the social deformation of desire and preference, (c) the charge that liberalism, by setting up definite norms to guide political thought, is bound to result in the tyranny of the 'normal' over the marginal or the subversive.

In Chapter 9, John Skorupski argues that liberty of thought and discussion have always been at the heart of the liberal outlook. In this paper Skorupski considers two conceptions of what free thought is: presuppositionless, or unconstrained. He aims to show that a commitment to the latter conception is fundamental to Mill's constructive empiricism, discusses how it ties together his epistemology and his ethics, and compares it to the discussion of free thought within German idealism.

Finally, in Chapter 10, Peter Singer discusses a number of aspects of Mill's thought that he deems to be of major importance today, focusing particularly on those areas where Mill's thought is most relevant to his own work and the philosophical and political controversies he is engaged in. The paper starts with a brief introduction where Singer discusses the main parallels between his own work and Mill's. Then Singer selects some works written by Mill and the respective issues on which he claims that Mill's work is particularly relevant today. Starting with *Utilitarianism*, he discusses briefly Mill's defence of 'Utility' or 'the Greatest Happiness Principle' in that book and distinguishes between Mill's version of utilitarianism ('the hedonistic version') and the one he (Singer) endorses ('preference utilitarianism'). He then moves on to the essay *On Liberty* and divides his analysis of its relevance today into two parts, dedicated to (a) the book's arguments for freedom of expression and opinion and (b) its defence of personal liberty in matters that do not cause harm to others. In the section dedicated to the former, Singer tests Mill's principles and arguments in *On Liberty* on a number of contemporary controversies (incarceration of Holocaust deniers, the publication of cartoons of the prophet Mohamed in 2006, etc.) and shows how crucial they are to contemporary debates. In the section on the latter (freedom of the individual) Singer again discusses Mill's famous 'simple principle' in *On Liberty* in the context of contemporary debates and issues – including debates he (Singer) is heavily embroiled with, such as that on voluntary euthanasia and assisted suicide. Moving to *The Subjection of Women*, Singer argues that it is 'a model of how to argue against a more or less universal social prejudice'. The next work by Mill to attract Singer's attention and praise is the essay 'On Nature'. Echoing Donald Winch's analysis in an earlier chapter, he draws attention to Mill's precautious environmentalist credentials. In the next section Singer discusses a part of Mill's 'Whewell on Moral Philosophy' where the issue of the treatment of animals is the focus, and traces a direct line of utilitarian thinking from Bentham thorough Mill to his own arguments on the issue. Finally, Singer briefly draws attention to the contemporary significance of Mill's main arguments in the 1859 essay 'A Few Words on Non-Intervention', one of Mill's main contributions to theorising on international relations, as we saw earlier in this introductory chapter.

The chapters in this volume do not purport to offer a unity of interpretation or a single uncontroversial discussion of Mill's ideas. But then, a most interesting incident occurred at the end of *The John Stuart Mill Bicentennial Conference*, at which preliminary versions of these papers were given. At some point a young woman (possibly a student and apparently a Mill fan) raised her hand and complained at the speakers' disagreements in their interpretations and assessments of Mill and at the fact that some of them were critical of certain aspects of Mill's thought. She took issue with the lack of consensus on him and concluded by saying 'aren't we here to celebrate him?'. What followed was perhaps the greatest tribute to Mill's legacy that he could possibly have hoped for. In the first and last instance where consensus occurred during the three-day Conference, all the participants in the Round Table one after another replied to the effect that they are not 'Millians', that 'there are no Millians' and that Mill would not have wanted there to be Millians, that he did not aspire to found a school of followers that would celebrate him. The message that came from all the participants was that Mill would have been deeply gratified at the disagreements and debates that continue to show the vitality of his thought.

Notes

1 J. S. Mill, *Autobiography*, in: John Stuart Mill, *The Collected Works of John Stuart Mill*, 33 vols, general editor F. E. L. Priestley and subsequently J. M. Robson, Toronto and London: The University of Toronto Press, 1963–91, hereafter referred to as: *CW*, Vol. I [*Autobiography and Literary Essays*], p. 87.

2 '*The John Stuart Mill Bicentennial Conference, 1806–2006*', that took place at University College London between 5 and 7 April 2006, assembled together more than 250 scholars and students of Mill's thought from scores of different countries from five continents.

3 R. Reeves, *John Stuart Mill: Victorian Firebrand*, London: Atlantic Books, 2007, pp. 481–82.

4   The phrase 'the Saint of Rationalism' is how William E. Gladstone later recalled he used to call Mill: M. St. John Packe, *The Life of John Stuart Mill*, London: Secker and Warburg, 1954, p. 455.

5   H. L. A. Hart, *Law, Liberty and Morality*, Oxford, Oxford University Press, 1963; see also the discussion in: S. Mendus, 'Private Faces in Public Places', in M. Kramer, C. Grant, B. Colburn and A. Hatzistavrou, eds, *The Legacy of H. L. A. Hart: Legal, Political and Moral Philosophy*, Oxford, Clarendon Press, 2008, pp. 299–313.

6   J. F. Stephen, *Liberty, Equality, Fraternity*, London: Smith Elder, 1873.

7   J. Hamburger, *John Stuart Mill on Liberty and Control*, Princeton: Princeton University Press, 1999.

8   See K. H. F. Dyson, *The State Tradition in Western Europe*, Oxford: Oxford University Press, 1980, pp. 186–202.

9   This was to be the common prejudice with respect to Mill's ethics until the 1960s and in some quarters it still continues.

10 M. Cowling, *Mill and Liberalism*, Cambridge: Cambridge University Press, 1963 (2nd edition, 1990); G. Himmelfarb, *On Liberty and Liberalism: The Case of John Stuart Mill*, New York: Alfred A. Knopf, 1974.

11 S. Collini, *Public Moralists*, Oxford: Clarendon Press, 1991, p. 341.

12 For earlier accounts of the vicissitudes of Mill's early reputation in the decades after his death see: S. Collini, 'From Dangerous Partisan to National Possession: John Stuart Mill in English Culture 1873–1933', in: Collini, *Public Moralists*, pp. 311–41; J. C. Rees, *Mill and his Early Critics*, Leicester: University College Leicester, 1956; G. L. Williams, 'Changing Reputations in the History of Political Thought: J. S. Mill', *Politics*, Vol. 15, No. 3 (1995), pp. 183–89; P. Nicholson, 'The reception and early reputation of Mill's political thought', in: J. Skorupski (ed.), *The Cambridge Companion to Mill*, Cambridge: Cambridge University Press, 1998, pp. 464–96. For an excellent introduction to Mill, including a survey of different interpretations and of his changing reputations see: W. Stafford, *John Stuart Mill*, Basingstoke: Macmillan, 1998.

13 On 'international political theory' see, for instance: C. Brown, *Sovereignty, Rights and Justice: International Political Theory Today*, Cambridge: Polity, 2002, pp. 1–14; D. Armitage, 'The Fifty Years' Rift: Intellectual History and International Relations', *Modern Intellectual History*, 1 (2004), 97–109; R. Jackson, *Classical and Modern Thought on International Relations: From Anarchy to Cosmopolis*, Basingstoke: Palgrave Macmillan, 2005, 1–16.

14 The third category of international theory writings Wight identified – in a now classic article – was '[t]he *parerga* of political philosophers, philosophers and historians. Among them he included 'J. S. Mill's essay on the law of nations.' M. Wight, 'Why is there no international theory?', in *Essays in the Theory of International Politics*, ed. H. Butterfield and M. Wight, London: George Allen & Unwin, 1966, p. 19. Apparently Wight had in mind *James* Mill's 'Law of Nations'.

15 Justin Rosenberg, quoted in: E. Keene, *International Political Thought: A Historical Introduction*, Cambridge: Polity, 2005, p. 160. Keene adds, in the same context, that 'it is the nineteenth-century liberals such as Mill who have probably suffered most.' (Ibid., p. 161).

16 Mill is absent from books such as: D. Boucher, *Political Theories of International Relations: From Thucydides to the Present*, Oxford: Oxford University Press, 1998; H. Williams, *International Relations in Political Theory*, Milton Keynes: Open University Press, 1992; H. Williams, M. Wright and T. Evans (eds), *A Reader in International Relations and Political Theory*, Buckingham: Open University Press, 1993.

17 Two notable exceptions were: M. Walzer, *Just and Unjust Wars: A Moral Argument with Historical Illustrations*, New York: Basic Books, 1977, pp. 87–97, 101; and C. R. Beitz, *Political Theory and International Relations*, Princeton, NJ: Princeton University Press, 1979, pp. 82, 84n, 85–87, 112–14 – both of which discussed briefly

some of Mill's main arguments in 'A Few Words on Non-Intervention' (1859). Mill's views on intervention were also briefly discussed in: R. J. Vincent, *Nonintervention and International Order*, Princeton, NJ: Princeton University Press, 1974, pp. 54–56, 61–63; and C. Holbraad, *The Concert of Europe: A Study in German and British International Theory 1815–1914*, London: Longman, 1970, pp. 162–65, 168, 170, 176. An anthology where Mill's main pronouncements on international politics were included and briefly commented upon was: A. Wolfers and L. W. Martin (eds), *The Anglo-American Tradition in Foreign Affairs: Readings from Thomas More to Woodrow Wilson*, New Haven: Yale University Press, 1956, pp. 206–20. The only article dealing directly with Mill's international thought before the recent emergence of interest was: K. E. Miller, 'John Stuart Mill's Theory of International Relations', *Journal of the History of Ideas*, 22:4 (1961), 493–514; for brief comments see also F. R. Flournoy, 'British Liberal Theories of International Relations (1848–98), *Journal of the History of Ideas*, 7:2 (1946), 195–217.

18 Leaving the even greater body of work on Mill and imperialism/colonialism aside (on which a few words will be said further on), some of the recent literature on Mill on international relations issues includes: G. Varouxakis, 'John Stuart Mill on Intervention and Non-Intervention', *Millennium: Journal of International Studies*, 26:1 (1997), 57–76; G. Varouxakis, *Mill on Nationality*, London: Routledge, 2002; E. Begby, 'Liberty, Statehood, and Sovereignty: Walzer on Mill on Non-Intervention', *Journal of Military Ethics*, 2:1 (2003), 46–62; J. J. Miller, 'Forced to be Free: Rethinking J. S. Mill and Intervention', *Politics and Ethics Review*, 1:2 (2005), 119–37; B. Jahn, 'Classical smoke, classical mirror: Kant and Mill in liberal international relations theory', in: B. Jahn (ed.), *Classical Theory in International Relations*, Cambridge: Cambridge University Press, 2006, pp. 178–203; M. Walzer, 'Mill's "A Few Words on Non-Intervention": A Commentary', in: N. Urbinati and A. Zakaras (eds), *J. S. Mill's Political Thought: A Bicentennial Reassessment*, Cambridge: Cambridge University Press, 2007, pp. 347–56; T. E. Schneider, 'J. S. Mill and Fitzjames Stephen on the American Civil War', *History of Political Thought*, 28:2 (2007), 290–304; G. Varouxakis, 'The international political thought of John Stuart Mill', in: I. Hall and L. Hill (eds), *British International Thinkers from Hobbes to Namier*, Basingstoke: Palgrave Macmillan, 2009, pp. 117–36.

19 See, e.g.: C. Brown, T. Nardin and N. Rengger (eds), *International Relations in Political Thought: Texts from the Ancient Greeks to the First World War*, Cambridge: Cambridge University Press, 2002, pp. 486–93; G. M. Reichberg, H. Syse, and E. Begby (eds), *The Ethics of War: Classic and Contemporary Readings*, Oxford: Blackwell, 2006, pp. 574–85.

20 See Jackson, *Classical and Modern Thought*, p. 14.

21 See also Brown, *Sovereignty, Rights and Justice*, pp. 48, 62, 77–80, 93–94, 174, 247–48; Keene, *International Political Thought*, pp. 160–64, 166–72.

22 Walzer, 'Mill's "A Few Words on Non-Intervention": A Commentary', pp. 348–49.

23 See, for instance, Chapter V, entitled 'Gladstone and Mill', in: L. T. Hobhouse, *Liberalism* (1911), in: L. T. Hobhouse, *Liberalism and Other Writings*, ed. by J. Meadowcroft, Cambridge: Cambridge University Press, 1994, pp. 49–55.

24 We are grateful to Ian Hall for this quote from Murray's letters. For more on Murray and his indebtedness to, and admiration for Mill see, e.g.: C. Stray (ed.), *Gilbert Murray Reassessed: Hellenism, Theatre, & International Politics*, Oxford: Oxford University Press, 2007, pp. 205, 249, 279 and *passim*. See also: J. Morefield, *Covenants Without Swords: Idealist Liberalism and the Spirit of Empire*, Princeton: Princeton University Press, 2004.

25 A. E. Zimmern, 'Nationality and Government' [1915, 1916], in: A. E. Zimmern, *Nationality & Government with other war-time essays*, London: Chatto & Windus, 1918, p. 46.

26 To give only a selection of recent works: U. Singh Mehta *Liberalism and Empire: A Study in Nineteenth-Century British Liberal Thought*, Chicago: The University of Chicago Press, 1999; B. Parekh, 'Decolonizing Liberalism', in: Aleksandras Shtromas (ed.), *The End of "Isms"? Reflections on the Fate of Ideological Politics after Communism's Collapse*, Oxford: Blackwell, 1994, pp. 85–103; B. Parekh, *Rethinking Multiculturalism: Cultural Diversity and Political Theory*, Basingstoke and London: Macmillan, 2000; E. M. Souffrant, *Formal Transgression: John Stuart Mill's Philosophy of International Affairs*, Lanham, MD: Rowman & Lttlefield, 2000; J. Pitts, *A Turn to Empire: The Rise of Imperial Liberalism in Britain and France*, Princeton: Princeton University Press, 2005, pp. 123–62; B. Schultz and G. Varouxakis (eds), *Utilitarianism and Empire*, Lanham, MD: Lexington Books, 2005; B. Jahn, 'Barbarian thoughts: imperialism in the philosophy of John Stuart Mill', *Review of International Studies*, 31 (2005), 599–618; M. Tunick, 'Tolerant Imperialism: John Stuart Mill's Defense of British Rule in India', *The Review of Politics*, 68 (2006), 586–611; B. Schultz, 'Mill and Sidgwick, Imperialism and Racism', *Utilitas*, 19:1 (2007), 104–30; K. Mantena, 'Mill and the Imperial Predicament', in: Urbinati and Zakaras (eds), *J. S. Mill's Political Thought*, pp. 298–318; K. Smits, 'John Stuart Mill on the Antipodes: Settler Violence against Indigenous Peoples and the Legitimacy of Colonial Rule', *Australian Journal of Politics and History*, 54:1 (2008), 1–15.

27 See D. Bell, 'Empire and International Relations in Victorian Political Thought', *Historical Journal*, 49 (2006), 281–98.

28 For criticisms of such interpretations see: G. Varouxakis, 'John Stuart Mill on race', *Utilitas*, 10:1 (1998), 17–32; G. Varouxakis, 'Empire, race, Euro-centrism: John Stuart Mill and his critics', in: Schultz and Varouxakis (eds), *Utilitarianism and Empire*, pp. 137–53.

29 For example, see: Tunick, 'Tolerant Imperialism'.

30 First published in *Fraser's Magazine*, LX (December 1859) and included by Mill to be reprinted in his collective volumes of selected essays under the title *Dissertations and Discussions*, Vol. III (1867), 153–78; now in: *CW*, XXI, pp. 109–24.

31 Walzer was meanwhile wrong in arguing that Mill did not discuss (and therefore did not advocate) what Walzer calls 'humanitarian intervention': Walzer, *Just and Unjust Wars*, p. 90. See an argument to the contrary in: Varouxakis, 'Mill on Intervention', pp. 72–73 (and n.80 and n.82).

32 For details see Varouxakis, 'Mill on Intervention', particularly pp. 61–67.

33 'The Spanish Question' [1837], *CW*, XXXI, pp. 359–88, particularly pp. 373–75; Mill, letter to James Beal, 17 April 1865, *CW*, XVI, p. 1033; 'The Westminster Election of 1865 [1]', *CW*, XXVIII, p. 17; 'Westminster Election 1865 [4]', *CW*, XXVIII, p. 39.

34 With the exception of Varouxakis, 'Mill on Intervention', particularly pp. 70–75.

35 First published in *Westminster Review*, LI (April 1849); reprinted in Mill's *Dissertations and Discussions*; now in *CW*, XX, pp. 317–63.

36 *CW*, I, p. 241; *CW*, XIV, p. 72.

37 *CW*, XX, pp. 344–48; *CW*, XIX, pp. 546–52.

38 See G. Varouxakis, 'Cosmopolitan Patriotism in J. S. Mill's Political Thought and Activism', in: Urbinati and Zakaras (eds), *J. S. Mill's Political Thought*, pp. 277–97; and Varouxakis, *Mill on Nationality*.

2 The primacy of the political and the problem of cultural authority in an age of transition

Bruce Kinzer

In the late 1820s J.S. Mill embarked on a quest to discover important truths that his education had failed to disclose. This enterprise called upon him to turn to sources towards which his father would not have directed him. It also involved an embrace of eclecticism: 'looking out for the truth which is generally to be found in errors when they are anything more than paralogisms, or logical blunders.'[1] Without abandoning his Benthamite foundations, he pursued his programme of internal culture, asked new questions, engaged with new ideas and personalities, and strove to enhance his understanding of the complexities attendant upon the search for truth. He had to work out not only what he *thought*, but what he *felt*, especially about himself and his place in the world. He wanted to be a figure of consequence, one who could make his mark in the realms of speculation and action. This personal ambition became intricately linked to a growing absorption in the challenges posed by the problem of authority in an age of transition. The lens through which he gazed at this problem had hard political surfaces.

A recurring and telling phrase in J.S. Mill's writings is 'the authority of the instructed'. The problem of authority was critically significant in a society experiencing rapid change. Only the 'instructed' could guide the uninstructed masses in the path of improvement. But who in England was fit to carry out this function? Not the products of the ancient universities, whose system of education aroused in Mill 'sentiments little short of utter abhorrence.'[2] That system, he held, did almost nothing to foster genuine intellectual cultivation; to suppose that England's university graduates merited deference from the uninstructed was preposterous. The English aristocracy had the leisure necessary to become instructed, but had neither the incentive nor the wisdom to use their leisure for this purpose. In a London Debating Society speech of 1826, Mill observed that 'talent cannot be acquired without trouble … Rank we know gives consideration. Property we know gives consideration … When a man can have as much consideration, without deserving it, as he could if he did, if his stupidity is no bar to his consideration, depend upon it he will cling to both with equal pertinacity.'[3] England's middle classes did not offer an attractive alternative to aristocratic leadership. They 'had but one object in life,' Mill told a correspondent in May 1829: 'to ape their superiors; for whom they have an open-mouthed & besotted admiration, attaching itself to the bad more than to the good points, being those they can more easily comprehend & imitate.'[4] The conditions needed for the formation of an instructed cohort did not yet exist in England. In a letter of November 1829 Mill wrote that 'great social sinister interests' saw to it that 'those, who would otherwise be the instructed classes, have no motive to obtain real instruction in politics and morals and are subjected to biasses from which the students of the physical sciences are exempt.' Such individuals, he said, 'can drive a trade in the ignorance and prejudices of others; they either write for the classes who have sinister interests, and minister to their selfishness and malevolence, or else, addressing themselves to the common people, they find in the well grounded discontent of the people against their institutions sufficient materials for acquiring popularity without either instructing their intellects, or cultivating right habits of feeling and judging in their minds.'[5] Only a young man confident that he ranked among the few of his nation's truly 'instructed' would feel competent to issue such judgements. John Mill had been so educated as to prepare him for a leading part in the political and moral reformation of English society.

His absorbing interest in political matters antedated and survived his espousal of eclecticism. Beliefs and principles essentially political in nature imbued the education James Mill had given his first-born. Political intent informed most of the younger Mill's early publications and activities. His *Autobiography* teems with paragraphs that discuss thought and action in political terms. His involvement in the 1820s with the *Westminster Review*, the *Parliamentary History and Review* and the London Debating Society followed from political preoccupations and ambitions. His musings on the problem of authority, his esteem for Samuel Taylor Coleridge as the seminal figure in the reaction against the eighteenth century, his encounter with contemporary continental thought (and with the Saint Simonians in particular) – all this, and more, held for J.S. Mill strong political import. In the sphere of theory he came to attach weight to considerations of which his father had been insufficiently mindful. Rather than viewing the introduction of representative democracy simply as a question of giving political expression to the self-interest principle, the younger Mill acknowledged the force of 'time, place, and circumstance'.[6] Whereas his father had grounded the case for a broad-based representative system in the vital need to protect the material interests of individuals, J.S. Mill thought it imperative to ask 'what great improvement in life and culture stands next in order for the people concerned, as the condition of their further progress, and what institutions are most likely to promote that'.[7] Yet he did not doubt that the premises invoked by his father in the latter's more theoretical writings possessed abundant explanatory power when it came to the circumstances of early nineteenth-century England. On practical political questions, Mill noted, he and his father 'were almost always in strong agreement'.[8] Both Mills believed that aristocratic predominance, 'the great demoralizing agency' in England, was 'an evil worth any struggle to get rid of'. The changes in J.S. Mill's speculative life during the late 1820s did not produce corresponding changes in his practical political creed. He remained, in his words, 'a radical and democrat, for Europe, and especially for England.'[9]

A continued allegiance to democratic radicalism blended well with his temperamental responsiveness to the gravitational pull of political action. In his imagination, heroic action most often happened in the political realm. Mill's withdrawal from the London Debating Society in 1829 did not signal a loss of political appetite. Indeed, the French Revolution of 1830, he says, 'roused my utmost enthusiasm, and gave me, as it were, a new existence.'[10] So excited was Mill by the overthrow of Charles X that he travelled to Paris during the second week of August, in the company of his friends J.A. Roebuck and G.J. Graham, to witness the unfolding of events. His feverish exhilaration bespoke a fascination with dramatic political action and susceptibility to democratic ardour. Was the 'spirit of the age' amenable to such enthusiasms?

Within months of his visit to Paris, Mill began a series of articles for the *Examiner* that he titled *The Spirit of the Age*. This series contended that change of a momentous character distinguished the nineteenth century. The era, as Mill put it, was one in which '[m]ankind have outgrown old institutions and old doctrines, and have not yet acquired new ones.'[11] The essays making up *The Spirit of the Age* explored the ramifications of this predicament, whose core was the problem of authority in an age of transition. Mill's treatment of this problem was certainly influenced by the eclecticism he had self-consciously cultivated in the years after his 'mental crisis'. The very title of the essays expressed an affinity with Romanticism and with the reaction against the Enlightenment. Scholars have rightly noted that *The Spirit of the Age* showed the weighty impression made on Mill by John Austin's theory of authority and by the Saint-Simonian conception of alternating 'organic' and 'critical' periods.[12] What has not been fully appreciated is Mill's massive concern with the disposition of political power in *The Spirit of the Age*. The search for authority could make no headway without a large-scale reform of England's political order.

The immediate context of Mill's 1831 series included a chain of political upheavals, the revolutions in France and Belgium being followed in short order by uprisings in Italy, Germany and Poland. In English politics, the long-lived (and increasingly decrepit) Tory ascendancy came to an abrupt end in November 1830, when the ministry led by the Duke of Wellington and Sir Robert Peel resigned in the wake of its defeat in the House of Commons. The force of circumstance – the threat of civil war in Ireland and the presence of a pro-Catholic majority in the House of Commons – had persuaded Wellington and Peel to introduce a bill for Catholic emancipation in early 1829. Its passage, with Whig support, enraged many Tories, who blamed their leaders for sponsoring a measure ruinous to the integrity of the Protestant Constitution in church and state. From this development J.S. Mill took heart, telling his friend Gustave d'Eichtal that 'the alteration of so important and so old a law as that which excludes Catholics from political privileges, has given a shake to men's minds which has loosened all old prejudices, and will render them far more accessible to new ideas and to rational innovations on all other parts of our institutions … As for the Tory party, it is broken; it is entirely gone.'[13] For years the Catholic question had dominated the domestic political scene. Its settlement opened critical space for the issue of parliamentary reform. The defeat of Wellington and Peel came soon after the former had declared his adamant opposition to a reform of the electoral system. The country receiving this declaration was already in an excited state. Thomas Attwood's Birmingham Political Union, dedicated to the cause of radical reform and supported by both the middle and working classes of the city, had been founded in December 1829. In the following months political unions sprang up in a great many towns. The accession of William IV prompted a general election in the summer of 1830, and parliamentary reform figured as one of the leading topics of discussion during this contest. Although inconclusive, the results brought no comfort to opponents of reform. The July Revolution in Paris gave further impetus to the movement for constitutional change. Upon the fall of Wellington and Peel, the new king, who had an open mind on the question of electoral reform, called upon Lord Grey to form a government. Grey, a Whig elder statesman, had a long-standing commitment to parliamentary reform (one dating from the 1790s), and the Whig-dominated coalition assembled near the close of 1830 clearly intended to move on the issue.

Worsening economic conditions heightened the political tension. A poor harvest in 1828 was followed by a worse one in 1829. A modest improvement in the yield of 1830 did not significantly mitigate the gathering effects of high bread prices, a slack demand for industrial goods, declining wages and rising unemployment. Extensive economic hardship bred widespread discontent, most spectacularly manifested in the spate of machine-breaking and arson that convulsed the agricultural counties of the south and east in the summer and autumn of 1830.[14] The mix of political agitation, social disorder and a generally sulky populace caused anxiety within the governing classes, whose disquiet did not perturb the eldest son of James Mill.

J.S. Mill claimed no originality for his assertion that 'the times are pregnant with change'; on the contrary, he observed that perception of this reality was 'already not far from being universal'.[15] Did awareness of an unfolding radical economic transformation inform Mill's conception of the change with which the times were pregnant? Not really. The rise of industrial society is not a theme of the transition Mill speaks of. In *The Spirit of the Age*, the Protestant Reformation is treated as the event marking the birth of the current era, and nothing Mill says elsewhere suggests that he ever thought otherwise. This notion matched the Saint-Simonian temporal scheme, which considered the Catholic Middle Ages the last 'organic' period in the history of European civilization. Mill observed: 'the age of transition arrived ... Mankind outgrew their religion, and that, too, at a period when they had not yet outgrown their government, because the texture of the latter was more yielding, and could be stretched.'[16] What event showed they had also 'outgrown their government'? The eruption of the great French Revolution, 'the first overt manifestation' of Europe's entering 'the state of transition'.[17] This 'overt manifestation', though a phenomenon of the eighteenth century, was the political expression of a movement of mind whose origins lay in the Protestant Reformation.

Mill did not overlook the obvious when he failed to give special significance to the effects of industrialization in his investigation of the problem of power and authority in an age of transition. Most economic historians now agree that the so-called Industrial Revolution of the late eighteenth and early nineteenth centuries was chiefly defined by a sizeable shift of workers from the agricultural into the industrial sector. The latter sector, however, was highly diverse in character, and the technology upon which most manufacturing relied remained labour-intensive. Attentive to the fact that an ever-increasing proportion of the wage-earning labour force was being employed outside the agricultural sphere, Mill was none the less disposed to see this development as the concomitant of an evolving commercial society. In England, the habits of getting and spending intrinsic to a market economy were well established long before the late eighteenth century. By the middle part of that century the agricultural sector, itself highly commercialized, was already providing for the country's food requirements without drawing upon the labour of a majority of the population. Mill had little personal experience of England's industrializing heartland, if Lancashire be taken as its location. He lived in the richest city in the world, and much of what he saw around him constituted the hub of an advancing commercial society, within which 'manufactures', as he understood the term, had long occupied an important place.

At the time Mill wrote *The Spirit of the Age* the construction of Britain's railway system was in its infancy; the agricultural sector accounted for a quarter of the working population and the number of people toiling as agricultural labourers was still on the rise (the ratio of males working as agricultural labourers to those working in all branches of the textile industry was roughly two to one); three-quarters of the population lived in communities of fewer than 20,000 inhabitants; over 90 per cent of the country's 'industrial workers' had no experience of factory employment. While the British economy was a good deal more 'industrialized' in 1831 than it had been in 1801, most of its vital elements would have been familiar to a London man of business of the mid-eighteenth century. Mill considered himself well-placed to grasp the essence of his era, remarking in *The Spirit of the Age* that a man 'may learn in a morning's walk through London more of the history of England during the nineteenth century, than all the professed histories in existence will tell him concerning the other eighteen'.[18]

The most momentous social change occurring between 1750 and 1831 was demographic. In 1750 the population of England (Wales and Scotland excluded) approached six million; in 1801 it stood at over eight million; by 1831 it had reached thirteen million. The social and economic ramifications of such a rate of population growth were profound. The relation of this unprecedented rise in population to industrialization, however, is problematic. Ireland, whose annual rate of population growth between 1750 and 1831 exceeded that of England, saw little in the way of urbanization and industrialization. Socially and economically, Ireland remained overwhelmingly rural and agrarian, subsistence agriculture retaining an ultimately disastrous prominence. J.S. Mill, in any case, never assumed that an expanding industrial sector would necessarily bring about an improvement in the standard of living experienced by the masses. Such an improvement, in his view, depended upon the labouring classes' restricting their own numbers, thereby enhancing the market value of their labour. The bearing of population growth on Mill's exploration of 'the spirit of the age' was cultural and political rather than economic, and involved 'the increase of the town-population, which brings masses of men together, and accustoms them to examine and discuss important subjects with one another'.[19] Mill's bland depiction of this evidently salutary development confirms that the crisis he apprehended in *The Spirit of the Age* did not stem from the alarming effects of industrialization.

In *The Spirit of the Age* Mill argued that established institutions and traditional elites had lost their hold over the minds of men. The incapacity of those in whom 'worldly power' and 'moral influence' had been concentrated stood nakedly exposed. The advance of civilization – an increase in the number of people enjoying a measure of material well-being, the rising level of literacy, the spread of elementary education, the growth of towns and the greater opportunities for the exchange of goods and ideas this growth afforded – had undermined the authority of a governing class whose initial fitness for rule had been forged in very different circumstances. Prevailing conditions, however, did not yet permit the formation of a new set of men, doctrines and institutions able to gain the assent and respect of the masses. This transitional state would eventually make way for a better order of things, a 'natural' state, in which political power and moral sway would rest in the hands of the fittest persons, whose authority society at large would unhesitatingly accept. Mill declared: 'the first men of the age will one day join hands and be agreed: and then there is no power on earth or in hell itself, capable of withstanding them.'[20] This assertion does not mean he looked forward to a time when 'the first men of the age' could coerce the multitude into submission. All individuals, Mill believed, should use the reason and judgement at their disposal. In so doing, they would probably see that it was in their interest to defer to the superior knowledge and understanding of others. The daily realities facing the vast majority of people could not be reconciled with the systematic examination of 'physical, moral, and social truths'.[21] When the minority qualified to undertake such investigations succeeded in placing the moral and social sciences on a footing with the physical sciences, the multitude would see the wisdom in trusting the authority of those who had mastered these pivotal fields of inquiry.

The theory of authority set forth in *The Spirit of the Age* owed more to John Austin than to the Saint-Simonians. James Mill had arranged for his eldest son to read Roman Law with Austin during the winter of 1821–22. Austin's powerful intellect and solemn character made a deep impression on the younger Mill. In the autumn of 1829 Austin delivered his first set of lectures as Professor of Jurisprudence and the Law of Nations in the recently created University of London. John Mill was among those who regularly attended these twice-weekly evening presentations, and he took extensive notes.[22] In his third lecture Austin delineated a theory of authority that prefigured, and markedly influenced, Mill's treatment of the issue in *The Spirit of the Age*. Austin asserted that 'an inquiry into the tendencies of actions embraces so spacious a field that none but the comparatively few, who study the science assiduously, can apply the principle [of utility] extensively to received or positive rules, and determine how far they accord with its genuine suggestions or dictates.'[23] Acknowledging that students of the subject had hitherto reached divergent conclusions, Austin conceded that a system of ethics perfect in conception and practice was unattainable. Substantial advance he did think possible, even likely; a dedication to impartial inquiry and the application of apt method and patient investigation, Austin urged, 'would thoroughly dispel the obscurity by which the science is clouded, and would clear it from most of its uncertainties.'[24] Furthermore, as experience and knowledge radiated more widely among the masses, they would be increasingly inclined to accept the guidance of the highly-instructed persons responsible for shaping and disseminating a coherent body of doctrine. A reasoned respect would then inform the deference offered by the multitude. 'Though most or many of their opinions would still be taken from *authority*, the authority to which they would trust might satisfy the most scrupulous reason.'[25] When Mill stated, in *The Spirit of the Age*, that 'reason itself will teach most men that they must, in the last resort, fall back upon the authority of still more cultivated minds, as the ultimate sanction of the convictions of their reason itself', he was himself falling back (a bit clumsily too) upon the authority of one whose mind he considered more cultivated than his own.[26]

Mill had no need to draw upon the thought of John Austin when explaining how those caught up in the evils of a transitional age could best promote the birth of a new age of authority. Throughout his formative years Mill had been taught that the power and influence of the landed classes stood as the major obstacle to progressive change. The reading he did in the late 1820s convinced him that the men who had initially acquired and sustained pre-eminence must have shown the qualities then required for effective rule. 'The possessor of power', he observed in *The Spirit of the Age*, 'was not in the situation of one who is rewarded without exertion, but of one who feels a great prize within his grasp, and is stimulated to every effort necessary to make it securely his own.'[27] This reading did nothing to shake his conviction that the political might of the aristocracy in the early nineteenth century corrupted public morality and hindered the march of mind. For generations England's titled nobility and gentry had held worldly power without being called upon to display the vigour and skill indispensable to the survival of their ancestors. Their energy had dissipated, and their ability had withered away. Meanwhile, the civilizing forces at work in English society had brought forth groups of men better fitted for the exercise of power than the territorial aristocracy. Conditions were not yet ripe for these men to claim and exercise the kind of authority Austin and Mill yearned to see created. They were ripe for ridding the political system of aristocratic dominance, the essential next step for advancing English society towards a more healthy state. 'Worldly power', Mill insisted, 'must pass from the hands of the stationary part of mankind into those of the progressive part.'[28]

The Spirit of the Age sternly maintained that a fundamental reform of England's political order was imperative. Referring to the country's traditional governing class, Mill asserted that 'their effect is now ... to degrade our morals, and to narrow and blunt our understandings: nor shall we ever be what we might be ... until our institutions are adapted to the present state of civilization, and made compatible with the future progress of the human mind.'[29] This adaptation would 'leave to no man one fraction of unearned distinction or unearned importance.'[30] Mill did not call this transformation a 'political' revolution because he knew such a term would conjure up violent images in the minds of his readers. Instead he called it 'a moral and social revolution,' one that would 'take away no men's lives or property.'[31] The discussion that followed, however, made clear that a sweeping redistribution of political power was the paramount precondition of this 'moral and social revolution'. Near the close of *The Spirit of the Age* Mill emphatically underscored this point. The 'higher classes', he announced, 'must ... be divested of the monopoly of worldly power, ere the most virtuous and best-instructed of the nation will acquire that ascendancy over the opinions and feelings of the rest, by which alone England can emerge from this crisis of transition, and enter once again into a natural state of society.'[32]

Although Mill lauded the blessings of a 'natural state of society', and lamented the woes of a transitional state, there are grounds for thinking he liked his chances in an age of change. Earned distinction was not a matter to which the young John Mill was personally indifferent. Once the aristocratic grip on political power had been broken – an event whose realization he thought might be near – opportunities to obtain great influence would open up for virtuous and well-instructed young men (among whom he surely counted himself). They could step forward to help construct the mental, moral and political edifice worthy of a 'natural' state. John Mill's generation, unlike his father's, might hope to see the dawn of the new era.

The Spirit of the Age included a striking commentary on the role of age and youth in transitional and natural states. A distinguishing trait of a natural state of society, Mill noted, was the great moral sway enjoyed by the aged. The community rightly valued their knowledge of human nature, their long practical acquaintance with matters of business, their far-reaching experience in the conduct of public affairs. In a time of transition, however, the experience and strongly-held convictions of the old were liabilities rather than assets. The turn taken by history in a transitional age placed a premium on society's capacity to 'change its opinions and its feelings.'[33] The 'greater flexibility of the young' counted for more than the fixed habits and principles of the old. Mill stipulated that 'their greater accessibility to new ideas and new feelings' made the young 'the sole hope of society.'[34] He hastened to add, in keeping with the sombre tone of *The Spirit of the Age*, that no solace could be had from this regrettable dependence on the young, who lacked the qualifications needed to make best use of the scope for action circumstances now presented. Yet even among the young there were exceptional cases. 'A young man *cannot*, unless his history has been a most extraordinary one, possess either that knowledge of life, which is necessary in the most difficult and important practical business, or that knowledge of the most recondite parts of human nature, which is equally necessary for the foundation of sound ethical and even political principles'.[35] The young man prepared to elucidate the *zeitgeist* presumably saw that his own 'history' had been a remarkable one. Beneath the lugubrious surface of *The Spirit of the Age* ran a current of heady expectation. The emergence of the 'natural state' was not imminent, and this, if one happened to be John Mill, was perhaps just as well.

Joseph Hamburger's justly influential book on J.S. Mill and the Philosophic Radicals asserts that Mill 'remained aloof from politics' in the early 1830s.[36] Hamburger holds that only after 1833 did Mill return to 'his old role as spokesman for Radicalism as a political program.'[37] In a letter written in late October 1831 – a time when much of the country was in an uproar over the Lords' rejection of the Second Reform bill – Mill told his friend John Sterling that he was himself 'often surprised' by 'how little' he cared about politics. One of the reasons he felt the need to say this to Sterling was that he had just treated him to a lengthy commentary on the politics of the day: 'You will perhaps think from this long prosing rambling talk about politics, that they occupy much of my attention'.[38] In March 1833 Mill wrote to Thomas Carlyle: 'For myself, I have well-nigh ceased to feel interested in politics.'[39] Sterling revered Coleridge; Carlyle admired Carlyle. Neither man had any use for 'politics', as James Mill understood the notion. John Mill was passing through his most acute phase of Carlylean intoxication – 'The Bad, God wot, is tumbling down quite as fast as is safe where there is nothing of Good ready to be put into its place'.[40] He had won Carlyle's good opinion, and he meant to keep it. An open display of engagement with mundane political matters would not further this end.

The fact is that the early 1830s saw a quickening of Mill's political pulse. His correspondence and extensive newspaper writings of the early 1830s evince powerful political preoccupations. In these years John Mill's journalistic activity kicked into high gear. Between July 1830 and the end of 1834 he contributed nearly 230 items to newspapers, the great majority of which carried political freight. Reaching a newspaper readership was important to a young man who viewed the press as a vital instrument of power in an age of transition. In February 1834 he affirmed, in 'Notes on the Newspapers', that

> The social position of the newspaper press in this country is altogether anomalous. In all the circumstances by which we are surrounded there is no more striking indication of a society in a state of moral revolution. If there be a law in human affairs which seems universal, it is, that the respect of mankind follows power, in whatsoever hands residing. In England, however, the seat of power has changed, and the respect of mankind has not yet found its way to the new disposers of their destiny. Nobody denies that the newspapers govern the country.[41]

This is not to say that Mill had a high opinion of most of those who wrote for the English press. In a letter to Gustave d'Eichtal of November 1829 he contrasted the state of the press in France and England. 'In France the best thinkers & writers of the nation, write in the journals & direct public opinion; but our daily & weekly writers are the lowest hacks of literature'.[42]

France was much on Mill's mind in the early 1830s. As the French Revolution of 1789 embodied the unmistakable political arrival of the age of transition, so the fall of Charles X in 1830 promised a new age of productive reform. Acting as the *Examiner*'s chief commentator on French affairs during the early 1830s, Mill kept readers of Albany Fonblanque's radical weekly informed of the developments shaping the political fortunes of France. Many aspects of French cultural and intellectual life had exerted a potent attraction for John Mill ever since his sojourn in France in 1820–21.[43] Astringently critical of English insularity and smugness, Mill worried that the character and significance of the Revolution of 1830 would be misrepresented by an ignorant and prejudiced English press. He believed the direction taken by events in France after July 1830 would have important consequences for the course of change both within and beyond French borders. In his *Examiner* articles he aimed to supply his contemporaries with a discriminating discussion of these events and a percipient analysis of their implications.[44]

Mill liked to think that his personal investment in such events was no bar to fashioning an acute analysis of their import. A strong romantic current flowed through John Mill's political veins. Radical action, when animated by the noble desire to create a free and virtuous political order dedicated to promoting the moral, mental and material improvement of the masses, gripped his imagination. In the part taken by the common people and the popular press of Paris during the July Days he saw an inspiring blend of bold action and righteous restraint. On 20 August 1830 John Mill began a long letter to his father with an extravagant tribute to the working classes of Paris.

> I have not heard one word of self-applause, nor boasting about the heroism ... of the people of Paris, nor any credit taken to themselves for having preserved order or avoided excesses; it does not seem to occur to them at all that they have done any thing extraordinary. They had but one idea, that of fighting for their legal rights, and the observance of the legal rights of others followed as an immediate corollary. The inconceivable purity and singleness of purpose ... which they all shew in speaking of these events, has given me a greater love for them than I thought myself capable of feeling for so large a collection of human beings, and the more exhilarating views which it opens of human nature will have a beneficial effect on the whole of my future life.[45]

The dispatching of the reactionary Bourbon regime with a minimum of violence instilled in him the hope that a constitutional government exemplifying what was best in the French character and intellect would emerge. Yet the social and political conditions that allowed for the removal of Charles X could not deliver the system Mill longed to see put in place.

The young Englishman so enraptured by what he believed the people of Paris had accomplished in the July Days soon felt the sobering effects of Louis Philippe's bourgeois monarchy. It could hardly be otherwise, deep disappointment being the inevitable outcome of inflated expectations. Mill identified wholeheartedly with what he deemed 'the popular party' in France. More a 'movement' than a 'party', its adherents pressed for a wide extension of the franchise for elections to the Chamber of Deputies, a greatly-reduced property qualification for candidates, and an elimination of the hereditary principle from the composition of the peerage. They also urged the creation of broad-based representative institutions at the municipal level. Mill vigorously supported these reforms, which he thought essential to securing good government. The men whose programme he strenuously endorsed, however, were not the men able to make the political running after the July Days. Writing to his father from Paris in late August, Mill expressed concern that the popular cause was already in jeopardy. 'Having effected their glorious object, they [the common people of Paris] calmly retired to their homes and resumed their accustomed avocations. The *educated* and the *rich* now came upon the stage ... The old generals and courtiers of Napoleon, the abettors and fautors of Charles, the rich bourgeois, all appeared in the character of place-hunting courtiers of Philippe. A spectacle more disgusting can hardly be imagined.'[46] What happened thereafter did not lessen his disgust. Louis Philippe and his political accomplices considered those without substantial resources unfit for participation in the new political order. Mill's article for the 19 September issue of the *Examiner* stated: 'The monied class has stepped into the place of both the King [Charles X] and of his allies, the emigrants [the aristocratic allies who had returned to France with the restoration of the Bourbons] and the clergy. When itself excluded from the Government, this class made common cause with the people. Now, however, it composes the Government: and being a narrow Oligarchy, it has the same interests with any other Oligarchy.'[47]

Incensed by the aggrandizement of the affluent and the well-connected, Mill defended those calling for large changes and excoriated their opponents. He ardently expressed his sympathies and enmities, as the following passage from an article written in mid-February 1831 illustrates: 'It is astonishing to us how the popular leaders find patience to bear up, without any attempts at retaliation, against the reproaches heaped upon them every day by an insolent and corrupt oligarchy, whose shameless greed of places and dignities has equaled or surpassed anything previously known even in the worst times of the Restoration.'[48] Louis Philippe's readiness to embrace the cause of this 'insolent and corrupt oligarchy' led Mill to invoke the prospect of further upheavals. The king's dismissal of magistrates who had revealed 'democratic inclinations' moved Mill to declare that 'Posterity at least will know, if contemporaries do not, on whose head the responsibility should rest of all the evils which may result from another struggle, followed by another convulsion.'[49] Mill held that the continued provocations of the new regime – its crass opportunism, its refusal to enact forward-looking legislation, its recurring resort to repressive measures when facing agitation and disturbance kindled by its own flagrant defects – had alienated the progressive forces that had brought down Charles X. Louis Philippe's government had 'made an enemy of every man in France, who either stirred, or would have dared to stir, a finger or a foot to place that Government where it is.'[50] Having entered a critical phase in an age of transition, French society needed at the helm leaders who understood the imperative of 'movement'. Instead, it found itself misgoverned by 'the Stationaries'.[51]

Mill gave his analysis a notable generational spin. He asserted that the dominion of Napoleon had corrupted the formative years of most of the men dominating the post-1830 French political scene. The despotism imposed by Napoleon had exceptional ambition and reach: 'no other despotism which we have known applied so great a power, or applied it so systematically, to the purpose of degrading the human mind.'[52] Bonaparte had muzzled the press and closed up all channels of public discourse; he had discouraged all scientific activity unrelated to the making of war and all investigations concerned with the first principles of the moral and political sciences; he had restored to the Catholic Church a predominant influence over the nation's educational system. It should come as no surprise, Mill observed, 'that men who were trained, and passed the best years of their lives, at a time when the human intellect was chained up, should be a puny race.'[53] The contrast between such men and those between the ages of twenty and thirty-five – *'jeune France'* – was stark. The latter had been educated in years when France had enjoyed 'comparatively free institutions' (Charles X's design to eviscerate these institutions and return France to the ways of the *ancien régime* had spurred the July Days). They had risen to maturity in a time of lively and open political discussion, a time when many new books were published and read. Their opportunities, idealism and serious pursuit of learning had determined that 'it is among them alone that fit successors will be found in point of intellect, to the best men whom France has produced in the former periods of its history.'[54] A pity it was that power should be exercised by the petty and self-serving men who had lined up with Louis Philippe rather than by those best able to guide the political destinies of France.

During the first half of the 1830s one Frenchman in particular engrossed John Mill's political imagination. Armand Carrel was the editor of the *National*, a radical newspaper founded in 1830. Born in 1800, and therefore only six years older than Mill, Carrel had joined with Adolphe Thiers and François Mignet to create an organ whose original purpose was the destruction of the Polignac ministry and the Bourbon monarchy.[55] When this end had been met, Thiers and Mignet – each in his own way – came to terms with Louis Philippe's bourgeois monarchy. Not so Carrel, who, until his death in a duel in 1836, employed his brilliant journalistic gifts to denounce the regime and to uphold the democratic cause. Mill had greatly admired Carrel's work before the two men met in November 1833, when Mill was in Paris with Harriet Taylor. A letter he wrote Carlyle on 25 November understandably made no mention of Harriet Taylor; of Carrel it had much to say.

> I knew Carrel as the most powerful journalist in France, the sole manager of a paper which while it keeps aloof from all *coterie* influence & from the actively revolutionary part of the republican body, has for some time been avowedly republican; & I knew that he was considered a vigorous, energetic *man of action*, who would always have courage & conduct in an emergency … Knowing thus much of him, I was ushered into the National office … I was introduced to a slight elegant young man with extremely polished manners … and apparently fitter for a drawing-room than a camp…But it was impossible to be five minutes in his company without perceiving that he was accustomed to *ascendancy*, & so accustomed as not to feel it; instead of that eagerness & impetuosity which one finds in most Frenchmen, his manner is extremely deliberate; without any affectation he speaks in a sort of measured cadence, & in a manner of which your words 'quiet emphasis' are more

characteristic than of any man I know: there is the same quiet emphasis in his writings: a man singularly free, if we may trust appearances, from self-consciousness; simple, graceful, almost *infantinely* playful as they all say when he is among his intimates, & indeed I could see that myself; & combining perfect self-reliance with the most unaffected modesty ...[56]

Mill turned from personal traits to political location, saying that Carrel held 'a midway position, facing one way towards the supporters of monarchy & an aristocratic limitation on the suffrage, with whom he will have no compromise, on the other towards the extreme republicans who have anti-property doctrines, and ... want a republic ... with something like dictatorship in their own hands'. Carrel, Mill added, did not see himself as qualified to occupy high political office. Journalism was his *métier*, Carrel declared, and his craft did not allow him time for 'study'. He considered himself 'profoundly ignorant of much upon which he would have to decide if he were in power; & could do nothing but bring together a body generally representative of the people, & assist in carrying into execution the dictates of their united wisdom.' Mill, however, demurred from Carrel's self-assessment, contending that he was 'the man who would certainly be President of the Republic if there were a republic within five years & the extreme party did not get the upper hand.'[57]

Carrel's example inspired Mill during the 1830s, when he sought to act the part of Carrel in an English context.[58] In his commemorative essay on Carrel, published in 1837, Mill proclaimed that the 'true idea of Carrel is not that of a literary man, but of a man of action, using the press as his instrument'.[59] The authority of the leader stemmed from his ability to fuse thought and action. According to Mill, 'the man to lead his age is he who has been familiar with thought directed to the accomplishment of immediate objects, and who has been accustomed to see his theories brought early and promptly to the test of experiment'. This individual would see 'at the end of every theorem to be investigated, a problem to be solved' and would have 'learned early to weigh the means which can be exerted against the obstacles which are to be overcome, and to make an estimate of means and of obstacles habitually a part of all his theories that have for their object practice, either at the present or at a more distant period.'[60] Carrel, in Mill's view, had been such a man.[61]

James Mill – who died the same year as Carrel – had himself been a leader of men, but of a kind different from what John Mill had in mind. The former had served as the efficient head of a school of Benthamites. Carrel, unlike James Mill, 'had an intellect capacious enough to appreciate and sympathize with whatever of truth or ultimate value to mankind there might be in all theories, together with a rootedly practical turn of mind, which seized and appropriated to itself such part only of them as might be realized, or at least might be hoped to be realized, in his own day.'[62] Although James Mill had an aptitude for practical action, he lacked the healthy expansiveness of intellect John Mill found in Carrel. For the younger Mill, Carrel brilliantly exemplified an era in French thought, one that saw the liberation of the French mind from both the classical conventions of the seventeenth century and the 'narrowness' of the eighteenth. The autobiographical content in Mill's characterization of the generational change that had occurred is plain. The period during which Carrel (and John Mill) had come of age had seen the French 'national intellect' move 'from the stage of adolescence to early maturity.' This development corresponded

> To that in an individual mind, when, after having been taught to think (as every one is) by teachers of some particular school, and having for a time exercised the power only in the path shown to it by its first teachers, it begins, without abandoning that, to tread also in other paths; learns to see with its naked eyes, and not through the eye-glasses of its teachers, and, from being one-sided, becomes many-sided and of no school.[63]

This metaphor says more about its author than about the state of the French 'national intellect'. Mill mythologized Carrel as the journal editor who became 'the most powerful political leader of his age and country'.[64] For the author of *The Spirit of the Age* in 1831, the English commentator on French affairs in the early 1830s, and the de facto editor of the *London and Westminster Review* not long thereafter, there was little to choose between the primacy of the political and the primacy of the personal.

Notes

1 J.M. Robson and J. Stillinger (eds), *Autobiography and Literary Essays*, in *The Collected Works of John Stuart Mill* (henceforth cited as *CW*), vol. 1, Toronto: University of Toronto Press, 1981, p. 156.
2 'Civilization', in J.M. Robson (ed.), *Essays on Politics and Society*, *CW*, vols. 18–19, Toronto: University of Toronto Press, 1977, vol. 18, p. 139.
3 'The British Constitution [2]', in J.M. Robson (ed.), *Journals and Debating Speeches*, *CW*, vol. 26, Toronto: University of Toronto Press, 1988, p. 382.
4 F.E. Mineka (ed.), *The Earlier Letters of John Stuart Mill 1812 to 1848*, *CW*, vols. 12–13, Toronto: University of Toronto Press, 1963, vol. 12, p. 32.
5 Ibid., p. 40.
6 Robson and Stillinger (eds), *Autobiography and Literary Essays*, *CW*, vol. 1, p. 177.
7 Ibid.
8 Ibid., p. 189.
9 Ibid., p. 177.
10 Ibid., p. 179.
11 A.P. Robson and J.M. Robson (eds), *Newspaper Writings*, *CW*, vols. 22–25, Toronto: University of Toronto Press, 1986, vol. 22, p. 230.
12 See especially R.B. Friedman, 'An Introduction to Mill's Theory of Authority', in J.B. Schneewind (ed.), *Mill: A Collection of Critical Essays*, Notre Dame, Indiana: Notre Dame University Press, 1969, pp. 379–425.
13 *Earlier Letters*, *CW*, vol. 12, p, 28.
14 For a valuable account of these disturbances in the English countryside, see Eric Hobsbawm and George Rudé, *Captain Swing: A Social History of the Great English Agricultural Uprising of 1830*, New York: Pantheon Books, 1968.
15 *Newspaper Writings*, *CW*, vol. 22, p. 228.
16 Ibid., p. 306.

17 Ibid., p. 292.
18 Ibid., p. 230.
19 Ibid., p. 279.
20 Ibid., p. 245.
21 Ibid., p. 242.
22 Other members of John Austin's first class included Charles Buller, Henry Cole, J.A. Roebuck, George Cornewall Lewis, John Romilly, Edward Strutt, C.P. Villiers and Edwin Chadwick. Chadwick and Cole excepted, all these young men would eventually enter the House of Commons, as would Mill himself, although long after the others. See Lotte and Joseph Hamburger, *Troubled Lives: John and Sarah Austin*, Toronto: University of Toronto Press, 1985, p. 56.
23 Austin's lectures were published in 1832 under the title *The Province of Jurisprudence Determined*. I have made use of the 1954 reprint edition (New York: Noonday Press). The passage quoted appears at p. 73 of this edition.
24 *Province of Jurisprudence Determined*, p. 79.
25 Ibid.
26 *Newspaper Writings*, *CW*, vol. 22, p. 244. In presenting this account of Mill's debt to John Austin relative to *The Spirit of the Age*, I have drawn heavily on Friedman's seminal essay, 'An Introduction to Mill's Theory of Authority', cited in note 12 above.
27 *Newspaper Writings*, *CW*, vol. 22, p. 280.
28 Ibid., p. 245.
29 Ibid., p. 282.
30 Ibid., p. 245.
31 Ibid.
32 Ibid., p. 316.
33 Ibid., p. 294.
34 Ibid., p. 295.
35 Ibid., p. 294.
36 Joseph Hamburger, *Intellectuals in Politics: John Stuart Mill and the Philosophic Radicals*, New Haven, Connecticut: Yale University Press, 1965, p. 86.
37 Ibid., p. 96.
38 *Earlier Letters*, *CW*, vol. 12, p. 78; the 'long prosing rambling talk' can be found at pp. 75–78.
39 Ibid., p. 145.
40 Ibid.
41 'Notes on the Newspapers', in J.M. Robson (ed.), *Essays on England, Ireland, and the Empire*, *CW*, vol. 6, Toronto: University of Toronto Press, 1982, p. 163.
42 *Earlier Letters*, *CW*, vol. 12, pp. 38–39.
43 John Mill's French experience of 1820–21 was made possible by an invitation from Sir Samuel Bentham and his family, who had taken up domicile at Pompignan, not far from Toulouse. For Mill's journal of his French sojourn, see Anna J. Mill (ed.), *John Mill's Boyhood Visit to France: A Journal and Notebook*, Toronto: University of Toronto Press, 1960.
44 For valuable commentaries on Mill's response to the Revolution of 1830, see Iris W. Mueller, *John Stuart Mill and French Thought*, Urbana, Illinois: University of Illinois Press, 1956, pp. 17–47; J. C. Cairns's introduction to J.M. Robson (ed.), *Essays on French History and Historians*, *CW*, vol. 20, Toronto: University of Toronto Press, 1985, pp. xlv-lviii and lx-lxii; Marion Filipiuk, 'Mill and France', in Michael Laine (ed.), *A Cultivated Mind: Essays on J.S. Mill Presented to John M. Robson*, Toronto: University of Toronto Press, 1991, pp. 94–98; Georgios Varouxakis, *Mill on Nationality*, London: Routledge, 2002, pp. 62–66; Georgios Varouxakis, *Victorian Political Thought on France and the French*, Houndsmill, Basingstoke, Hampshire: Palgrave, 2002, pp. 58, 59, 60, 62–63, 65.
45 *Earlier Letters*, *CW*, vol. 12, pp. 55–56.

46 Ibid., p. 60.
47 *Newspaper Writings, CW*, vol. 22, p. 132.
48 Ibid., p. 262.
49 Ibid., p. 263.
50 Ibid., p. 298.
51 Ibid., p. 297.
52 Ibid., p. 154.
53 Ibid., p. 155.
54 Ibid., p. 156.
55 See Cairns's introduction to *Essays on French History and Historians, CW*, vol. 20, p. xii.
56 *Earlier Letters, CW*, vol. 12, pp. 194–95.
57 Ibid., pp. 195–96.
58 For an illuminating discussion of Carrel's exemplary status for Mill, see Ann P. Robson and John M. Robson, 'Private and Public Goals: John Stuart Mill and the *London and Westminster*', in Joel H. Wiener (ed.), *Innovators and Preachers: The Role of the Editor in Victorian England*, Westport, Connecticut: Greenwood Press, p. 232 and pp. 235–37.
59 *Essays on French History and Historians, CW*, vol. 20, p. 171.
60 Ibid., p. 174.
61 The exalted esteem in which Mill held Carrel was expressed to Sir William Molesworth in a letter Mill wrote in September 1837: 'I never admired any man as I did Carrel; he was to my mind the type of philosophic radical *man of action* in this epoch' (Francis E. Mineka and Dwight N. Lindley [eds], *The Later Letters of John Stuart Mill 1849 to 1873*, vols. 14–17, Toronto: University of Toronto Press, 1972, vol. 17, p. 1978).
62 *Essays on French History and Historians, CW*, vol. 20, p. 174.
63 Ibid., pp. 182–83.
64 'Fonblanque's England under Seven Administrations', in *Essays on England, Ireland, and the Empire, CW*, vol. 6, p. 380.

3 Competing theories of character formation

James vs. John Stuart Mill *

Terence Ball

Toward the end of *A System of Logic* (1843) – the first (and longest) of John Stuart Mill's many books – he sketches an outline of, and justification for, what he calls 'Ethology, or the science of character formation.'[1] This is to be the intermediate science or linch-pin of the moral sciences, linking the micro-level laws of individual psychology with the macro-level laws of sociology. Mill obviously sets great store by this new bridging 'science.' He stresses its centrality and importance, indeed its indispensability, in explaining why human beings behave as they do. And yet, oddly – so the long-standing scholarly consensus has it – Mill never attempted to develop this new science of Ethology. Mill's younger contemporary and associate Alexander Bain noted that after his *System of Logic* Mill's 'next book ... was to be on the new science, first sketched in the *Logic*, and there called "ethology." With parental fondness, he cherished this project for a considerable time; regarding it as the foundation and cornerstone of Sociology ... In fact, it never came to anything; and he seems shortly to have dropped thinking of it.'[2] Bain is hardly alone. He stands, indeed, at the head of a long line that stretches into our own day. As one modern commentator puts it, 'Mill enthusiastically advocates ethology but never really begins to construct even the rudiments of such a science.'[3] As another remarks, Mill 'regretted all his life that he had not been able to contribute more to its progress,' other than by merely introducing the idea in his *Logic*.[4] Another adds that 'Mill never managed to make any progress with this proposed study.'[5] 'Mill's own failure to contribute to this science [of ethology] was a source of disappointment and embarrassment to him,' says a prominent modern defender.[6] Because his new science was never actually constructed, it was 'aborted' before it could be born.[7] By the mid-1840s Mill 'gave up ... his attempt to found the new science of Ethology.'[8] Mill's most recent biographer goes further still, saying that 'Mill never even began constructing the ethology.'[9] It accordingly became his 'forgotten science.'[10] Mill's proposed work on Ethology was perhaps 'the greatest book Mill never wrote.'[11] Mill's hoped-for science of ethology was, in short, a flash in the pan, and nothing ever came of it.

My aim here is to challenge this long-standing scholarly consensus. It is indeed true that Mill never wrote a treatise on Ethology, or the science of character formation. He did, however, write four books dealing with apparently disparate topics but – so I shall argue – tied together by their common ethological concerns.

These comprised two case studies, an ethological account of the formation of civic character, and, not least, an essay on liberty as the wellspring of vivid and vigorous individual characters. The two case studies are concerned with the deformation and potential reformation of character. The first is an in-depth study of a single individual, namely Mill himself; that book is his *Autobiography*. The second is a study of the malformation and potential reformation of the characters of half the human race, namely women; that book is *The Subjection of Women*. The third of Mill's ethological studies deals with civic education, that is, the formation of civic character; that work is *Considerations on Representative Government*. Fourth and finally, Mill conducts an inquiry into the conditions conducive to the formation of strong and vigorous individual characters. Those conditions – free thought, unfettered discussion and the liberty to develop one's individual capacities to their fullest – are just those described at length and lauded in *On Liberty*. Taken together, and viewed from the new angle I propose here, these apparently disparate works may all be viewed as 'ethological' enquiries and even as works of *applied ethology*. Each is concerned with the conditions under which character is formed, or more precisely, deformed and perchance reformed. Without ever having written a systematic treatise on ethology, Mill nevertheless did undertake four important studies in applied ethology and thus contributed extensively and memorably to the science of character formation.

My route to this conclusion begins with a brief account of James Mill's and Robert Owen's hard-determinist theory of character formation which the younger Mill's science of ethology was meant to repudiate and replace. I next consider what Mill meant by ethology and why he thought it so central to the moral sciences. I then offer a re-reading of his *Autobiography* in light of its main themes and Mill's own, albeit brief, account of character formation in his *System of Logic*. This is followed by a re-reading of *The Subjection of Women* through the lens supplied by his *System of Logic*, and the science of Ethology more especially. I turn next to Mill's *Considerations on Representative Government* which, I contend, is in part a treatise on political ethology or the formation of civic character. I then suggest how all these works help to illuminate Mill's intentions in writing *On Liberty*.

1. James Mill and Robert Owen on the formation of character

The younger Mill's ethology was not only or merely meant to be a theory of character formation, but an account of the ways in which one may contribute to the formation of one's own character. His is, in short, a theory of character *self*-formation that is directed against James Mill's and Robert Owen's hard-determinist view that one's character is necessarily formed *for* one by others, and not by oneself. I begin therefore by briefly recounting the main tenets of the Owenite creed of character formation, since it jibed with the elder Mill's own views on that subject – views which the younger Mill repudiated, albeit in the fillially pious guise of a critique of Owen's views.

Robert Owen claimed that a person's character is "formed *for* him, and not *by* him." This deterministic (one might even say fatalistic) doctrine is articulated most fully in Owen's *A New View of Society: or, Essays on the Principles of the Formation of the Human Character* (1813). Owen held that

> children are, without exception, passive and wonderfully contrived com-pounds, which, by due preparation and accurate attention, founded on a correct knowledge of the subject, may be formed collectively into any human character ... They all partake of that plastic nature or quality, which, by per-severance under judicious management, may be ultimately moulded into the very image of rational wishes and desires.[12]

'Train any population rationally,' Owen adds, 'and they will be rational.' To this end he advocates 'a national system of formation of character.'[13] This end may be easily achieved inasmuch as human beings are merely 'living machines' which can be made to perform predictably and reliably.[14]

'The greatest of all errors, Owen insists, is 'the notion that individuals form their own characters.'[15] Indeed the chief tenet of the Owenite creed is

> That the character of man is, without a single exception, always formed for him; that it may be, and is chiefly, created by his predecessors; that they give him ... his ideas and habits, which are the powers that govern and direct his conduct. Man, therefore, never did, nor is it possible he ever can, form his own character.[16]

In a lengthy review of Owen's *New View of Society* in William Allen's *Philanthropist* James Mill praised and heartily endorsed Owen's deterministic theory, and reiterated his agreement in later essays, including 'Education' and 'Prisons and Prison Discipline.' 'Human beings,' wrote Mill, 'are the creatures of the circumstances in which they are placed.' Indeed, 'almost everything which constitutes character [is] the offspring of the impressions which, from sources over which he has no control, are made upon the individual.'[17] Mill adds that 'the character of every man is bad to the most enormous pitch of depravity, or good to the highest degree of excellence, exactly as it has been operated upon by circum-stances' in his early formative years.[18] The character of even the most depraved adult criminal was formed during his childhood:

> If a man's character, and even his opinions, are the unavoidable results of the circumstances in which he has been placed, he is not the object of any hostile feeling on account of them. They were not produced by circumstances over which he had any control. If they are bad, he deserves our pity; but hatred is altogether unreasonable.[19]

The upshot is that laws and their enforcement via punishment are attempts, af-ter the fact of character (mal)formation, to alter the dispositions of misfits and malefactors. The reach of the law and the power of punishment to reform, i.e. reform, misformed characters is very limited indeed.[20] Mill holds that 'laws are ... imperfect substitutes for the defects of character,' and 'no laws, where character is universally depraved, can save society from wretchedness.' Individual 'character, in proportion as it is good, really supplies the place of laws.' Therefore it is

> the first consideration of public wisdom, to ascertain in what degree it is possible to operate on the improvement of human character. This lies at the foundation of every thing. No law, or set of laws, ... can boast of a comprehensiveness and efficiency equal to this. Every other branch of legislation, in truth, sinks into insignificancy in the comparison.[21]

'Character' *peut tout.*

The elder Mill, like Owen, gave pride of place to 'character' and to the role of (as we might now say) socialization during early childhood. The human mind is a store of 'associations' of ideas that derive from experience.[22] And those associations first formed in childhood are, for better or worse, the most indelible and determinative of adult character:

> It seems to be a law of human nature, that the first sensations experienced produce the greatest effects; more especially, that the earliest repetitions of one sensation after another produce the deepest habit; the strongest propensity to pass immediately from the idea of the one to the idea of the other. Common language confirms this law, when it speaks of the susceptibility of the tender mind.[23]

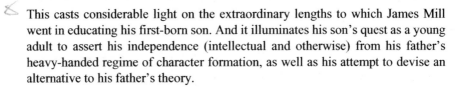 This casts considerable light on the extraordinary lengths to which James Mill went in educating his first-born son. And it illuminates his son's quest as a young adult to assert his independence (intellectual and otherwise) from his father's heavy-handed regime of character formation, as well as his attempt to devise an alternative to his father's theory.

2. Ethology: J.S. Mill's science of character formation

In the late 1820s Mill began sketching the outline for the book that became *A System of Logic.* He laboured over his *Logic* for twelve years, finally publishing it in 1843. He later deemed the *Logic* and *On Liberty* to be the most important and probably most enduring of his books.[24] Judging from the obituaries that appeared after his death, his contemporaries believed the *Logic* to be much the more important of the two.[25] We, on the other hand, are much more likely to read and regard *On Liberty* as the more important; few, indeed, now read his *Logic.* One of my aims here is to help redress the balance and to suggest that it is an error to overlook the *Logic* and its importance in our understanding of Mill's other, better-known works, including *On Liberty.*

Staunch rationalist that he was, Mill regarded pernicious political doctrines as the result of flawed reasoning. (Not for nothing did Gladstone call Mill the 'Saint of Rationalism.'[26]) Faulty deductions, false inferences, mistaken associations, imprecise or misleading words – these were among the props and mainstays of unexamined prejudice and unreasoning custom. Mill's aim was to 'rectify' these and other 'operations of the understanding ... But whatever may be the practical value of a true philosophy of these matters, it is hardly possible to exaggerate the mischiefs of a false one.' The mischief was wrought, more particularly, by the then-fashionable philosophy of 'intuitionism' as defended by that stalwart of English conservatism William Whewell, among others. 'There never was such an instrument devised for consecrating all deep seated prejudices.'[27] Mill hoped to oppose this sort of sclerotic conservatism by exposing, criticizing and offering a defensible alternative to the faulty modes or methods of reasoning upon which such conservatism rested. His *Logic*, then, had an avowedly political purpose. It was not, however, to be partisan in any narrowly sectarian sense. 'Logic,' Mill held, 'is common ground on which the partisans of Hartley and of Reid, of Locke and of Kant, may meet and join hands.'[28] Or so he hoped. In subsequent editions, Mill tried repeatedly to reply to and 'meet and join hands' with conservative critics. To his great disappointment, and no one else's surprise, this meeting of minds on the neutral field of 'logic' failed to materialize.

So much, then, for a brief history of the reception of and reaction to Mill's *Logic*. A book launched with high hopes had a chequered history and conveyed a mixed message. And nowhere was this ambivalent admixture more evident than in the sixth and final book of the *System of Logic*.

Mill begins Book VI by decrying 'the backward state of the Moral Sciences' as compared with the swift and cumulative advances of their natural or physical counterparts. He 'hope[s] to remove this blot on the face of science.' Although 'the most effectual mode of showing how the sciences of Ethics and Politics may be constructed would be to construct them,' his more modest ambition is merely 'to point out the way' in good Lockean underlabourer fashion by clearing away some of the logical confusions and semantic rubbish that have impeded the progress of the moral sciences; to show that the methods of the physical sciences are indeed applicable to the moral sciences; and to sketch the outlines of the new science that he calls Ethology.

Polar star or *idee fixe*, the formation of character became for Mill an abiding preoccupation.[29] As Bain rightly remarks, 'He was all his life possessed of the idea that differences of character, individual and national, were due to accidents and circumstances that might possibly be, in part, controlled; on this doctrine rested his chief hope for the future.'[30] It appears that Mill's preoccupation with character and how it is formed was itself overdetermined. In one sense this was a concern inherited from his father and Robert Owen. Mill's emphasis on character was also a staple of Victorian ethical-political discourse.[31] And, not least, that preoccupation can also be traced to his (and his father's) very Greek – and more particularly Platonic – concern with *paideia*, or the cultivation of character and intellect.[32]

The first two tasks that Mill sets himself are parts of a larger whole. He aims, firstly, to show that character is formed causally, by 'antecedent circumstances.' But he also tries to show that the causal formation of one's character does not mean that one is powerless to change one's character. Briefly, Mill's argument is this: It is sometimes said that if 'the actions of human beings, like all other natural events, [are] subject to invariable laws,' then human freedom or 'free will' is an illusion; and if we are not free, then we are automatons devoid of responsibility for our actions. We are unfree creatures caught in the net of causal and nomological necessity. Mill sets out to show that this claim rests on a series of semantic and other confusions surrounding 'the doctrine called Philosophical Necessity.' That doctrine,

> correctly conceived, ... is simply this: that, given the motives which are present to an individual's mind, and given likewise the character and disposition of the individual, the manner in which he will act might be unerringly inferred; that if we knew the person thoroughly, and knew all the inducements which are acting upon him, we could foretell his conduct with as much certainty as we can predict any physical event.

From this it does *not* follow that the person is the helpless slave of antecedent causes or circumstances. And why? Because, says Mill, we can change circumstances by adding our own wishes or volitions to the antecedent conditions that causally determine our conduct. 'That wish being ... a *new antecedent*' we thereby alter the outcome of a causally connected chain of events.[33]

My concern here is not with the logical validity of Mill's argument, but with its bearing on the question of character formation. The third of Mill's tasks is to sketch in rough outline the contours of the new science of ethology. This requires, among other things, refuting what might be termed the hard-determinist or even fatalistic doctrine of character formation and putting in its place an alternative theory of the self-formation or cultivation of character that is entirely consistent with the doctrine of philosophical necessity, properly understood. The fatalistic theory is well represented, Mill says, by the Owenite 'sect' to which his father and Bentham both belonged after their fashion. This supplies Mill with his target and stalking-horse. The Owenite doctrine that one's character, once formed for one by others, is formed finally and forever, Mill rejoins, 'is a grand error,' resting as it does on the misunderstanding of the doctrine of philosophical necessity that he had just refuted and corrected. 'His character is formed by [antecedent] circumstances ... but his own desire to mould it in a particular way is one of those circumstances, and by no means one of the least influential.' Just as those who initially moulded our character '*for* us' acted as they did because (in part) they willed or wished to mould us as they did, so can we re-mould or re-make our characters according to antecedent causes that include our wish to change who and what we are. 'If they could place us under the influence of certain circumstances, we, in like manner, can place ourselves under the influence of other circumstances. We are exactly as capable of making our own character, *if we will*, as others are of making it for us.'[34]

To the Owenite who replies that our will is no less the product of 'external causes' that are beyond our control, Mill counters that our characters are the product not only of an 'education' planned and carried out by others but also, *pace* Owen and James Mill, of contingent 'experience' and chance. Now among the attributes of the latter is the ever-present possibility of accident and of consequences unforeseen and unintended by our educators and – not least – neither willed nor intended by us. These include 'experience of the painful consequences of the character we previously had' or of 'some strong feeling of admiration or aspiration, accidentally aroused.'[35] (Keep these two sources of motivation in mind, for we shall encounter them again, in Mill's *Autobiography*.)

Whatever its subject matter, any science worthy of the name must in Mill's view be a science of causal and nomological necessity. We explain any event, whether it be a volcanic eruption or a human action, by deducing a description of it from premises that include all appropriate laws or general principles, along with a statement of the relevant antecedent conditions. Mill subscribes, in sum, to what later came to be called the deductive-nomological or 'covering-law' model of scientific explanation.[36] From this it follows that, if there is to be a science of character formation, it must be a science of causes and laws. It must be predicated on the doctrine of philosophical necessity, correctly understood. And a correct understanding of that doctrine, as applied to the moral sciences, Mill insists, requires that we recognize an individual's wishes or desires as being among the antecedent circumstances that cause his character and conduct to be what they are.

I cannot here consider Mill's proposed science of ethology in great detail. Suffice it to say that it is to be an intermediary science, linking psychology and its micro-level 'laws of the mind' with sociology and its macro-level laws concerning collectivities or classes of individuals. Psychology's 'general laws of the mind' are laws of association, *à la* Locke, Hartley and Hume (and of course James Mill): If an 'idea' or 'mental impression' A is invariably associated with another impression B, then the experience or recollection of the one will invariably call the other to mind.[37] To put it crudely, such laws are determinative of how and what we *think*. The laws of sociology are determinative of how we *act* in the aggregate, in concert with others and on the basis of beliefs formed by processes of association. Between these two sciences, and linking them, is the intermediate science of ethology. This new science is concerned with the types or kinds of characters formed via association and under different antecedent circumstances. People with different formative experiences will have different characters; and people with different characters will act in different ways, both individually and in conjunction with others. Ethology is, in short, the bridge or *via media* between psychology and sociology.

A science is thus formed, to which I would propose to give the name of Ethology, or the Science of Character, from *ethos*, a word more nearly corresponding to the term "character" as I here use it ... The name is perhaps etymologically applicable to the entire science of our mental and moral nature; but if, as is usual and convenient, we employ the name Psychology for the science of the elementary laws of mind, Ethology will serve for the ulterior science which determines the kind of character produced in conformity to those general laws by any set of circumstances, physical and moral ... Ethology is the science which corresponds to the art of education in the widest sense of the term, including the formation of national or collective character as well as individual.[38]

'Ethology,' Mill adds, 'is still to be created.' Its laws are to be derived from the elementary laws of psychology as applied to experience. 'The inference given by theory as to the type of character which would be formed by any given circumstances must be tested by specific experience of those circumstances wherever obtainable.'[39] And to this end Mill turned first to himself and the circumstances that had formed, and (as he thought) to some degree deformed, his own character.

3. Case 1: Mill's *Autobiography*

At first glance Mill's *Autobiography* appears to have a rather curious structure. It consists of seven chapters. The first five chronicle the author's life to 1830, when he was twenty-four; the sixth covers the years 1830–38, taking the author to age thirty-two. The relatively short seventh and final chapter – 'The Remainder of my Life' – deals summarily with the last thirty-three years of Mill's life. Although momentous indeed – these were the years that saw the publication of all his major works, his marriage, his election to and participation in Parliament – the second half of Mill's life is given short shrift. Why?

Mill himself supplies the answer. He calls his *Autobiography* the 'record of an education which was unusual and remarkable.'[40] By 1838 (and arguably as early as 1830) Mill's education was complete and his character fully formed. Because (as Mill says at the beginning of the final chapter) 'I have no further mental changes to tell of ... I shall therefore greatly abridge the chronicle of my subsequent years,' that is, the second half of his life.[41] The *Autobiography* deals almost exclusively with his early years, when his character was being formed (and to some degree deformed) by his father and subsequently re-formed by himself.

Mill's early education was meticulously planned and sternly supervised by his dour and demanding father. James Mill eagerly embraced Helvetius' dictum, *l'education peut tout*, and – as we have already seen – agreed with Robert Owen (among others) that 'character' is formed early and by 'circumstances.'[42] He subscribed wholeheartedly to Owen's dictum that our characters are formed for us and not by us. Under the right circumstances a child's character will be well-formed, and for life; but under the wrong circumstances his character will be stunted and misshapen, making for a life of misery, misconduct, perhaps even of crime.[43] James Mill was determined that his first-born son's character would be carefully moulded and shaped by the right circumstances, that is, by those that he deemed right and good.

A stern taskmaster, the elder Mill made few if any concessions to childish tastes and predilections, much less limitations. John Mill was largely kept away from other children, lest they be a bad influence. He was discouraged from playing games or engaging in other frivolous and time-wasting entertainments. As Mill later lamented to Caroline Fox, 'I never was a boy, never played at cricket.'[44] His friend J.A. Roebuck recalled his first impressions on meeting the 19 year-old Mill. He 'was the result of a most strict and extraordinary training. He was armed at all points … In his childhood and youth he had no playfellows.' 'He had never played with boys; in his life he had never known any, and we [i.e. Roebuck and George John Graham] were the first companions he had ever mixed with.'[45] Even then the elder Mill disapproved of this mixing.[46]

The pedagogical regimen to which the young Mill was subjected was, to say the least, both stringent and demanding. By age three he was learning Greek, and Latin by eight. He would later insist that his was not an education of 'cram' and that a great deal of good resulted from it.[47] But he lived in constant fear of his father's rebuke. In passages deleted (at Harriet Taylor Mill's insistence) from the final version of his *Autobiography* Mill wrote that 'mine was not an education of love but of fear.'[48]

> I thus grew up in the absence of love and in the presence of fear: and many and indelible are the effects of this bringing-up in the stunting of my moral growth … To have been, through childhood, under the constant rule of a strong will, certainly is not favourable to strength of will. I was so much accustomed to expect to be told what to do, either in the form of direct command or of rebuke for not doing it, that I acquired a habit of leaving my responsibility as a moral agent to rest on my father, my conscience never speaking to me except by his voice … I thus acquired a habit of backwardness, of waiting to follow the lead of others, an absence of moral spontaneity, an inactivity of the moral sense and even to a large extent, of the intellect … – for which a large abatement must be made from the benefits, either moral or intellectual, which flowed from any other part of my education.[49]

His father's influence was felt in the young Mill's every thought and attitude. 'My education,' Mill wrote, 'was wholly his work.'[50]

He had been trained by his father to be an analyst and reformer of society, and at first he relished the role he had been assigned. 'From the winter of 1821, when I first read Bentham, … I had what might truly be called an object in life; to be a reformer of the world.'[51] Bentham's principle of utility 'gave unity to my conceptions of things. I now had opinions; a creed, a doctrine, a philosophy; in one among the the best senses of the word, a religion; the inculcation and diffusion of which could be made the principal outward purpose of a life.'[52]

And then this reasoning machine rebelled, or at any rate sputtered and ceased to function as before. In his early twenties Mill underwent 'a crisis in my mental history' – an understated way of saying that he had a mental breakdown. Beginning in the Autumn of 1826, Mill fell into a depression, further deepened by an awful discovery:

> In this frame of mind it occurred to me to put the question directly to myself, 'Suppose that all your objects in life were realized; that all the changes in institutions and opinions which you are looking forward to, could be completely effected at this very instant: would this be a great joy and happiness to you?' And an irrepressible self-consciousness distinctly answered, 'No!' At this my heart sank within me: the whole foundation on which my life was constructed fell down ... I seemed to have nothing left to live for.[53]

As 'the dry heavy dejection of the melancholy winter of 1826–27' dragged on, Mill continues, 'I frequently asked myself if I could, or if I was bound to go on living, when life must be passed in this manner. I generally answered to myself, that I did not think I could possibly bear it beyond a year.'[54] These feelings he kept hidden from his father.

Much of Mill's melancholy was due to his fear that, as his friend John Sterling once confided to him, Mill might be 'a "made" or manufactured man, having had a certain impress of opinion stamped on me which I could only reproduce.'[55] The fear by which he was haunted had a philosophical source:

> during ... my dejection the doctrine of what is called Philosophical Necessity weighed on my existence like an incubus. I felt as if I was scientifically proved to be the helpless slave of antecedent circumstances; as if my character and that of all others had been formed for us by agencies beyond our control, and was wholly out of our own power. I often said to myself, what a relief it would be if I could disbelieve the doctrine of the formation of character by circumstances ...[56]

'Philosophical Necessity' was precisely the Owenite doctrine to which James Mill subscribed and that he had applied in forming his son's mental and moral character. The younger Mill believed that his character had in fact been formed for him, not by him. He felt himself an automaton devoid of autonomy, of free will, and of all feeling. He was, to revert to his own words in the *Logic*, 'experienc[ing] the painful consequences of the character' formed for him by his father.[57]

Fortunately the cloud began to lift, if only gradually and, on Mill's own account, accidentally. In the depths of his depression 'a small ray of light broke in upon my gloom. I was reading, accidentally, Marmontel's Memoirs, and came to the passage which relates his father's death, the distressed position of the family ... A vivid conception of the scene and its feelings came over me, and I was moved to tears.'[58] It is noteworthy that by his own account Mill did not wish for or will this experience; it simply happened, and 'accidentally' at that. Feelings over which he had no control 'came over' him and 'moved' him. He was, to revert to the words of the *Logic*, motivated 'by some strong feeling of admiration or aspiration, accidentally aroused.'[59]

'From this moment' of unwilled and accidental arousal of feeling, Mill writes, 'my burthen grew lighter. The oppression of the thought that all feeling was dead within me, was gone. I was no longer hopeless: I was not a stock or a stone. I had still, it seemed, some of the material out of which all worth of character, and all capacity for happiness, are made.'[60] Out of this material Mill began, as he believed, to remould and remake his own character along his own lines and as he saw fit. The motivations – the causal impetus – for beginning this process of self-transformation came not from his tightly controlled 'education' but from contingent 'experience' and were, moreover, precisely those supplied by Mill in his answer to the Owenite in the *Logic*.

If these be the causes, what then were the effects? 'The experiences of this period [of depression] had two very marked effects on my opinions and character.' The first was 'to adopt a theory of life, very unlike that on which I had before acted.' This theory required that Mill cease his self-interrogation about whether he was happy. 'Ask yourself whether you are happy and you cease to be so.' Mill's second move was to cultivate his capacity to feel as well as to analyze. 'The cultivation of the feelings became one of the cardinal points' in his new 'ethical and philosophical creed.'[61] Mill came to the realization that 'the habit of analysis' that his father had inculcated 'has a tendency to wear away the feelings.'[62] Henceforth, Mill would nurture his feelings by, among other things, pondering the poetry of Wordsworth and Coleridge (in which his father took no interest at all).[63] Unlike his early education, in which he had no choice of teacher, Mill now had and exercised his freedom to choose whose teaching he would follow. In his quest for a 'new way of thinking' and for weaving 'my new fabric of thought,' he chose Wordsworth as guide and teacher, and 'found the fabric of my old and taught opinions giving way in many fresh places.'[64] The experience was evidently exhilarating.

Mill's *Autobiography* can be read as – and arguably is intended to be – an ethological tale. The pegs on which he hangs his narrative are to be found in his account of Ethology and of Liberty and Necessity in Book VI of his *System of Logic*. Those dry logical bones are the skeleton which takes on flesh in the *Autobiography*. Taking himself as a case study, he shows how one man's partially deformed character was reformed, rounded out and made whole. Moreover, he shows by example how a character originally formed by 'circumstances' outside one's control can be re-formed according to one's own wishes and will (and with a little luck). A manufactured man can revolt against his manufacturer. He can re-make and re-mould his own character. An automaton may yet, through his own efforts, become autonomous. Or, to put the point in Kantian terms, Mill's *Autobiography* tells how one young man traversed the distance from heteronomy to autonomy. This young man was in this respect more fortunate than the vast majority of his female counterparts.

4. Case 2: *The Subjection of Women*

Whilst his *Autobiography* supplies a case study of a single individual, Mill's *Subjection of Women* is concerned with the deformation and reformation of the characters of fully half the human race. From their earliest years girls are taught to be submissive, self-sacrificing, amusing but not overly bright, and, above all, attractive to the opposite sex. Great emphasis is placed on physical appearance and very little on intellectual cultivation. To the extent that their 'mental cultivation' is attended to, its purpose is nothing short of perverse: it is to turn young women into willing slaves. Mill repeatedly compares the status of women to that of slaves, the latter being more fortunate than the former:

> Men do not want solely the obedience of women, they want their sentiments. All men, except the most brutish, desire to have, in the woman most nearly connected with them, not a forced slave but a willing one ... They have therefore put everything in practice to enslave their minds. The masters of all other slaves rely, for maintaining obedience, on fear ... The masters of women wanted more than simple obedience, and they turned the whole force of education to effect their purpose. All women are brought up from the very earliest years in the belief that their ideal of character is the very opposite to that of men; not self-will, and government by self-control, but submission, and yielding to the control of others.[65]

Circumstances are so arranged that young women's options are limited and their choices channeled into the approved path of marriage and motherhood. If they are to be wives and mothers they must first find a husband; and that requires that their characters be formed for the purpose of attracting a mate. Under these circumstances 'it would be a miracle if the objective of being attractive to men had not become the polar star of feminine education and formation of character.'[66]

Mill insists repeatedly that the features thought to be part of women's 'nature' or are 'natural' to women are in fact utterly artificial. They are the result of the education, or rather miseducation, that moulds women's minds and characters according to men's designs. They thus become little better than human hot-house plants, bred for men's purposes and pleasures:

> What is now called the nature of women is an eminently artificial thing – the result of forced repression in some directions, unnatural stimulation in others ... No other class of dependents have had their character so entirely distorted from its natural proportions by their relation with their masters; ... but in the case of women, a hot-house and stove cultivation has always been carried on ... for the benefit and pleasure of their masters. Then, because certain products of the general vital force sprout luxuriantly and reach a great development in this heated atmosphere and under this active nurture and watering, while other shoots from the same root, which are left outside in the wintry air, with ice purposely heaped all round them, have a stunted growth ... ;

men, with that inability to recognise their own work which distinguishes the unanalytical mind, indolently believe that the tree grows of itself in the way they have made it grow, and that it would die if one half of it were not kept in a vapour bath and the other half in the snow.[67]

Women, thinking and acting according to their own supposed 'natures,' are in fact acting according to the precepts programmed into them from childhood onward. Their very characters are 'made' or 'manufactured' according to men's specifications.

Mill emphasizes the role of ethology in criticizing and combating the conventional view of women's 'real' or 'natural' character. But this science is still in a primitive state. Mill laments 'the unspeakable ignorance and inattention of mankind in respect to the influences which form human character.'[68] What is needed, he insists – echoing his call a quarter-century earlier for a science of Ethology – is

an analytic study of the most important department of psychology, the laws of the influence of circumstances on character ... The profoundest knowledge of the laws of the formation of character is indispensable to entitle any one to affirm even that there is any difference, much more what the difference is, between the two sexes considered as moral and rational beings; and since no one, as yet, has that knowledge (for there is hardly any subject which, in proportion to its importance, has been so little studied), no one is entitled to any positive opinion on the subject. Conjectures are all that can at present be made; conjectures more or less probable, according as more or less authorised by such knowledge as we yet have of the laws of psychology, as applied to the formation of character.[69]

What the proper cultivation and formation of female character might produce remains in the realm of conjecture. 'Their [real] capabilities,' Mill laments, 'nobody knows, not even themselves, because most of them have never been called out.'[70] There is, however, empirical evidence that some claims about the supposed shortcomings of the female character are clearly and demonstrably false. For example, claims about women's inaptitude for politics and public life are controverted by the example of Queen Elizabeth and other female monarchs.[71] Their characters were formed for the purposes of public life, and in that capacity they clearly excelled. Does it not then follow, Mill asks, that other women, if given the right education and upbringing, might also contribute to the common or civic life? Is society not at present depriving itself of the talents of half its members? And if so, is society not then progressing much more slowly than it otherwise might? Sexual inequality, in short, not only deprives women of the opportunity of developing and using their talents; it also deprives the larger society of the benefit of those talents.

Although the deformation and possible re-formation of female character is Mill's main theme in *The Subjection of Women*, he also emphasizes the ways in which sexual inequality corrupts and deforms men's characters. Male children, like female ones, are moulded from the first by their experiences in the family. 'The family, justly constituted, would be the real school of the virtues of freedom.' But the un-justly constituted and deeply inegalitarian patriarchal family is little better than 'a school of despotism' in which boys learn early and easily that they are women's natural superiors.[72] 'There is nothing which men so easily learn as this self-worship: all privileged persons, and all privileged classes, have had it.'[73] Boys learn early to imitate their fathers and denigrate their mothers and sisters:

> ... when a boy is differently brought up [from his sisters] how early the no-tion of his inherent superiority to a girl arises in his mind; how it grows with his growth and strengthens with his strength; how it is inoculated by one schoolboy upon another; how early the youth thinks himself superior to his mother, owing her perhaps forbearance, but no real respect; and how sublime and sultan-like a sense of superiority he feels, above all, over the woman whom he honors by admitting her to a partnership of his life. Is it imagined that all this does not pervert the whole manner of existence of the man, both as an individual and as a social being?[74]

The moral of Mill's tale is distinctly ethological: women's and men's characters are corrupted and deformed by sexually inegalitarian institutions and practices. If their characters are to be improved, the modes of mental and moral cultivation must be changed. The marriage contract must be made an agreement between equals, and marriage a partnership of equals. 'The equality of married persons before the law, is not the sole mode ... but it is the only means of rendering the daily life of mankind, in any high sense, a school of moral cultivation.'[75] Another mode would be to enfranchise women.[76] Yet another would be to open almost all offices and occupations to women, so that little girls might aspire to alter-natives (or perhaps additions) to marriage and motherhood.[77] In these and other ways women's characters might become very different from what humans have heretofore known. The resulting benefit would redound not only to women but to humankind at large.

5. Case 3: Representative government

We have so far considered two ethological case studies involving the formation of individual characters – Mill himself in the *Autobiography* and females in *The Subjection of Women*. Important though individual character is, it does not suf-fice for civic purposes, as Mill contends in *Considerations on Representative Government*, published two years after *On Liberty*. The members of modern dem-ocratic societies must also attend to the formation and cultivation of their civic characters. For it is as citizens that they are able to act collectively and in concert. Indeed, individual and civic character are two sides of the same coin. Mill holds that 'the influence of the form of government upon character' cannot be overes-timated.[78] Consider, he says, two broad regime types – despotic and democratic – and the ways in which each shapes (and are in turn shaped by) the character of its members. Despotic government requires passive subjects, and the inculcation of passivity is there the hallmark of what passes for education. Among 'the distinctive mischiefs of despotism' is its failure to 'bring into sufficient exercise the individual faculties, moral, intellectual, and active, of the people.'[79] Under even the mildest of despotisms it is not only intelligence that is stifled and stunted:

> Their moral capacities are equally stunted. Wherever the sphere of action of human beings is artificially circumscribed, their sentiments are narrowed and dwarfed in the same proportion. The food of feeling is action ... Let a person have nothing to do for his country, and he will not care for it ... Leaving things to the Government, like leaving them to Providence, is synonymous with caring nothing about them, and accepting the results, when disagreeable, as visitations of Nature.[80]

'Passive subjects' unaccustomed to active public life are apt to take into account only their own narrowly circumscribed material interests. 'The intelligence and sentiments of the whole people are given up to the material interests, and, when these are provided for, to the amusement and ornamentation of private life.'[81]

Representative government, by contrast, requires active and attentive citizens; and such citizens must possess active characters – characters formed in part through the activity of participating in and contributing to the wider community to which they belong. This is the 'school' in which one's civic character is formed. 'Citizenship, in free countries, is partly a school of society in equality.'[82] It is through debating and deliberating with one's equals – one's fellow citizens – that one is schooled in the civic arts. One can only 'develop by exercise the active capacities and social feelings of the individual citizen.'[83]

Much as Mill decried the 'mischiefs' of despotism, he did not deny that democracy may have its own distinctive mischiefs, as he notes in *On Liberty* and elsewhere; but the greatest benefit it bestows upon its citizens is a heightened sense of civic competence, moral responsibility and the cultivation of *active* virtue. Active citizens have active characters, and passive subjects passive characters. The former attend to the public business as well as their own, the latter only to their own narrowly circumscribed 'worldly' or 'material interests.'[84]

Mill's point is not that the protection or promotion of one's worldly or material interests is illegitimate; it is, rather, that it is *insufficient* – that it does not suffice as an approximation of a higher, more civic ideal. It is, rather, revelatory of a character that is decidedly less than it could be, that falls well short of the more robust and demanding ideal of vigorous, virtuous, active citizenship. Echoing the ethological theme of the *Logic* Mill then asks 'a still more fundamental [question], namely, which of two common types of character, for the general good of humanity, it is more desirable should predominate – the active, or the passive type; that which struggles against evils, or that which endures them; that which bends to circumstances, or that which endeavours to make circumstances bend to itself.' And this in turn leads to the question as to how – and under what conditions – these more vigorous character-types might be formed. Once again Mill's answer is clear: 'the passive type of character is favoured by the government of one or a few, and the active self-helping type by that of the Many' – that is, by democracy.[85] The sort of 'action' that is 'the food of feeling,' Mill says elsewhere, 'can only be learned in action.' Just as 'we do not learn to read or write … by being merely told how to do it, but by doing it,' so likewise do we learn to be democratic citizens and 'active characters' by being active, by engaging in political activities.[86]

This is all part of an educational – or ethological – process of civic character formation that takes place in a variety of venues. Consider, for example, an ordinary citizen's service as a juror or in some other minor, albeit important, office or,

> still more salutary, … the moral part of the instruction afforded by the participation of the private citizen in public functions. He is called upon, while so engaged, to weigh interests not his own; to be guided, in case of conflicting claims, by another rule than his private partialities; to apply, at every turn, principles and maxims which have for their reason of existence the common good … He is made to feel himself one of the public, and whatever is for their benefit to be for his benefit.[87]

What is this, if not Mill's Goethian ideal of 'many-sidedness' applied to a more specifically civic context? Just as the richest and most robust individual characters are complex and many-sided, so also are the best civic characters capable of taking on and appreciating the perspectives of others.[88] The many-sidedness of individual character translates, in a more civic idiom, into the public-spiritedness of characters created and schooled in the give-and-take of civic engagement. But, Mill remarks in a passage reminiscent of Tocqueville's earlier warning about the dangers of the 'individualism' that degenerates so easily and so readily into *egoisme*,

> Where this school of public spirit does not exist, scarcely any sense is entertained that private persons … owe any duties to society, except to obey the laws and submit to the government. Every thought or feeling, either of interest or of duty, is absorbed in the individual and in the family. The man never thinks of any collective interest, of any objects to be pursued jointly with others, but only in competition with them, and in some measure at their expense. A neighbour, … since he is never engaged in any common undertaking for joint benefit, is therefore only a rival. Thus even private morality suffers, while public is actually extinct. Were this the universal and only possible state of things, the utmost aspirations of the lawgiver or the moralist could only stretch to make the bulk of the community a flock of sheep innocently nibbling the grass side by side.[89]

Such passive and sheep-like characters are created under conditions of political lassitude and inactivity. The more vigorous types are formed from and fed on the food of action – of political participation, in short.

Notes

* This chapter was originally a paper presented at the John Stuart Mill bicentennial conference, University College London, 7 April 2006. I have tried out these ideas and this interpretation of Mill's meaning in conversations over many years with Richard Dagger, Mary Dietz, William Thomas, the late John Rees and the late John Robson, with whom I am happy to share credit or blame, or both. I am also grateful for the questions, comments and criticisms raised by members of the audience at the UCL conference.

1 J. S. Mill, *A System of Logic* in Mill, *Collected Works* [*CW*], ed. J. M. Robson, Toronto: University of Toronto Press, 1974, vol. VIII, Bk. VI.

2 A. Bain, *John Stuart Mill, A Criticism, with personal recollections*, London: Longmans Green & Co., 1882, p. 78.

3 D. Thompson, *John Stuart Mill and Representative Government*, Princeton: Princeton University Press, 1976, p. 152, n. 48.

4 A. Ryan, *John Stuart Mill*, London: Routledge, 1974, p. 88.

5 S. Collini, 'Introduction' to J. S. Mill, *On Liberty and Other Writings*, Cambridge: Cambridge University Press, 1989, p. xix.

6 J. Gray, *Mill on Liberty: A Defence*, London: Routledge & Kegan Paul, 1983, p. 83.

7 J. M. Robson, *The Improvement of Mankind: The Social and Political Thought of John Stuart Mill*, Toronto: University of Toronto Press, 1968, p. 141.

8 M. St. John Packe, *The Life of John Stuart Mill*, London: Secker and Warburg, 1954, p. 295.

9 N. Capaldi, *John Stuart Mill: A Biography*, Cambridge: Cambridge University Press, 2004, p. 177.

10 N. Capaldi, 'Mill's Forgotten Science of Ethology,' *Social Theory and Practice*, 2 (1973), pp. 409–20.

11 W. L. Sumner, remarks made at the 1992 Utilitarianism Conference, University of Western Ontario, March 1992.

12 R. Owen, *A New View of Society: or, Essays on the Principle of the Formation of the Human Character*, London, 1813, 2nd Essay, pp. 2–3. (References are to the first edition, in which each essay is paginated individually.)

13 Ibid., 2nd Essay, p. 36.

14 Ibid., 3rd Essay, p. 5.

15 Ibid., 4th Essay, p. 71.

16 Ibid., 3rd Essay, p. 23. This entire passage is printed in boldface in the first edition.

17 J. Mill, 'Essays on the Formation of Human Character,' *Philanthropist*, III, 10 (1813), pp. 93–119, at p. 96.

18 Ibid., p. 98.

19 Ibid., p. 113.

20 I have discussed James Mill's theory of punishment in my *Reappraising Political Theory: Revisionist Studies in the History of Political Thought*, Oxford: Clarendon Press, 1995, ch. 7.

21 J. Mill, 'Essays on the Formation of Human Character,' p. 97.

22 James Mill's most extensive elaboration of his associationist theory of mind is his *Analysis of the Phenomena of the Human Mind*, 2nd edition, ed. J. S. Mill, London: Longmans, Green, Reader & Dyer, 1869, 2 vols.

23 J. Mill, 'Education,' in *James Mill: Political Writings*, ed. T. Ball, Cambridge: Cambridge University Press, 1992, p. 175.

24 J. S. Mill, *Autobiography*, Oxford: Oxford University Press, 1971, p. 150.

25 J. M. Robson, 'Introduction' to J.S. Mill, *A System of Logic*, in J.S. Mill, *CW*, vol. VII, xlix. Compare Bain (*John Stuart Mill*, p. 91): By 1848, with the *Logic* and *Political Economy* behind him, Mill's 'greatest works [were] now completed.' So much, then, for *On Liberty* (1859), *Representative Government* (1861) and *The Subjection of Women* (1869)!

26 Quoted in J. Morley, *The Life of William Ewart Gladstone*, London: Macmillan, 1903, 3 vols., II, p. 544.

27 J. S. Mill, *Autobiography*, p. 134.

28 *Logic*, in *CW*, vol. VII, p. 14. Mill, like Jurgen Habermas in our day, really did believe in 'the forceless force of the better argument.' See J. Habermas, 'Wahrheitstheorein,' in *Wirklichkeit und Reflexion*, Pfullingen: Neske, 1973, p. 239.

29 *CW*, VIII, Bk. VI, ch. 1, pp. 833–35.

30 Bain, op. cit., p. 79. On the centrality of 'character' in Mill's works, see Janice Carlisle, *John Stuart Mill and the Writing of Character*, Athens: University of Georgia Press, 1991.

31 See, e.g., Samuel Smiles, *Character*, London, 1871, and, more generally, S. Collini, *Public Moralists: Political Thought and Intellectual Life in Britain, 1850–1930*, Oxford: Oxford University Press, 1991, ch. 3.

32 'I have ever felt myself, beyond any modern that I know of except my father, ... a pupil of Plato, and cast in the mould of his dialectics.' *The Early Draft of John Stuart Mill's Autobiography*, ed. J. Stillinger, Urbana: University of Illinois Press, 1961, p. 48. Mill's emphasis on *paideia* is especially evident in the very late 'Inaugural Address Delivered to the University of St. Andrews' (1867), *CW*, XXI, pp. 217–57.

33 *Logic*, *CW*, VIII, pp. 837–38.

34 Ibid., p. 840.

35 Ibid., pp. 840–41.

36 The phrase was coined by one of the model's leading critics, W. H. Dray, *Laws and Explanation in History*, Oxford: Oxford University Press, 1957.

37 J. Mill, *Analysis of the Phenomena of the Human Mind*, I, ch's 2–3.

38 *Logic*, *CW*, VIII, p. 869. Elsewhere Mill describes a 'science secondaire que j'ai nommée Ethologie, c.à.d. de la théorie de l'influence des diverses circonstances extérieures, soit individuelles, soit sociales, sur la formation du caractère morale et intellectuel. Cette théorie, base nécessaire de l'education rationelle, me paraît aujourd'hui la moins avancée de toutes les spéculations scientifiques un peu importantes.' J.S. Mill to A. Comte, 30 October 1843, in *CW*, XIII, p. 604.

39 *Logic*, *CW*, VIII, 872, 874.

40 *Autobiography*, p. 3.

41 Ibid., p. 132.

42 J. Mill, 'The Formation of Human Character,' op. cit.; and 'Education,' op. cit.

43 J. Mill, 'Prisons and Prison Discipline,' in *Political Writings*, pp. 195–224. See further my *Reappraising Political Theory*, ch. 7.

44 C. Fox, *Memories of Old Friends*, 2nd ed., London: Smith, Elder, 1882, 2 vols., I, pp. 63–64.

45 *Life and Letters of John Arthur Roebuck*, ed. R. E. Leader, London: Edward Arnold, 1897, pp. 36, 28.

46 James Mill disliked and disapproved of Roebuck's high-spiritedness and sense of humour – it was he who dubbed the three young friends the 'Trijackia, all of us being named John' – as well as his love of poetry and talent as a sketch artist and painter. To these sources of dislike was added another: 'His [J. S. Mill's] father took occasion to remark to myself especially, that he had no great liking for his son's new friends. I, on the other hand, let him know that I had no fear of him who was looked upon as a sort of Jupiter Tonans. James Mill looked down on us [i.e., Graham and himself] because we were poor, and not greatly allied [i.e., socially well-connected], for while in words he was a severe democrat, in fact and in conduct he bowed down to wealth and position.

To the young men of wealth and position who came to see him he was gracious and instructive, while to us he was rude and curt, gave us no advice, but seemed pleased to hurt and offend us. This led to remonstrance and complaint on the part of John Mill, but the result was that we soon ceased to see John Mill at his home.' Thereafter the Trijackia met instead at the home of George Grote, where they were welcomed by the eminent historian of Greece and his kindly wife. Roebuck, op. cit., pp. 28–29.

47 *Autobiography*, p. 20.
48 *Early Draft*, p. 66.
49 Ibid., 183–85.
50 *Autobiography*, p. 82.
51 Ibid., p. 81.
52 Ibid., p. 42.
53 Ibid., p. 81.
54 Ibid., pp. 84–85.
55 Ibid., p. 93.
56 Ibid., p. 101.
57 *Logic, CW*, VIII, p. 841.
58 *Autobiography*, p. 85.
59 *Logic, CW*, VIII, pp. 840–41.
60 *Autobiography*, p. 85.
61 Ibid., pp. 85–86.
62 Ibid., p. 83.
63 Ibid., p. 11.
64 Ibid., pp. 89–90, 92, 94.
65 J. S. Mill, *The Subjection of Women* (1869) in Mill, *On Liberty and Other Writings*, ed. Collini, op. cit., p. 132.
66 Ibid., p. 133.
67 Ibid., p. 139.
68 Loc. cit.
69 Ibid., p. 140.
70 Ibid., p. 141.
71 Ibid., p. 170.
72 Ibid., p. 160.
73 Ibid., p. 158.
74 Ibid., p. 197; cf. also p. 158.
75 Ibid., p. 159.
76 Ibid., p. 168–69.
77 Ibid., pp. 199–203.
78 J. S. Mill, *Considerations on Representative Government*, in J. S. Mill, *Utilitarianism, Liberty, and Representative Government*, ed. A.D. Lindsay, New York: Dutton, 1951, p. 283.
79 Ibid., p. 325.
80 Ibid., p. 274.
81 Ibid., pp. 274–75.
82 *Subjection of Women*, p. 160.
83 *Representative Government*, p. 324.
84 *Logic, CW*, VIII, p. 890.
85 *Representative Government*, pp. 283, 288.
86 Mill, 'De Tocqueville on Democracy in America,' *London Review*, II (October 1835), p. 100; *CW*, XVIII, p. 63.
87 *Representative Government*, p. 291.
88 The *locus classicus* of this view is Aristotle's *Politics*, Bk. III, ch. 11 (1281 b); and among its most prominent modern articulations is H. Arendt, *The Human Condition*, Chicago: University of Chicago Press, 1958, ch. 5.

89   *Representative Government*, p. 291.
90   *Autobiography*, p. 150.
91   *On Liberty*, p. 59.
92   Ibid., p. 57.
93   Ibid., p. 14. For a brilliant explication of Mill's views on 'harm to interests,' see J. C. Rees, 'A Re-reading of Mill on Liberty,' *Political Studies* 8 (1960), pp. 113–29.
94   Including Mill's friend Caroline Fox: 'I am reading that terrible book of John Mill's on liberty, so clear, and calm, and cold: he lays it on one as a tremendous duty to get oneself well contradicted, and admit always a devil's advocate into the presence of your dearest, most sacred Truths, as they are apt to grow windy and worthless without such tests, if indeed they can stand the shock of argument at all. He looks you through like a basilisk, relentless as Fate … Mill makes me shiver, his blade is so keen and so unhesitating.' *Memories of Old Friends*, vol. II, pp. 269–70.
95   See the exchange between John Rawls and Jurgen Habermas in *Journal of Philosophy* 92 (1995), pp. 109–80.
96   Just as Mill did when, as MP for Westminster, he introduced a bill for the enfranchisement of women: see *Autobiography*, pp. 179–80. On this and other aspects of Mill's parliamentary career, see B. L. Kinzer, A. P. Robson and J. M. Robson, *A Moralist In and Out of Parliament: John Stuart Mill at Westminster, 1865–1868*, Toronto: University of Toronto Press, 1992. See, further, my *Reappraising Political Theory*, ch. 8.

4 Wild natural beauty and the religion of humanity

Mill's 'green' credentials

Donald Winch

We must needs think ... that there is something out of joint, when so much is said of the value of refining and humanizing tastes to the labouring people – when it is proposed to plant parks and lay out gardens for them, that they may enjoy more freely nature's gift alike to rich and poor, of sun, sky, and vegetation; and along with this a counter-progress is constantly going on, of stopping up paths and enclosing commons. Is not this another case of giving with one hand, and taking back more largely with the other? We look with the utmost jealousy upon any further enclosure of commons. In the greater part of this island, exclusive of the mountain and moor districts, there certainly is not more land remaining in a state of natural wildness than is desirable.[1]

1. Introduction

My epigraph comes from an article Mill wrote on 'the claims of labour' three years before he published his *Principles of Political Economy*. It contains an attack on 'legalized spoliation', Mill's description of enclosure of the commons in Britain, and was written fully two decades before he played a part alongside Henry Fawcett and others in founding the Commons Preservation Society in 1866. When Mill drew up the programme of the Land Tenure Reform Association three years later, the aims of commons preservation were incorporated in a clause insisting that waste lands, and those lands requiring an Act of Parliament to enclose them, should be permanently reserved for national purposes, leaving the less fertile land around cities to be 'retained in a state of wild natural beauty, for the general enjoyment of the community, and encouragement in all classes of healthful rural tastes, and of the higher order of pleasures'.[2] Protecting the rights of all people to enjoy nature from the dual threat posed by population pressure and the predations of urban landowners united Mill's environmentalist concerns with the long-standing anti-landlord opinions of a Ricardian economist who was also a philosophic radical.

Mill had been a keen amateur botanist since youth; he had acquired this hobby, along with a taste for mountain scenery, during his first visit to the Pyrenees as a fourteen-year old. Botanizing was the main activity he undertook during his extensive walking tours, enabling him to become an amateur expert on the flora of Britain. The hobby was often pursued near to home in the Surrey hills, but one of the most important walking tours he undertook, undoubtedly, was the one that resulted in a visit to Wordsworth in the Lake District in 1831. This pilgrimage was undertaken with vivid recollections of Wordsworth's earlier poems in mind, and the poet's didactic tourist guide, a *Description of the Scenery of the Lakes in the North of England,* in hand.[3]

Memories of the visit left a small but significant mark on Mill's *Principles of Political Economy.* It had taken place before Mill immersed himself in the literature on land tenure throughout Europe, largely prompted by a search for a solution to the problems revealed by the Irish famine. Mill's observations on the condition of the Lakeland yeomen or 'statesmen' and Wordsworth's brief paean to the 'perfect Republic of Shepherds and Agriculturists' in his depiction of them, were recalled when Mill was advocating replacement of the cottier system by peasant proprietorship as a partial solution to Irish problems. The Lakeland 'statesmen' are cited as an example of what could have been achieved in England if the yeoman ideal had not given way to the native prejudice in favour of *grande culture* as the only means of feeding a rising population.

Mill was signalling a major departure from the political economy on which he had been raised, which operated with a model that took for granted the superiority of the tripartite system of ownership and reward embodied in English agriculture, according to which landowners received rents paid by tenant farmers who pursued profit on their capital and employed wage labour in order to do so. The memory of his visit to the Lake District remained with Mill when marshalling evidence in favour of peasant proprietorship on a pan-European scale and against the background of his official knowledge of peasant agriculture in India gained as an employee of the East India Company. It is worth remembering Mill's remark on the similarities of India and Ireland: 'those Englishmen who know something of India, are even now those who understand Ireland best'.[4]

Mill credited Wordsworth with giving poetic form to what he described as 'one of the strongest of [his] pleasurable susceptibilities – the love of rural objects and natural scenery'.[5] But Mill's environmental interests not only pre-date Wordsworth's influence, they have a deeper and decidedly un-romantic provenance as well: they derive directly from the neo-Malthusian anxieties that pervade many of his most characteristic political and economic opinions. Reconciling Wordsworth with Malthus – reconciling a romantic ecology with one based squarely on political economy – was not, at first sight, an easy task. But it is not a bad description of what Mill achieved as an environmentalist, and the rest of this paper will be devoted to showing how he did so, and why the result differs from the more straightforward Wordsworthian version of ecology that was later to be embodied in the National Trust's approach to conservation in Britain.

2. The effects of technological change

For Mill, the law of diminishing returns in agriculture and other activities involving the use of natural resources was 'the most important proposition in political economy'.[6] It was an essential part of the Ricardian theory of economic growth and income distribution that provided the theoretical backbone of his *Principles*. Along with its partner, neo-Malthusianism, it remained an article of faith with Mill from his earliest jousts with critics of political economy in the 1820s to his later engagements with socialists in his posthumous chapters on the subject. Half a century after he had been arrested for distributing birth control literature as a teenager, Mill continued to believe that restraining the Malthusian devil was essential to any prospect for a permanent rise in working-class living standards. Mill's interest in peasant proprietorship and in some experiments in cooperative socialism derived strength from his belief that parental irresponsibility would be more clearly perceived and hence controlled under those arrangements. Removing the burden of large families on women was, of course, an integral part of his feminism, and feminism was linked with environmentalism because Mill was convinced that 'as in so many other things ... women will be much more unwilling than men to submit to the expulsion of all beauty from common life'.[7] While men, he believed, were prone to stress the productive uses of land, women were more likely to be impressed by the beauty of an unspoiled landscape.

Neo-Malthusianism accounts too for Mill's disqualification from membership of what John Ruskin was later to describe and dismiss as the 'steam-whistle party', those who celebrated industrial and scientific progress and entertained optimistic visions of the prospects held out by further technological innovation. Any optimism Mill felt about social improvement based on technological change was hedged around with qualifications, chief among them being those connected with population.

> Hitherto it is questionable if all the mechanical inventions yet made have lightened the day's toil of any human being. They have enabled a greater population to live the same life of drudgery and imprisonment, and an increased number of manufacturers and others to make fortunes. They have increased the comforts of the middle classes. But they have not yet begun to effect those great changes in human destiny, which it is in their nature and in their futurity to accomplish. Only when, in addition to just institutions, the increase of mankind shall be under the deliberate guidance of judicious foresight, can the conquests made from the powers of nature by the intellect and energy of scientific discoverers, become the common property of the species, and the means of improving and elevating the universal lot.[8]

On this subject one could say that the public moralist was at war with the political economist, though it would be more accurate to cite it as a case where the abstract 'science' had no authority over the 'art' of public policy and the choice of the ultimate ends of social existence. Worship of the 'idol' of production, that 'disposition to sacrifice every thing to accumulation' and the 'exclusive and engrossing selfishness which accompanies it', was one of Mill's earliest strictures on the mentality of his fellow countrymen.[9] He added the 'dollar-hunting' habits of Americans later, and classified America alongside Britain as the two chief examples of the 'industrial' mentality. Mill was asserting a gospel of leisure over Carlyle's gospel of work: for what could be laudable about work for work's sake? In a more sane society, the labour effort involved in satisfying the demand for luxury would be questioned. In a more just society the burden of physical labour would be distributed more fairly. Mill thought the price paid for superior English productivity was too high when measured by the loss of pleasure from relaxation and self-cultivation.

The importance Mill attached to the law of diminishing returns, despite recognizing ways in which its operation could be suspended, places him among those who thought the trajectory of economic growth in 'old' countries would eventually have to be asymptotic, confined within limits, rather than exponential or open ended. As E. A. Wrigley, speaking from the viewpoint of historical demography, has pointed out, under these conditions control over birth rates was required to ensure the maintenance of rising living standards.[10] Consciously or unconsciously, steam-whistlers took the view that all bottlenecks could be overcome by technologies that enabled inorganic materials and processes to act as substitutes for those based on natural resources. Mill was one of the earliest political economists to stress environmental limits and costs when discussing economic growth. Indeed, it could be argued that it took more than a century for the argument to be stated in anywhere near such a fundamentalist fashion. Mill's way of conducting the case took its cue from the concept of a stationary state as the *ne plus ultra* of economic growth, an integral part of earlier debates on growth provoked by Adam Smith and continued by Malthus and Ricardo. But it was part and parcel of Mill's personal diagnosis of the current state of the British economy that he believed it now to be 'within a hand's breadth' of the stationary state, and only prevented from entering that state by periodic 'revulsions' in which capital was invested abroad or wasted in speculative enterprises at home.[11] It was on the basis of this diagnosis that Mill accepted Edward Gibbon Wakefield's case for systematic colonization involving the export of capital and labour to 'new' colonies capable of providing employment for her surplus population and of meeting Britain's need to import cheap food and raw materials.

Systematic colonization was a solution for the short and middle term. In the long run, instead of wishing only to see the onset of the stationary state postponed, Mill invited his progressive-minded readers to embrace a positive vision of stationarity in which, although there would be no net additions to population size or the capital stock, all future improvements in technology would be directed towards the reduction of effort and improvements in the quality of life. In other words, Mill's stationary state was to be a virtuous version of an idea that had been used by his mentors as a bogeyman to support those measures, such as free trade and the reduction of public expenditure, that would sustain private capital accumulation and widen, if not remove, the organic bottleneck to further accumulation and growth. One lengthy quotation from Mill's defence of a zero-growth society conveys the substance of those environmentalist values he believed to be under threat from further economic growth.

> There is room in the world, no doubt, and even in old countries for a great increase of population, supposing the arts of life to go on improving, and capital to increase. But even if innocuous, I confess I see little reason for desiring it. The density of population necessary to enable mankind to obtain, in the greatest degree, all the advantages both of cooperation and of social intercourse, has, in all the most populous countries, been attained. A population may be too crowded, though all be amply supplied with food and raiment. It is not good for man to be kept perforce at all times in the presence of his species. A world from which solitude is extirpated, is a very poor ideal. Solitude, in the sense of being often alone, is essential to any depth of meditation or of character; and solitude in the presence of natural beauty and grandeur, is the cradle of thoughts and aspirations which are not only good for the individual, but which society could ill do without. Nor is there much satisfaction in contemplating the world with nothing left to the spontaneous activity of nature; with every rood of land brought into cultivation, which is capable of growing food for human beings; every flowery waste or natural pasture ploughed up, all quadrupeds or birds which are not domesticated for man's use exterminated as his rivals for food, every hedgerow or superfluous tree rooted out, and scarcely a place left where a wild shrub or flower could grow without being eradicated as a weed in the name of improved agriculture. If the earth must lose that great portion of its pleasantness which it owes to things that the unlimited increase of wealth and population would extirpate from it, for the mere purpose of enabling it to support a larger, but not a better or a happier population, I sincerely hope, for the sake of posterity that they will be content to be stationary, long before necessity compels it.[12]

The final remark about 'necessity' may suggest a grim Malthusian version of the asymptotic nature of growth, but the rest of the passage has little or no connection with what one would normally associate with an economic analysis of optimal population size. It is also worth bearing in mind that when Mill first wrote this passage, the population of England, Scotland and Wales – though it had increased faster than ever before (or since) during the first decades of the nineteenth century – was still no more than 18 million. The language is clearly a 'romantic' one and the emphasis on the 'spontaneous activity of nature' and of 'solitude in the presence of natural beauty and grandeur' marks it as a Wordsworthian evaluation of the benefits of communing with nature.

3. Nature, political economy and religion

Mill was prepared to enjoy the raptures conjured up by Wordsworth's nature poetry, but he needed to give the metaphysics which underlay them a more solid basis of his own construction – one that consorted better with utilitarian ethics, his interest in the natural and moral sciences, and his hopes for a religion of humanity. Although the romantic influence contributed an important emotional dimension to Mill's environmentalism, it came as a supplementary revelation to the central tenets of his utilitarian upbringing. When listing the subjects on which he remained at odds with philosophic Tories, Mill mentioned ethics and religion, beliefs that account for the gulf separating his environmentalist ethic from that associated with Wordsworth and his more orthodox followers.

It would be impossible to envisage a Wordsworthian ethic that did not include a profound belief in a Christian deity. We have no direct evidence of Wordsworth's reaction to his meetings with his youthful admirer, though Mill reported that he was impressed by what his host had to say about 'states of society and forms of government'.[13] Even if Mill concealed or diluted some of his opinions, these topics were bound to be divisive. Opposition to Malthusianism, for example, was an enduring feature of the Lake poets' views on politics and morals. Malthus's depiction of the laws of nature as requiring constant exertion to avoid misery and vice proved especially challenging to Wordsworth's more benevolent view of Nature's healing qualities.[14] By coincidence, a few weeks before Mill arrived in the Lake District, Wordsworth had been condemning the influence of Malthus on current Poor Law debates, a position he was to expound more fully in a postscript to the 1835 edition of his poems, where the malign connection between political economy and the Poor Law Amendment Act was noted, and the virtues of 'a christian government standing *in loco parentis* towards all its subjects' extolled.[15] This was, of course, a version of the paternalist position that Mill was to attack in his *Principles*, after Carlyle had published heroic versions of it in *Chartism* and in *Past and Present*.

Like Coleridge and Southey, Wordsworth loosely associated much that he disliked about the modern world with utilitarianism and political economy. When opposing the extension of the railway into the heart of the Lake District in 1844, for example, he employed the conventional charge that utilitarianism served 'as a mask for cupidity and gambling speculations'.[16] He also expressed the hope that since man did not live by bread alone, political economy would not be allowed to decide whether the Lake District would be violated by working-class day-trippers from Manchester in search of cheap amusements. Mill's support for the Commons Preservation Society on grounds of the benefits it would bring to the working classes may suggest a different set of priorities, though Wordsworth too hoped that Manchester's operatives could learn to appreciate natural beauty closer to home, in their 'neighbouring fields'. Epping Forest, Hampstead Heath, Wimbledon Common and Banstead Downs may not have the 'sublime' connotations of the Lake District, but their preservation as open spaces was as much of a public achievement as any later associated with the National Trust, the body that grew out of the Commons Preservation Society and was founded by some of Wordsworth's followers in 1895 with conservation of the Lake District very much a first priority.[17]

Speaking purely as an economist, Mill was always in favour of strict parliamentary regulation of the monopoly powers of the railway companies. This included choice of routes, with their environmental impact on sites of natural beauty and botanical interest forming one of the criteria. In good radical fashion he contrasted lack of concern with damage to the environments open to the poor with parliamentary willingness to spend £11,000 on two Correggios for the new National Gallery. Mill was aware that such comments could arouse a chorus of denunciation of political economists and utilitarians for lacking imagination and taste, to which his response was that a 'sense of beauty' scarcely existed in Britain, and that purchase of the Correggios was a case of judging quality by price, a common aristocratic failing. He pilloried the urban developer who had succeeded in enclosing part of Hampstead Heath, and attacked the Archbishop of Canterbury, William Howley, for enclosing part of the Addington hills near Croydon. Incitement of the citizens of Croydon to 'sally out with axe in hand' to level the fences erected by the Archbishop 'to exclude them from what was morally as much their birthright as any man's estate is his' might well have compounded Mill's teenage offence of distributing birth control literature.[18]

Being thoroughly acquainted with the conventional objections to utilitarianism as a narrow selfish ethic, Mill was keen to demonstrate that his version of the doctrine provided equivalent, usually superior, answers to questions that involved our concern for others, including past and future generations. One way in which he accomplished this can be found in his articles later published as *Utilitarianism*, the first part of which is an extended exercise in comparing utilitarian moral criteria with those furnished by more conventional Christian accounts of morality. Mill took the high moral ground here by portraying Christ's teachings as containing the essence of utilitarian ethics: 'To do as one would be done by, and to love one's neighbour as oneself, constitute the ideal perfection of utilitarian morality', freed from the 'selfish' and immoral doctrines of personal reward and punishment that were part of the teachings of the corrupted Pauline Church.[19] This functional interpretation came without the central message that Christians would draw from Christ's sacrifice. Mill seems to have arrived at this conclusion in 1833 when he read the New Testament seriously for the first time. To Carlyle he wrote that he had 'unbounded reverence' for the Christ of the gospels when contrasted with the 'namby-pamby Christ of the poor modern Christians'.[20] Compared with this, Mill's altruistic religion of humanity entailed more strenuous demands on personal character to make the right kind of disinterested choices involving private and public good. He denied that he wrote in any 'hostile spirit' towards Christianity, but warned that 'good ethics and good metaphysics will sap Christianity if it persists in allying itself with bad'.[21]

The full extent of Mill's religious unorthodoxy was not disclosed until he published *Auguste Comte on Positivism* in 1865 and his stepdaughter released the *Three Essays on Religion* after his death. Readers of the former would have noticed Mill's commendation of the idea that 'a religion may exist without belief in a God, and that a religion without a God may be, even to Christians, an instructive and profitable object of contemplation'. Comte's concept of a Grand Etre entailed veneration for the collective existence embodied in the past, present and future of humanity; and it included a duty of care for those 'animal races which enter into real society with man' as well. Mill's Benthamite training would have extended this category to include all animals capable of suffering pain, whether or not they had a connection with man.[22] The botanist in Mill gave him reason for condemning Comte's 'overweening presumption' in proposing that all animals and plants that could not be justified for existing human use should be eliminated:

> As if any one could presume to assert that the smallest weed may not, as knowledge advances, be found to have some property serviceable to man. When we consider that the united power of the whole human race cannot reproduce a species once eradicated – that is what is once done, in the extirpation of races, can never be repaired; one can only be thankful that amidst all which the past rulers of mankind have to answer for, they have never come to the measure of the great regenerator of Humanity; mankind have not yet been under the rule of one who assumes that he knows all there is to be known, and that when he has put himself at the head of humanity, the book of human knowledge may be closed.[23]

The *Three Essays on Religion* were as much a part of the joint legacy with Harriet as the *Autobiography, On Liberty* and *The Subjection of Women*. Having exercised caution on the subject of religion in his published writings, Mill would have thought it cowardly not to leave a record of their views on this subject. He admired the courage of infidels such as Richard Carlile or George Jacob Holyoake in taking punishment for their beliefs, even though he could not respect all of the arguments they employed to defend infidelity. The reception given to Mill's posthumous essays by Christians and secular admirers alike proves how wise he was not to court publicity for his views during his lifetime. Agnostic admirers, led by John Morley, regretted the unnecessary concessions to Christianity, especially those in the last-written of the essays, that on 'Theism', with its conclusion that the rational sceptic was permitted an imaginative form of hope that God exists even if he was denied adequate grounds for belief. Although this essay was regarded by some of Mill's friends as 'hard to reconcile with his former self', there was little that was truly novel in the other two. The most polished of them, 'Nature', confirmed what he had maintained in his *Examination of the Philosophy of Sir William Hamilton,* as well as in less formal writings, namely that Mill diverged sharply from more conventional approaches to Nature's wonders and the lessons it was capable of teaching humanity. Nature could be malign as well as benign: 'nearly all the things which men are hanged or imprisoned for doing to one another, are nature's every day performances'.[24] If the results of natural laws were taken as evidence of the existence of God, the only conclusion any respecter of inductive evidence could draw would be that omnipotence and benevolence could not both be attributes of the deity. The idea that following Nature has any moral as opposed to prudential force receives some severe handling. At best the evidence supported the idea of a deity with limited powers who needed the active support of human creatures in the Manichaean struggle between good and evil, where evil was moral rather than natural and therefore fell within the scope of 'enlightened infidelity' to overcome. A religion of this kind, with the life of Christ acting as moral inspiration, was 'excellently fitted to aid and fortify that real, though purely human religion, which sometimes calls itself the Religion of Humanity and sometimes that of Duty'.[25]

The original importance of Christianity to environmentalism derives from its role in pointing to the providential aspect to Nature, the one embodied in pre-Darwinian notions of purpose, harmony and design. If Nature contained God's message of peace and order then there were powerful reasons for protecting it from man's overweening pride in his own scientific knowledge. Christian environmentalists could fortify secular notions of despoliation with charges of sacrilege. When Mill reproved Comte for his attitude towards plants that had no current human use, his case was confined to pointing out the uncertainty attached to existing scientific knowledge. Similarly, while Mill recognized the elevated pleasures of communing in solitude with nature, they did not require him to believe in God. When Christian aesthetes such as Ruskin deployed the ideas of infinity, unity, repose, symmetry, purity, moderation and adaptation to ends in a theory of beauty, Mill simply appropriated them, with due acknowledgment, as proof of the normal processes of psychological association and recollection. In any version of utilitarianism that recognized qualitative differences in pleasure they deserved special status for their superior character and capacity to grant 'deeper delight to the imagination'.[26] But there was no need to invoke a deity to explain such emotions. Mill was looking for a secular and science-based environmental ethic that was adapted to a post-Christian era. The pleasures and terrors of the sublime in nature were the effect of sheer scale and power when compared with what fell within the range of human achievement. But aesthetic uplift from such feelings could be purchased at the expense of ethical discrimination. As he said in a deadly aside that may have had Ruskin's position in view: '[t]hose in whom awe produces admiration may be aesthetically developed, but they are morally uncultivated'.[27] Finally, while Mill may have made some concessions to Christianity that his followers could not accept, he was not willing to admit that Epicurean short-sightedness was a defect in non-Christian versions of religion when it came to judging the results of human action on the environment.

> … the supposition, that human beings in general are not capable of feeling deep and even the deepest interest in things which they will never live to see, is a view of human nature as false as it is abject. Let it be remembered that if individual life is short, the life of the human species is not short; its indefinite duration is practically equivalent to endlessness; and being combined with indefinite capability of improvement, it offers to the imagination and sympathies a large enough object to satisfy any reasonable demand for grandeur of aspiration. If such an object appears small to a mind accustomed to dream of infinite and eternal beatitudes, it will expand into far other dimensions when those baseless fancies shall have receded into the past.[28]

As they used to say in the old Westerns, 'them's fightin' words'. And if we judge by the continued capacity of Mill's religion of humanity to arouse the ire of Christians and libertarians, they still are. On this occasion I offer them as additional proof, if such is needed, for Bruce Kinzer's contention about the primacy of the political in Mill.

Notes

1 J.S. Mill, 'The claims of labour' (*Edinburgh Review*, 1845), in: J. S. Mill, *CW*, IV, p. 384.
2 See 'Land tenure reform' in *CW*, V, pp. 689–95.
3 For the journal Mill kept while in the Lake District see *CW*, XXVII. The best accounts of the episode can be found in the editorial introduction to this volume and Anna J. Mill, 'John Stuart Mill's visit to Wordsworth, 1831', *Modern Language Review*, XLIV (1949), pp. 341–50.
4 England and Ireland in *CW*, VI, p. 519.
5 *Autobiography* in *CW*, I, p. 150.
6 *Principles of Political Economy* in *CW*, II, p. 174.
7 Letter to Charles W. Wilkinson, 24 October, 1869 in *CW*, XVII, p. 1659.
8 *Principles* in *CW*, III, 756.
9 Letters to D'Eichthal, 15 May and 8 October, 1829 in *CW*, XII, pp. 31 and 37.
10 See E. A. Wrigley *Continuity, chance and change; the character of the industrial revolution in England*, 1988.
11 *Principles, CW*, III, p. 746.
12 *Principles, CW*, III, 756.
13 Letter to Sterling, 20–22 October, 1831, in *CW*, XII, p. 81.
14 For detailed examination of the ambiguities of Wordsworth's relationship with Malthus, see the study by Philip Connell, *Romanticism, Economics and the Question of 'Culture'*, 2001, Chapter 1.
15 See letter to Lady Beaumont, 8 July, 1831 in the *Letters of William and Dorothy Wordsworth*, edited by A. G. Hill, (Oxford, 1978–88), V, pp. 405–6; and the *Prose Works of William Wordsworth*, edited by W. J. B. Owen and J. W. Smythe, 3 vols. (Oxford, 1974), III, pp. 240–48.
16 See *Prose Works*, III, p. 352.
17 On the foundation of the National Trust see G. Murphy, *Founders of the National Trust*, 1987; and J. Gaze, *Figures in a landscape; a history of the National Trust*, 1988. On the practical conservationist activities of Wordsworthians see the final chapter in S. Gill, *Wordsworth and the Victorians*, 1998. See too Jonathan Bate, *Romantic ecology; Wordsworth and the environmental tradition*, 1991; and for a general study of Victorian environmentalism, see James Winter, *Secure from rash assault; sustaining the Victorian environment*, 1999.
18 See Mill's *Notes on the Newspapers* in *CW*, VI, pp. 249–50, 328.
19 *Utilitarianism* in *CW*, X, p. 218.
20 Letter to Carlyle, 5 October, 1833, *CW*, XII, p. 182.
21 Letter to Bain, 14 November, 1859, *CW*, XV, pp. 645–46.
22 For Bentham's defence of animal rights see his *Introduction to the principles of morals and legislation*, Chapter XVII.
23 *Auguste Comte and Positivism* in *CW*, X, 357–58.
24 *Three essays on religion* in *CW*, X, p. 385.
25 Ibid., X, p. 488.
26 See Mill's references to Ruskin's *Modern painters* in the notes on his reissue of James Mill's *Analysis of the Phenomena of the Human Mind* in *Miscellaneous Writings, CW*, XXXI, pp. 224–26.
27 *Three essays on religion* in *CW*, X, p. 384.
28 Ibid., *CW*, X, p. 420.

5   Parallel lives in logic

The Benthams and the Mills

Frederick Rosen

1. Introduction

By parallel lives in logic, I am alluding to the logical works of four men: Jeremy Bentham and his nephew, George Bentham, on the one hand, and James Mill and his son, John Stuart Mill, on the other. If parallel lines do not meet, then parallel lives in logic may also not meet.

This essay is concerned with several problems in intellectual history, where biography, texts, contexts and philosophy combine to illuminate three curious puzzles concerning John Stuart Mill. Mill's reputation in his lifetime was established in part as a logician, largely through the publication of the two-volume *System of Logic Ratiocinative and Inductive* (1843), which dominated the study of logic in Britain and elsewhere for many years (see *CW*, VII, VIII).[1] In spite of this success, Mill failed to appreciate developments, which also began in his lifetime, in fact, around the same time as he published his *Logic*, in mathematical and symbolic logic by Augustus De Morgan, George Boole, W.S. Jevons and others, which transformed the modern study of the subject.[2] If we look at a remark by the editor of a recent edition of Boole's *The Mathematical Analysis of Logic* (1847), one notes immediately that the list of distinguished names, which defines the modern development of the subject, does not include Mill:

> Boole's work freed logicians, once and for all, from the endless repetition of a few principles, mostly derived from Aristotle, and, by example, challenged them to develop their subject in new directions. Many gifted thinkers, among them John Venn, William Stanley Jevons, Charles Sanders Peirce, Ernst Schröder, Alfred North Whitehead, and Bertrand Russell, rose to the challenge, and the vast and autonomous subject of modern logic gradually emerged from their combined efforts. It is a glorious success story.[3]

If it is arguable that all serious contemporary discussions of the theme of liberty begin with Mill's *On Liberty*, the same cannot be said of logic. The puzzle concerns why Mill failed to anticipate or why he rejected the modern study of the subject.[4]

The second puzzle concerns the relationship between Jeremy Bentham and James Mill. The traditional view of Bentham and Mill is that the former was a demanding and possessive master and the latter, the faithful disciple.[5] According to Mariangela Ripoli, the view of Mill (largely created by Leslie Stephen) is that of 'a thinker of little originality' who was a spokesman for and populariser of Bentham and, additionally, an important link between Bentham and J.S. Mill.[6] This view of James Mill has, of course, been challenged, not least of all by his son.[7] In his essays, 'Remarks on Bentham's Philosophy' (1833), 'Bentham' (1838) and 'Coleridge' (1840) (*CW*, X, pp. 3–18, 75–115, 117–63), the younger Mill tended to reduce Bentham's accomplishments to those of the practical side of legal science and reform, while his father's achievements in associationist psychology were proclaimed as the metaphysical response to the attack on eighteenth-century philosophy by the followers of the 'German' school in the nineteenth century (*CW*, X, pp. 80–81, 129–30). Thus, for the young Mill, his father was clearly the more important philosopher, at least in the field of psychology.

However much James Mill appeared to present himself as Bentham's lieutenant in practical politics, in philosophy he seemed to take a more independent line. Even though they shared the same room for their studies in the vast Ford Abbey between 1814 and 1818,[8] and at a time when Bentham had returned to philosophy, relations were not entirely harmonious. Mill even threatened to leave Ford Abbey in September 1814:

> I see that you have extracted umbrage from some part of my behaviour; and have expressed it by deportment so strongly, that I have seriously debated with myself whether propriety permitted that I should remain any longer in your house. I considered, however, that I could not suddenly depart, without proclaiming to the world, that there was a quarrel between us; and this, I think, for the sake of both of us, and more especially of the cause, which has been the great bond of connection between us, we should carefully endeavour to avoid. The number of those is not small who wait for our halting. The infirmities in the temper of philosophers have always been a handle to deny their principles; and the infirmities in ours, will be represented as by no means small, if in the relation in which we stand, we do not avoid shewing to the world that we cannot agree.

Mill continued by declaring himself to be a 'fervent disciple', 'the master's favourite disciple', and that there was 'no body at all so likely to be your real successor as myself'. He gave the following reasons to justify this declaration:

> ... I hardly know of any body who has so completely taken up the principles, and is so thoroughly of the same way of thinking with yourself ... [T]here are very few who have so much of the necessary previous discipline, my antecedent years have been wholly occupied in acquiring it ... I am pretty sure you cannot think of any other person whose whole life will be devoted to the propagation of the system.[9]

3. Parallel work

In 1823 and 1826 George Bentham made two trips from France to London, both of which involved his work in logic. In late 1822 he returned to the translation of the appendix to *Chrestomathia* in anticipation of completing it prior to a visit to England with his two sisters, Clara and Sarah, which was planned for 1823.[21] Though an 'appendix', the 'Essay on Nomenclature and Classification' was a considerable work (approximately 140 pages in the new edition of the *Collected Works*) and a major task of translation and understanding.[22] On the way to London, George and his sisters stopped at Paris, where he completed the *Essai sur la Nomenclature et Classification des Arts et Sciences* and arranged for its publication by Bossange Frères, the firm which had already published a number of the redactions of Bentham's writings, edited by his friend, Etienne Dumont.[23] After a stay of six weeks in Paris to complete this task, where George's labours were relieved by an active social life and frequent visits to the theatre, he and his sisters arrived in London, where he received a warm welcome from his uncle. The elder Bentham, who had not seen young George for nine years, found him 'much altered from a short fat boy, nicknamed "Devonshire Dumpling", to a thin young man of 5 ft 11½ in'.[24]

George Bentham and his sisters left London in early August and returned to their home in France by the autumn of 1823. In early 1826 he planned another trip to London, this time with his parents as well as the two younger sisters.[25] Samuel Bentham had not seen his brother since 1814, and both he and George were anxious to establish George's future prospects as his uncle's main heir. George Bentham's great love was science and, particularly, botany, but he had to earn a living and needed a profession. Jeremy Bentham engaged him to assist with his various projects and George began to meet with him first for dinner and then to work with him from eight to eleven in the evening twice a week. George seemed happy to accept this arrangement partly to secure his own interest and become close to his uncle and partly to 'counteract the influence of some of those about him who use it to no good' (probably referring to John Bowring).[26] He continued with this arrangement until Bentham's death in 1832, but there was no proper settlement or even a salary that would relieve the pressure on George to succeed in a profession. Bentham somehow believed that George could earn his fortune by editing his papers and writing articles for the *Westminster Review*. This view was not shared by George (or by his father, Samuel, or Lord Colchester, Samuel's and Jeremy's stepbrother, who was also advising the young, future botanist), and at the age of 26, he entered Lincoln's Inn to pursue a career in law.[27]

In his various meetings with his uncle, George began to consider editing Bentham's various manuscripts on logic. At first he thought that he might edit them in French and publish them with Bossange as a sequel to the Dumont redactions and his own earlier translation from *Chrestomathia*. He feared that his grasp of English was not good enough to succeed with the logic, and, additionally, he learned that 'James Mill had a work on Logic in contemplation, founded in a great measure on J. Bentham's papers, which both he and his son had studied'.[28] Nevertheless, he began to edit Bentham's unpublished manuscripts in logic, which, according to George Bentham, had not been examined since they were written in 1811, except for the use of some of them in *Chrestomathia*.[29] By a curious coincidence, John Stuart Mill had begun to edit Bentham's writings on evidence to produce the massive *Rationale of Judicial Evidence* (1827) in five substantial volumes. In 1826, therefore, George Bentham and J.S. Mill were working in parallel. Both were busily engaged on editorial work on what were arguably the most philosophical of Bentham's writings. Both completed their labours in 1827, when their respective works were published, presumably at Jeremy Bentham's expense, by Hunt and Clarke, the publishers and booksellers, which proceeded into bankruptcy shortly afterwards. Nevertheless, it should be noted that Jeremy Bentham was delighted with both works.

4. Crisis and logic

If we look at the work of George Bentham and J.S. Mill at this time we might be tempted to conjecture that, despite the differences in their ages, they had become close friends and colleagues. But while the parallel lives were in close proximity, they did not meet.

In 1825 John Stuart Mill helped form a society, called the 'Society of Students of Mental Philosophy', which met at the home of George Grote in Threadneedle Street twice a week in the morning from 8:30 to 10:00 (see *CW*, VII, p. liii). Although they probably began their study of logic in 1826, with the publication of Whately's *Elements of Logic*, at the same time as George Bentham began his work on logic, Bentham does not appear to be associated with this group. James Mill, however, is mentioned as providing a copy of Phillipus Du Trieu's *Manductio ad Logicam*, which the group reprinted and used in place of the *Artis Logicae Compendium* of Henry Aldrich (see *CW*, VII, p. liv; I, p. 125). Thus, not only are Mill and Bentham studying logic in London at the same time, but both are studying Whately's *Elements of Logic*, with George Bentham to write probably the first substantial critique of Whately's influential work and Mill to write a year later an important sympathetic review.[30]

Mill considered this period as being very influential in the development of his career in logic. In the following quotation, one can read what I call Mill's Socratic declaration of faith, expressed as a dramatic intellectual awakening of a young man of twenty years:

> I have always dated from these conversations my own real inauguration as an original and independent thinker. It was also through them that I acquired, or very much strengthened, a mental habit to which I attribute all that I have ever done, or ever shall do, in speculation; that of never accepting half-solutions of difficulties as complete; never abandoning a puzzle, but again and again returning to it until it was cleared up; never allowing obscure corners of a subject to remain unexplored, because they did not appear important; never thinking that I perfectly understood any part of a subject until I understood the whole (*CW*, I, p. 127).

But Mill was not an ordinary young man of twenty years of age. He might well have looked back to the earlier intellectual awakening in France, when, albeit at the age of fourteen, he began his study of logic. However, nothing concerning this earlier exploration of logic appears in the *Autobiography*.

At the same time as this dramatic awakening took place, Mill was also suffering from his much-discussed mental crisis. Because I have had considerable experience of editing Bentham's works, I have assumed over the years that Mill's extraordinary efforts to edit and publish in five volumes in a few short years Bentham's *Rationale of Judicial Evidence* must have led to his mental crisis. Robson has also taken this view.[31] However, when one considers his numerous other activities at this time, the morning meetings to discuss logic, the debating societies in which he participated, his new position in the East India Company, and numerous other writings, one might also conclude that Mill actually thrived on hard work and constant intellectual engagement.

Perhaps there was another reason for the mental crisis of 1826. His only discussion of his mental state, besides the chapter in the *Autobiography*, which tends to describe his feelings rather than analyse them, is the letter to John Sterling in 1829. Their friendship was then in jeopardy following a particularly acrimonious debate (concerning Bentham), which led to both of them resigning from the London Debating Society. In a successful attempt to repair the breach, Mill referred to his mental crisis and to the loneliness that had accompanied him through life. This is the only discussion of it surviving in his published correspondence:

> By loneliness I mean the absence of that feeling which has accompanied me through the greater part of my life, that which one fellow traveller or one fellow soldier has towards one another – the feeling of being engaged in the pursuit of a common object, and of mutually cheering one another on, and helping one another in an arduous undertaking. This, which after all is one of the strongest ties of individual sympathy, is at present, so far as I am concerned, suspended at least, if not entirely broken off. There is now no human being (with whom I can associate on terms of equality) who acknowledges a common object with me, or with whom I can cooperate even in any practical undertaking without the feeling, that I am only using a man whose purposes are different, as an instrument for the furtherance of my own (*CW*, XII, p. 30).[32]

If we apply these sentiments to Mill's relationship with George Bentham, the results are striking. Both began their study of logic together, and both were engaged in serious and substantial editorial work on Jeremy Bentham's writings, and yet there is little cooperation or even sympathy between them. If Mill felt alone and depressed within the circle he shared with Jeremy and George Bentham, his work in logic reflected his feelings. In what might be called his Coleridgean moment he embraced the newly published *Elements of Logic* of Whately virtually at the same time as George Bentham developed his critique, based on the ideas of Jeremy Bentham. Thus, at that time, Mill dramatically ceased to have 'a common object' or reason for cooperation with the one person working on logic whom he had known since childhood.[33]

5. Debate on logic

With the bankruptcy of Hunt and Clarke, only sixty copies of Bentham's *Outline* had been published. The stock had been seized by creditors, and George Bentham, disappointed at the lack of response to his work and the state of the publishers, allowed the back stock to be sold as waste paper.[34] John Stuart Mill was approached to review the book in the *Westminster Review*, just after his review of Whately's *Elements* appeared in 1828, but in a very self-assured letter for a young man of twenty-two, he turned down Bowring's request.[35] George Bentham abandoned the study of logic, but the story does not end in 1827–28.[36] In his numerous and important writings on botany, George developed a rigorous use of names and classifications. In the frequently reprinted *Handbook of The British Flora*, for example, one can see evidence of his use of a form of bifurcation in the various classifications. But he neither referred directly to his uncle's work in this field nor to the *Outline*.[37] Nevertheless, as Marion Filipiuk has carefully chronicled in her excellent edition of his *Autobiography*, he paid close attention (without making any public statement) to the various debates, which took place during the nineteenth century over the quantification of the predicate.[38]

What is meant by the quantification of the predicate? As Jevons wrote, '*to quantify the predicate is simply to state whether the whole or part only of the predicate agrees with or differs from the subject*'.[39] For some logicians, the Aristotelian syllogism contained some ambiguity regarding propositions. For example, in the proposition, all humans are mortal (taking the form all A are B), it is not clear if it means that all A are all B or all A are some B. That is to say, it might mean that all humans are all mortals or that all humans are some mortals. Though it is commonly believed that the latter is meant (as there are other mortals besides humans), it is not clear from the notation.

The discovery of this ambiguity was considered by Jevons 'the most fruitful one made in abstract logical science since the time of Aristotle ...'.[40] The debate over the quantification of the predicate accompanied the dramatic development in logic by writers like De Morgan and Boole, who sought to express logical relations in symbolic or algebraic form and hence to break out of the modes of expression of logical relations in use since Aristotle.[41] But, paradoxically, although Boole wrote at the beginning of *The Mathematical Analysis of Logic* (1847) that he was inspired to return to his topic by the debate between Sir William Hamilton and De Morgan over the quantification of the predicate,[42] and hence one can see a link between the development of modern logic and this precise issue, much of the debate was concerned less with the doctrine than with who discovered it.

Sir William Hamilton claimed that he had done so, and wrote that 'touching the principle of an explicitly *Quantified Predicate*, I had by 1833 become convinced of the necessity to extend and correct the logical doctrine upon this point'.[43] He then proceeded to accuse De Morgan, who had developed a similar doctrine, of plagiarism. De Morgan presented a long appendix to *Formal Logic* (1847) providing a detailed account of the controversy.[44] According to Heath, his editor, 'the consensus of De Morgan's correspondents, and of fair-minded persons generally – so far as they professed to understand the issue – was that Sir William had had a good deal the worst of it, and that the whole affair was unseemly and should never have arisen'.[45] Although the dispute had the positive effect of stimulating Boole to develop his theories, and De Morgan called his 'Appendix' his 'final reply' to Hamilton, the controversy was by no means at an end.

Hamilton had numerous successful students, and one of them, Thomas Spencer Baynes, published *An Essay on the New Analytic of Logical Forms* in 1850 in which he supported Hamilton's theories as well as his claims to originality.[46] This publication then sparked an intervention in the *Athenaeum* by William Warlow who credited two chapters of George Bentham's *Outline* with the development of the same doctrine.[47] From the end of December 1850 to the end of March 1851, when the editor called a halt to the controversy and refused to publish Warlow's third note on the subject, George Bentham's original notation to quantify the predicate was considered an important early discussion of this theme.[48]

The next development in this controversy took place two decades later when Herbert Spencer was publishing a series of essays on 'The Study of Sociology' in the *Contemporary Review*. In one essay, devoted to anti-patriotism in sociology, a critique of Matthew Arnold's view that the English, unlike the French, were deficient in ideas, Spencer turned to the important developments in logic in Britain in the nineteenth century to support his thesis that Arnold had undervalued the contribution of the British to philosophy.[49] Here, he mentioned the work of Sir John Herschel, Mill, Alexander Bain, De Morgan, Boole and George Bentham. On deductive logic, he wrote:

Deductive logic, too, has been developed by a further conception. The doctrine of the quantification of the predicate, set forth in 1827 by Mr. George Bentham, and again set forth under a numerical form by Professor De Morgan, is a doctrine supplementary to that of Aristotle; and the recognition of it has made it easier than before to see that Deductive Logic is a science of the relations implied by the inclusions, exclusions, and overlappings of classes.[50]

To this statement, Spencer added a footnote:

Most readers of logic will, I suppose, be surprised on missing from the above sentence the name of Sir William Hamilton. They will not be more surprised than I was myself on recently learning that Mr. George Bentham's work, *Outline of a New System of Logic*, was published six years before the earliest of Sir W. Hamilton's logical writings, and that Sir W. Hamilton reviewed it. The case adds another to the multitudinous ones in which the world credits the wrong man; and persists in crediting him in defiance of the evidence.[51]

It is true that Hamilton reviewed George Bentham's *Outline* (and, indeed, it was the only review) in 1833, the same year in which he claimed, as we have seen, to develop his own doctrine.[52] Thus, at the same time as he was accusing De Morgan of plagiarism, Hamilton could be fairly accused of plagiarism from George Bentham. Spencer's remarks were probably taken from Jevons's *Elementary Lessons in Logic: Deductive and Inductive* (1870), where he claimed that Bentham's work on the quantification of the predicate preceded that of Hamilton.[53] Jevons was soon to re-enter this debate, as he did earlier in the *Athenaeum*.

First, however, Baynes re-entered the field and actually quoted at length from his earlier essay in the *Athenaeum*. Baynes's arguments were somewhat paradoxical. On the one hand, he tried to diminish the importance of Bentham's discovery. He claimed that Bentham's fixing symbols of quantity to the subject and predicate of propositions had been anticipated in the history of logic. But to obviate the criticism that Sir William Hamilton had not made a discovery at all, he claimed that while Bentham had applied a 'technical rule', Hamilton had developed a 'scientific principle', and this was a novel discovery. Baynes mentioned that Hamilton was the first 'to appreciate truly its value, and apply it to a new and more perfect development of the science …'.[54]

Jevons accepted none of this and returned to the controversy by claiming that George Bentham was 'the first discoverer' of this logical principle, at least in Britain in the nineteenth century. He rejected claims by Baynes that Bentham had merely employed a technical terminology in a few pages by arguing that it was the foundation of his treatment of propositions and syllogisms.[55] As for Hamilton's plagiarism, he wrote:

> Out of the fruitful principle of the quantified form of the proposition, Hamilton developed one system of syllogisms, clearly foreshadowed by Bentham; Archbishop Thomson developed independently nearly the same system; De Morgan developed another and essentially different system; Boole, on the very same principle, a still more different system, probably more valuable than any of the others. Now, of these four eminent men, Hamilton is the only one who can be shown to have had, or probably had any knowledge of Bentham's book; and yet Hamilton is the one commonly credited with the discovery.[56]

6. The work of De Morgan and others

Although Mill's *Logic* was published in 1843, prior to these debates, he revised his work as he produced various editions. In the 1851 edition he took note of the controversy between Hamilton and De Morgan, which he then revised and expanded into a more substantial footnote in 1856 (see *CW*, VII, pp. 170n.–3n.). He also considered the issue in his *An Examination of Sir William Hamilton's Philosophy* (1865) (see *CW*, IX, pp. 395–403). In the 1851 note he mentioned the dispute in passing, and took a dismissive position regarding its significance. 'The "quantification of the predicate"', he wrote, 'an invention to which Sir William

Hamilton attaches so much importance as to have raised an angry dispute with Mr. De Morgan respecting its authorship, appears to me, I confess, as an accession to the art of Logic of singularly small value' (*CW*, VII, p. 170n.). Mill remained silent regarding George Bentham and the various claims made on his behalf. In 1851, however, he concentrated on De Morgan, and in an important statement with a bearing on the development of modern logic, he questioned the point of what De Morgan was attempting to achieve:

> It is of course true that "All men are mortal" is equivalent to "Every man is *some* mortal." But as mankind certainly will not be persuaded to "quantify" their predicates in common discourse, they want a logic which will teach them to reason correctly with propositions in the usual form, by furnishing them with a type of ratiocination to which propositions can be referred, retaining that form. Not to mention that the quantification of the predicate, instead of being a means of bringing out more clearly the meaning of the proposition, actually leads the mind out of the proposition into another order of ideas. For when we say, All men are mortal, we simply mean to affirm the attribute mortality of all men; without thinking at all of the *class* mortal in the concrete, or troubling ourselves about whether it contains any other beings or not. It is only for some artificial purpose that we even look at the proposition in the aspect in which the predicate also is thought of as a class name, either including the subject only, or the subject and something more (*CW*, VII, pp. 170n., 173n.).

Mill concluded that De Morgan's work 'was worth doing once (perhaps more than once, as a school exercise); but I question if its results are worth studying and mastering for any practical purpose' (*CW*, VII, p. 172n.). Nevertheless, it is arguable that Mill himself was somewhat confused over this issue. If the doctrine of the quantification of the predicate was of little significance, except perhaps as a school exercise, how did it have the power, in Mill's own words, to 'lead the mind out of the proposition, into another order of ideas'? If this was the case, it would seem to be an important issue to assess this new 'order of ideas' to establish its significance for logic. Although he knew that numerous logicians dismissed Aristotle's syllogistic logic in favour of a wholly inductive form, or, perhaps more significantly, some logicians (including De Morgan, Jeremy Bentham and George Bentham) dismissed the foundational role of the syllogism, while still utilizing aspects of Aristotle's logic, such as the material on fallacies, an emphasis on classification, and reasoning itself. Mill believed that the whole of the Aristotelian system (with the addition of a superior theory of induction) had to be accepted as foundational. Mill then linked this acceptance with a rejection of what he called 'technical forms of reasoning'. From his perspective, the Aristotelian syllogism was complete, sufficient, and close to what common understanding required. He could not imagine further developments within the Aristotelian system that would improve it without losing the supposed link with ordinary language and common understanding.

In his critique of Hamilton, Mill continued in the same vein. If Baynes thought that Hamilton had completed 'the plan of the mighty builder, Aristotle', by laying 'the top-stone' on the fabric whose foundation stone was laid two thousand years earlier, Mill believed that no such 'top-stone' was either needed or even helpful.[57] He attacked the complexity of Hamilton's conceptualisation of the syllogism, which, in Mill's view, showed a misunderstanding of the purpose of the syllogism. Mill understood Hamilton to have constructed a theory to indicate how we must think in order for our thought to be valid. For Mill, however, the syllogism did not teach one how one must reason, but rather it provided 'a test of the validity of reasonings, by supplying forms of expression into which all reasonings may be translated if valid, and which, if they are invalid, will detect the hidden flaw'(*CW*, IX, p. 398). Although a quantified predicate might conceivably assist in this process, in fact, as Mill demonstrated, the existing syllogistic theory covered all of the so-called ambiguities, even though it might require several propositions to cover the ground. Nevertheless, these quantified forms removed the syllogism from common understanding and common language. Mill asked:

> Does he, when he judges that all oxen ruminate, advert even in the minutest degree to the question, whether there is anything else which ruminates? Is this consideration at all in his thoughts, any more than any other consideration foreign to the immediate subject? One person may know that there are other ruminating animals, another may think there are none, a third may be without any opinion on the subject: but if they all know what is meant by ruminating, they all, when they judge that every ox ruminates, means exactly the same thing. The mental process they go through, as far as that one judgment is concerned, is precisely identical; though some of them may go on further, and add other judgments to it (*CW*, IX, pp. 396–97).

To insist that every ox is some ruminator simply deflects the mind from this common understanding, requiring one to consider another issue, whether there are other ruminators, when one is concerned simply with whether or not all oxen ruminate. In Mill's view:

> As all reasoning, except in the process of teaching Logic, will always be carried on in the forms which men use in real life; and as the only purpose of providing other forms, is to supply a test for those which are really used; it is essential that the forms provided should be forms into which the propositions expressed in common language can be translated – that every proposition in logical form, should be the exact equivalent of some proposition in the common form (*CW*, IX, p. 398).

Mill went on to claim that the proposition, all As are all Bs failed to be expressed in this common form, but could be expressed in common language as two separate judgments, e.g., All As are Bs and All Bs are As. 'The sole purpose of any syllogistic forms', he concluded, 'is to afford an available test for the process of drawing inferences in the common language of life from the premises in the same common language; and the ordinary forms of Syllogism effect this purpose completely' (*CW*, IX, p. 403). Although the new forms may be of some theoretical interest, they were of little utility in practice and added unnecessary complexity to existing logical forms.

7. Conclusion

We have considered Mill's position with regard to the quantification of the predicate at some length in part to raise the question again of his neglect of George Bentham's *Outline*. One might argue that Bentham's employment of a new technical notation in his account of propositions and the syllogism was different from, and less ambitious than, that of De Morgan and Hamilton. It is also possible that Mill's concentration on Hamilton as his main opponent in philosophy and his critique of an a priori philosophy that, in this instance, led nowhere, took him away from the important issues whose resolution eventually led to modern symbolic logic. Where Mill did confront the issue of technical forms, he thought of their use as either of little importance (as a school exercise) or a threat to rationality itself. Boole seemed to realize this peculiarity in Mill when he began to develop the application of algebra and other symbolic forms to logic. Although Boole did not seek to supersede common reason, he believed that logic differed from other sciences, because 'the perfection of its method is chiefly valuable as an evidence of the speculative truth of its principles'.[58] Without such a view, he thought that logic became the veneration of Aristotle. Mill was equally critical of such a position and developed new principles (e.g. in the fields of induction and fallacies), which were never considered by Aristotle and the scholastic tradition. But for a number of reasons he also felt strongly identified with traditional logic and the syllogism. This identification with traditional logic perhaps made him blind to new moves in logic, apart from those of Whately (who, paradoxically, was regarded as a traditionalist by George Bentham),[59] and led him to reject George Bentham's work (as well as that of Jevons, De Morgan and Boole).

We can now see some of the basis for Mill's reluctance to embrace the development of modern logic. In part, it is based on Mill's otherwise admirable desire to place 'the common language of life', as well as natural science and mathematics, under the heading of logic, and, particularly, a logic of truth. Mill might have found a source for some of his logical ideas and for the emphasis on truth and its transparency in the various appendices to Jeremy Bentham's *Chrestomathia*. Of particular interest is appendix VIII, 'Geometry and Algebra', which first appeared in the Bowring edition of Bentham's works in 1843, and was edited (at the suggestion of Southwood Smith) by no less a figure than De Morgan.[60] What prevented Mill from examining this material (as far as we know) may well have been the hardened parallel lines that separated the Mills (both father and son) from the Benthams (both uncle and nephew). We may never know what drove Mill to ignore and dismiss these earlier and important sources, and to adopt the Coleridgean, Whately, as an inspiration and guide to the development of his own logical ideas. But we can see here that the parallel lives in logic did exist, and Mill's omission from the cannon of modern logic may well be dependent on its influence.[61]

Notes

1   References to *CW* are to: J.S. Mill, *The Collected Works of John Stuart Mill*, ed. J.M. Robson, 33 vols., Toronto: University of Toronto Press and London: Routledge & Kegan Paul, 1963–91.
2   See G. Scarre, *Logic and Reality in the Philosophy of John Stuart Mill*, Dordrecht: Kluwer Academic Publishers, 1989, pp. 1ff.
3   J. Slater, 'Introduction' to G. Boole, *The Mathematical Analysis of Logic*, Bristol: Thoemmes Press, 1998, p. xi.
4   See Scarre op. cit., p. 2; J. Passmore, *A Hundred Years of Philosophy*, 2nd ed., London: Duckworth, 1966, pp. 11–12.
5   See E. Halévy, *The Growth of Philosophic Radicalism*, trans. Mary Morris, London: Faber and Faber, 1928, p. 308; L. Stephen, *The English Utilitarians*, 3 vols., London: Duckworth, 1900, ii., pp. 7ff.
6   M. Ripoli, 'The Return of James Mill', *Utilitas* 10, 1998, 105–6; T. Ball, 'Introduction' to James Mill, *Political Writings*, Cambridge: Cambridge University Press, 1992, p. xv.
7   See also Halévy, op. cit., p. 307.
8   A. Bain, *James Mill: A Biography*, London: Longmans, Green and Co., 1882, p. 135.
9   J. Bentham, *The Correspondence of Jeremy Bentham, Volume 8, January 1809 to December 1816*, ed. S. Conway, Oxford: Clarendon Press, 1988, p. 417.
10 Ibid., pp. 153, 155.
11 See J. Mill, *Political Writings*, ed. T. Ball, Cambridge: Cambridge University Press, 1992, pp. 139–94.
12 See Bain, op. cit., pp. 142–44; Ripoli, op. cit., pp. 111ff.
13 See J. Bentham, *Chrestomathia*, ed. M.J. Smith and W.H. Burston, Oxford: Clarendon Press, 1983; G. Bentham, *Outline of a New System of Logic with A Critical Examination of Dr. Whately's 'Elements of Logic'*, Bristol: Thoemmes Press, 1990.
14 J. Mill, *Analysis of the Phenomena of the Human Mind*, 2 vols., London: Baldwin and Cradock, 1829, i. pp. 309–12, 313–20, ii. pp. 1–135, 136–40, 141–42.
15 Ibid., ii. pp. 311–12.
16 G. Bentham, *Autobiography 1800–1834*, ed. M. Filipiuk, Toronto: University of Toronto Press, 1997, p. 9.
17 Ibid., p. 63.
18 See J. Bentham, *Chrestomathia*, op. cit., pp. 139–276; G. Bentham, *Autobiography*, op. cit., p. 69.
19 See M. Filipiuk, 'John Stuart Mill and France', *A Cultivated Mind, Essays on J.S. Mill Presented to John M. Robson*, ed. M. Laine, Toronto: University of Toronto Press, 1991, pp. 81ff.
20 See also A. Mill, 'Introduction', *John Mill's Boyhood Visit to France*, Toronto: University of Toronto Press, 1960, pp. xv, xix; T. Inoue, 'The Week-Long Blank in J.S. Mill's Sojourn in France: A Notebook Rediscovered', *Notes and Queries*, 250, 2005, 57–65 (New Series Vol. 52).
21 G. Bentham, *Autobiography*, op. cit., pp. 97–98; J. Bentham, *The Correspondence of Jeremy Bentham, Volume 11, July 1824 to June 1828*, ed. C. Fuller, Oxford: Clarendon Press, 2000, pp. 170–72.
22 J. Bentham, *Chrestomathia*, op. cit., pp. 139–276.
23 G. Bentham, *Autobiography*, op. cit., pp. 100–101, 458n.2.

24 Ibid., p. 104. Besides enjoying an active social life, George set out to explore gardens and to travel throughout England and Scotland mainly taking an interest in botanical matters. At an early point in his visit (30 March 1823), he recorded a trip to Hackney with John Bowring, J.S. Mill and Richard Doane, Bentham's amanuensis who had visited France in 1819–20, just prior to the visit by Mill, to see the spectacular Loddiges's hothouses and gardens, filled with tropical palms and flowers. The event provides some evidence that, despite their mutual dislike of Bowring, Mill and George Bentham were happy to be together at this time and indulge their shared interest in botany and horticulture. See ibid., pp. 108–9.

25 Ibid., pp. 234ff.

26 Ibid., p. 244.

27 See ibid., pp. 245–46.

28 Ibid., p. 244.

29 According to Bentham's manuscripts, he wrote on logic at various dates from 1795 but, particularly, from 1811 and during the period at Ford Abbey (1814–18).

30 See G. Bentham, *Outline of a New System of Logic*, op. cit.; *CW*, XI, pp. 1–35).

31 See J.M. Robson, 'John Stuart Mill and Jeremy Bentham, with some Observations on James Mill', *Essays in English Literature from the Renaissance to the Victorian Age, Presented to A.S.P. Woodhouse*, ed. M. MacLure and F.W. Watt, Toronto: University of Toronto Press, 1964, 258; *The Improvement of Mankind, The Social and Political Thought of John Stuart Mill*, Toronto: University of Toronto Press and London: Routledge & Kegan Paul, 1968, p. 22.

32 See M. Green, 'Sympathy and Self-Interest: The Crisis in Mill's Mental History', *Utilitas* 1, 1989, 259–77.

33 In 1843 Mill acknowledged that he had not forgotten George Bentham's work as a logician by sending him a copy of his own *System of Logic*. See *CW*, XIII, p. 577. Nevertheless, most further exchanges were concerned more with botany than with logic.

34 G. Bentham, *Autobiography*, op. cit., p. 271.

35 'Your letter, which I received this morning, is a more good-natured one than I fear mine was. I am much obliged to you for not being offended at my *taking huff* as I did, and I will now tell you exactly what I think of Mr. George Bentham's book – and what I am ready to say of it, if you think that it would be more satisfactory to Mr. Bentham than an entire omission. I do not think that Mr. G.B.'s book affords any proof of want of talent – far from it – but many of haste, and want of due deliberation. This mistake was, it seems to me, that of supposing that he was qualified to write on such a subject as logic after two or three months' study, or that so young a logician was capable of maintaining so high a ground as that of a critic upon Whately. The consequences of his mistake have been twofold: first of all, he has produced nothing but minute criticism, which even when most just, is particularly annoying to the person criticized when so much stress appears to be laid upon it. This minute criticism is often just, sometimes very acute, but frequently, also, if I am not mistaken, altogether groundless. Instead of this, a good critic on Whately should have laid down as a standard of comparison, the best existing or the best conceivable *exposition of the science*, & examined how far Whately's book possesses the properties which should belong to *that*. In the second place, Mr. George Bentham seems not to be aware, that Dr. Whately is a far greater master of the science than *he* is, & that the public will think the disproportion still greater than it is. It would therefore have been wiser in him not to have assumed the tone of undisputed & indisputable superiority over Whately, which marks a greater part of his critique. To be entitled to do this, a writer should not only *be* superior, but *prove* himself to be superior, in knowledge of the subject, to the author whom he criticizes. He should let the people see that if he differs from Whately, it is not because W. knows more than he but because he knows more than W. I have put this more strongly, and enlarged upon it more fully to you than I should do in the W.R. But I should think it wrong, in noticing the book, not to say something of this sort' (*CW*, XII, pp. 23–24).

Part of the tension evident in Mill's letter might be accounted for by the position of Bowring in the life of Jeremy Bentham. George Bentham and J.S. Mill shared the widespread antipathy towards Bowring among Bentham's older friends like James Mill and Francis Place, which had reached a high point in 1826 with revelations of Bowring's involvement in the Greek loan scandal and his taking refuge in Bentham's house (see F. Rosen, *Bentham, Byron and Greece: Constitutionalism, Nationalism, and Early Liberal Constitutional Thought*, Oxford: Clarendon Press, pp. 265ff.). For George Bentham, Bowring 'retains the same command over the whole of my Uncle's actions, and which power he has the art to preserve by the grossest flattery and the most egregious nonsense and stories that he makes my uncle swallow' (G. Bentham, *Autobiography*, op. cit., p. 236; cf. F. Rosen, 'John Bowring and the World of Jeremy Bentham', *Sir John Bowring 1792–1872, Aspects of his Life and Career*, ed. J. Youings, Plymouth: The Devonshire Association, 1993, pp. 13–28). He feared that Bowring was making himself wealthy from funds supplied by Bentham for his various schemes and would exhaust the fortune he should receive (as Bentham's main heir) at the time of his uncle's death. For George Bentham, even the *Westminster Review*, established by Bentham with Bowring as editor, 'is going to the dogs – because Bowring is Editor' (G. Bentham, *Autobiography*, op. cit., p. 236). Although J.S. Mill had no higher estimation of Bowring, like his father (who had earlier been offered the editorship of the *Westminster Review*), he was a supporter of the review and was willing to write for it (see *CW*, I, pp. 93, 95–97, 101). In the spring of 1828, however, both he and his father stated that they would not continue to write under Bowring's editorship, and J.S. Mill ended his relationship with the journal (*CW*, I, p. 135). No direct connection with the Bowring–J.S. Mill exchange of letters over George Bentham's book was made by Mill in the *Autobiography*, even though the events took place at roughly the same time. The anger in Mill's letters, however, may well have reflected this falling out with Bowring, as much as his dissatisfaction with George Bentham's book.

It might also be worth considering the falling out between the Mills and Benthams in 1827, when George Bentham was sent by Jeremy to collect books from James Mill's house from a list of nearly 600 that presumably had been borrowed by Mill (see Robson, 'John Stuart Mill and Jeremy Bentham', op. cit., p. 252; J. Bentham, *The Correspondence of Jeremy Bentham, Volume 12, July 1824 to June 1828*, ed. L. O'Sullivan and C. Fuller, Oxford: Clarendon Press, 2006, pp. 320–21). I am indebted to Dr. Kevin O'Rourke for reminding me of this incident.

36 Cf. Bentham, *Correspondence*, volume 12, op. cit., pp. 310–11; see B. Daydon Jackson, *George Bentham*, London: Dent, 1906, p. 57.

37 See G. Bentham, *Handbook of the British Flora*, London: Lovell, Reeve, 1858, p. vii.

38 See G. Bentham, *Autobiography*, op. cit., pp. 271, 484–86.

39 W.S. Jevons, *Elementary Lessons in Logic: Deductive and Inductive*, London: Macmillan, 1870, p. 183, original in italics.

40 W. S. Jevons, 'Who Discovered the Quantification of the Predicate?', *Contemporary Review*, 21, 1872–73, 823.

41 See Slater, 'Introduction', op. cit., p. viii.

42 G. Boole, *The Mathematical Analysis of Logic*, ed. J. Slater, Bristol: Thoemmes Press, 1998, p. 1.

43 W. Hamilton, *Discussions on Philosophy and Literature, Education and University Reform. Chiefly from the Edinburgh Review*, 2nd ed., enlarged, London and Edinburgh: Longmans, Brown, Green and Longmans, Maclachlan and Stewart, 1853, p. 650.

44 A. De Morgan, *Formal Logic: or, The Calculus of Inference, Necessary and Probable*, London: Taylor and Walton, 1847, pp. 297–323.

45 P. Heath, 'Introduction', A. De Morgan, *On the Syllogism and Other Logical Writings*, London: Routledge & Kegan Paul, 1966, p. xv.

46 T.S. Baynes, *An Essay on the New Analytic of Logical Forms*, Edinburgh: Sutherland and Knox, London: Simpkin, Marshall, 1850.

47 W. Warlow, *Athenaeum*, 21 December 1850, p. 1351.
48 See G. Bentham, *Autobiography*, op. cit., pp. 484–85.
49 See H. Spencer, 'The Study of Sociology. IX. – The Bias of Patriotism', *Contemporary Review*, 21, 1872–73, 487ff.
50 Ibid., pp. 489–90.
51 Ibid., p. 490n.
52 W. Hamilton, *Discussions*, op. cit., p. 650.
53 W.S. Jevons, *Elementary Lessons in Logic*, op. cit., p. 187.
54 T.S. Baynes, 'Mr. Herbert Spencer on Sir William Hamilton and the Quantification of the Predicate', *Contemporary Review*, 21, 1872–73, 798.
55 W.H. Jevons, Who Discovered the Quantification of the Predicate?', op. cit., pp. 822–23.
56 Ibid., p. 823.
57 *CW*, IX, p. 385, quoting Baynes, *An Essay on the New Analytic of Logical Forms*, op. cit., p. 80.
58 G. Boole, *The Mathematical Analysis of Logic*, op. cit., p. 2.
59 G. Bentham, *Outline of a New System of Logic*, op. cit., p. viii.
60 See J. Bentham, *Chrestomathia*, op. cit., pp. xxv-xxvi, 330–94.
61 I am indebted to the splendid edition of George Bentham's *Autobiography*, expertly edited by Marion Filipiuk for much information regarding George Bentham and the debate over the quantification of the predicate. My thanks also to Georgios Varouxakis for valuable suggestions and assistance.

6   John Stuart Mill and virtue ethics

Wendy Donner

Introduction

John Stuart Mill's utilitarianism has some interesting connections and indebtedness to the tradition of virtue ethics. I explore some of these linkages against the backdrop of an interpretive framework that I have developed in several other writings.[1] In other writings I have examined Mill's value theory, a variant of qualitative hedonism, in part by comparing it with the quantitative hedonism of Jeremy Bentham.[2] I have argued that Mill holds that those qualities or kinds of happiness that develop and exercise the higher human capacities and faculties are the most valuable. His conception of the good for humans is analyzed in terms of certain core excellences of development and self-development. Mill's liberalism underpins his baseline conviction that activities involving the development and exercise of these excellences over the span of entire human lifetimes are stable and enduring sources of highly valuable satisfactions and worthwhile lives. Societies owe it to their members to offer the liberal cultural context and educational venues so that they may avail themselves of the opportunities to realize these excellences, in multifarious forms as appropriate in pluralistic societies.[3] Mill's elaborate liberal philosophy of education, featuring promotion of processes of development and self-development, is best read as prescribing a programme for inculcating and cultivating the mental and moral virtues he regularly extols. Education and self-development train the human capacities of reason, emotion and sympathy as well as higher order capacities like autonomy, individuality, sociality and compassion. The 'competent judges' that Mill invokes in *Utilitarianism* as being in an excellent position to assess and compare the value of different kinds or qualities of happiness and models of life are members of society who have been so educated. Mill combines a liberal commitment to egalitarianism with the insight gleaned from Greek virtue ethical traditions that a flourishing human life depends upon an education which trains the excellences of self-development.

I begin here by looking at the structure of Mill's moral philosophy, as he explains it, primarily in *A System of Logic* and *Utilitarianism*. I argue that Mill's philosophy has a doctrine of Virtue to complement his theory of Morality. They both have their due place in the practices of life that promote happiness, and they should not be regarded as competitors. Mill's theory is comprehensive, but he argues that morality should not be regarded as being entrusted with the entire mandate for utility promotion. Mill scrutinizes with deep suspicion those 'moralists by profession' who believe otherwise and are overly enthusiastic about the province of morality in the Art of Life. He suspects that those with despotic tendencies, who love wielding power over others and are the enemies of liberty, are rather quick to resort to their favoured tools of coercion and thus end up undermining rather than promoting happiness. In the *Logic*, Mill lays out the three departments of the Art of Life – 'Morality, Prudence or Policy, and Aesthetics; the Right, the Expedient, and the Beautiful or Noble'.[4] The distinction between Morality or Duty, on the one hand, and Nobility or Virtue, on the other, plays a crucial role in Mill's theory and yet this distinction is often underplayed in discussions of his philosophy. In the absence of this understanding, it is not surprising that confusion sometimes follows concerning Mill's arguments and commitments. For example, blurring the distinction between Duty and Virtue can lead to mistaken readings in which virtue is incorrectly taken to be obligatory, resulting in the false conviction that it is permissible to coerce people to be more virtuous.

The art of life, morality and the doctrine of virtue

Virtue ethicist Sarah Broadie poses a challenge to Mill's utilitarianism. She laments that although the concept of the highest good or *summum bonum* is the determining idea of ancient ethics, it has been pushed aside in modern ethical theories. She holds Mill and his legacy responsible for this state of affairs. Her imputation may seem odd, since Mill points out the importance of the concept of the *summum bonum* in the early passages of *Utilitarianism*. He certainly seems to share her concern as he also laments 'the little progress which has been made in the decision of the controversy respecting the criterion of right and wrong. From the dawn of philosophy, the question concerning the *summum bonum*, or, what is the same thing, concerning the foundation of morality, has been accounted the main problem in speculative thought'.[5] Broadie is not impressed and she charges Mill with sidelining the concept of the highest good, making it into something that is useful for only one purpose: 'the philosophical assumption [is] that being the highest good is the same as, or at the very least is essentially connected with, being the standard of right and wrong'.[6] But in this statement Broadie puts side-by-side two very different claims about the purported relation between the good and the standard of right and wrong. Broadie presents her claims about Mill's complicity with confidence. She says that whether Mill is interpreted as an act or as a rule utilitarian, the error remains. Mill's readers, she says, have acquiesced in this. His readers and commentators also ignore the idea of the highest good, 'presumably because they do not consider there is anything for the highest good to be or do apart from being, or functioning as, the mythological ... determinant of ... morality'.[7]

Despite Broadie's confidence, her pronouncement would be shocking news to Mill. Could he have foreseen that Book VI of *A System of Logic*, where he carefully lays out the structure of the moral arts and sciences in his thought, would be so thoroughly misunderstood? Since the *Logic* was a standard text in his day, he could reasonably expect reader familiarity with arguments about the structure of his moral philosophy. Regrettably, this familiarity is often lacking in current discussions of his utilitarianism.

Let us turn our attention to the *Logic*, where Mill examines the principle of utility, the first principle of Teleology. In the last chapter of Book VI of this work, Mill separates out the domain of morality from the broader domain of the moral arts. The principle of utility is the foundation of all of the many practical arts of human nature and society. It should be noted that sometimes Mill uses the phrase 'moral arts and sciences' to refer to the entire span of the practical arts of living and the term 'morality' to point out one compartment of this. Care is needed, then, not to conflate these two. It is here that he says that 'ethics, or morality, is properly a portion of the art corresponding to the sciences of human nature and society'.[8] He says that there is a 'body of doctrine, which is properly the Art of Life, in its three departments, Morality, Prudence or Policy, and Aesthetics; the Right, the Expedient, and the Beautiful or Noble, in human conduct and works'.[9] All other practical arts are subordinate to this. The subordinate arts require the arbitration of the general principle of Teleology to decide questions of precedence or weighing. Practical reasoning requires a first principle of Teleology. 'There must be some standard by which to determine the goodness or badness, absolute and comparative, of ends, or objects of desire.'.[10] Arguing against moral sense theories, he says that the principles of these theories, even if true, 'would provide only for that portion of the field of conduct which is properly called moral. For the remainder of the practice of life some general principle, or standard, must still be sought; and if that principle be rightly chosen, it will be found, I apprehend, to serve quite as well for the ultimate principle of Morality, as for that of Prudence, Policy, or Taste'.[11] He concludes that this general principle and test is that of 'conduciveness to the happiness of mankind ... the promotion of happiness is the ultimate principle of Teleology'.[12]

Morality, the subject of the essay *Utilitarianism*, inhabits but a portion of the Art of Life. It occupies an even smaller portion of the entire realm of the moral arts, in which it is one of dozens. In the earlier chapters of Book VI of the *Logic*, Mill explores the methods of some of these other moral arts and sciences, including psychology, ethology (the science of the formation of character), education, politics, political philosophy, government, economics, sociology, political economy and history. When Mill says that the promotion of happiness is the ultimate principle of Teleology, he means what he says. The principle of utility is the foundation of morality, but it performs that same function for all of the dozens of practical moral arts. When Mill argues that we ought to promote happiness, he is not speaking about a moral ought, but about a general value ought. He promotes utilitarianism as furnishing the guiding principle of the practical arts of the good life. The principle of utility is a principle of the good, and to interpret it as being a principle of right, rather than as the principle that provides the foundation of morality, is to invite misunderstanding.

It is important, then, not to misunderstand the difference between Morality and Virtue (two of the three components of the Art of Life) in Mill's theory. The

Art of Life, a bedrock element of Mill's moral philosophy, is usually ignored in explorations of his thought, even though his reliance upon its components affects almost everything he writes about the arts of living well. Seen in this light, utilitarianism is most accurately depicted as a 'theory of life on which this theory of morality is grounded'.[13] This comment from the early pages of *Utilitarianism* may seem quite mysterious unless it is read in the context of Mill's reasonable expectation that readers of *Utilitarianism* would know that he was drawing on discussions of the Art of Life in the *Logic*. In *Utilitarianism*, the ascribed book in which he examines Morality, Mill articulates his method for demarcating the sphere of Morality from the rest of the Art of Life and the other moral arts. In Chapter V of *Utilitarianism*, Mill analyzes in detail the structure of his moral philosophy, and scrutinizes the relation of justice and utility. First he carves out the place of the category of Morality within the Art of Life by marking it off from 'the remaining provinces of Expediency and Worthiness'.[14] He says,

> We do not call anything wrong, unless we mean to imply that a person ought to be punished in some way or other for doing it ... This seems to be the real turning point of the distinction between morality and simple expediency. It is a part of the notion of Duty in every one of its forms, that a person may rightfully be compelled to fulfill it ... There are other things ... which we wish that people should do, which we like or admire them for doing, perhaps dislike or despise them for not doing, but yet admit that they are not bound to do; it is not a case of moral obligation ... we say that it would be right to do so and so, or merely that it would be desirable or laudable, according as we would wish to see the person whom it concerns, compelled, or only persuaded and exhorted, to act in that manner.[15]

This quote is familiar to readers of Mill's work. However, his full agenda is not always appreciated. This quote differentiates the dominion of Morality from the other spheres of the Art of Life. However, the principles determining the division are motivated by Mill's intention both to demarcate and to limit the powers of morality. Many insights concerning the structure of Mill's theory flow from grasping his intentions on this structural question. Mill's evaluation of Auguste Comte's and Jeremy Bentham's overzealous advocacy of the powers of morality shed light on his agenda. In 'Auguste Comte and Positivism' Mill skewers Comte for being too fervent about morality. Comte is a 'morality-intoxicated man' who wants to expand the authority of morality and transform all practical issues into moral concerns.[16] Comte is prone to the erroneous Calvinist predilection of thinking that

> [W]hatever is not a duty is a sin. It does not perceive that between the region of duty and that of sin, there is an intermediate space, the region of positive worthiness. It is not good that persons should be bound, by other people's opinion, to do everything that they would deserve praise for doing. There is a standard of altruism to which all should be required to come up, and a degree beyond it which is not obligatory, but meritorious. It is incumbent

on every one to restrain the pursuit of his personal objects within the limits consistent with the essential interests of others. What those limits are, it is the province of ethical science to determine; and to keep all individuals and aggregations of individuals within them, is the proper office of punishment and of moral blame. If in addition to fulfilling this obligation, persons make the good of others a direct object of disinterested exertions, postponing or sacrificing to it even innocent personal indulgences, they deserve gratitude and honour, and are fit objects of moral praise. So long as they are in no way compelled to this conduct by any external pressure, there cannot be too much of it; but a necessary condition is its spontaneity ... Such spontaneity by no means excludes sympathetic encouragement ... The object should be to stimulate services to humanity by their natural rewards; not to render the pursuit of our own good in any other manner impossible, by visiting it with the reproaches of other and of our own conscience. The proper office of those sanctions is to enforce upon every one, the conduct necessary to give all other persons their fair chance: conduct which chiefly consists in not doing them harm, and not impeding them in anything which without harming others does good to themselves. To this must of course be added, that when we either expressly or tacitly undertake to do more, we are bound to keep our promise. And inasmuch as every one, who avails himself of the advantages of society, leads others to expect from him all such positive good offices and disinterested services as the moral improvement attained by mankind has rendered customary, he deserves moral blame if, without just cause, he disappoints that expectation. Through this principle the domain of moral duty, in an improving society, is always widening. When what once was uncommon virtue becomes common virtue, it comes to be numbered among obligations, while a degree exceeding what has grown common, remains simply meritorious.[17]

He continues,

Demanding no more than this, society, in any tolerable circumstances, obtains much more; for the natural activity of human nature, shut out from all noxious directions, will expand itself in useful ones ... But above this standard there is an unlimited range of moral worth, up to the most exalted heroism, which should be fostered by every positive encouragement, though not converted into an obligation ... Nor can any pains taken be too great, to form the habit, and develop the desire, of being useful to others and to the world, by the practice, independently of reward and of every personal consideration, of positive virtue beyond the bounds of prescribed duty.[18]

Mill argues that Comte is not alone in his efforts to expand the moral domain of duty beyond its reasonable and legitimate borders. Comte's companion is none other than Jeremy Bentham, Mill's utilitarian predecessor. In 'Bentham', Mill argues that Bentham, if not morality-intoxicated, at the very least makes too much of morality. Bentham's

[O]ne-sidedness, belongs to him not as a utilitarian, but as a mor; profession, and in common with almost all professed moralists, whe; ligious or philosophical: it is that of treating the *moral* view of actic characters, which is unquestionably the first and most important m looking at them, as if it were the sole one: whereas it is only one of three, by all of which our sentiments towards the human being may be, ought to be, and without entirely crushing our own nature cannot but be, materially influenced. Every human action has three aspects: its *moral* aspect, or that of its *right* and *wrong*; its *aesthetic* aspect, or that of its *beauty*; its *sympathetic* aspect, or that of its *loveableness*. The first addresses itself to our reason and conscience; the second to our imagination; the third to our human fellow-feeling. According to the first, we approve or disapprove; according to the second, we admire or despise; according to the third, we love, pity, or dislike. The morality of an action depends on its foreseeable consequences; its beauty, and its loveableness, or the reverse, depend on the qualities which it is evidence of ... It is not possible for any sophistry to confound these three modes of viewing an action; but it is very possible to adhere to one of them exclusively, and lose sight of the rest. Sentimentality consists in setting the last two of the three above the first; the error of moralists in general, and of Bentham, is to sink the two latter entirely. This is pre-eminently the case with Bentham: he both wrote and felt as if the moral standard ought not only to be paramount (which it ought), but to be alone; as if it ought to be the sole master of all our actions, and even of all our sentiments.[19]

The department of morality has authority over conduct concerning the area of rules of duty. Mill's definition of moral duty in *Utilitarianism* is set out in terms of moral rules whose violation incurs coercion and sanctions. A crucial implication of this is that if conduct fails to maximize the good it does not follow that it is morally wrong. Many, many actions in numerous arenas do not maximize the good and yet under Mill's schema they are not morally wrong. Morality is a restricted domain in Mill's theory; in particular, the range of morally wrong acts is more limited than in Comte's or in Bentham's systems. Morally wrong acts, in Mill's system, are those that by definition are liable to punishment and coercion. Mill's theory conceptually links punishment, coercive sanctions and moral duty. Most actions in the domains of the practical arts do not have this link to legitimate coercion. Failure to appreciate the significance and the implications of the distinction between morality and the other two compartments of the Art of Life leads to the untenable position that morality has authority over large areas of practical life. Repudiating this stance as exhibiting intoxication with morality, Mill's contains morality's authority. In this way, by 'demanding no more than this, society ... obtains much more'. The domain of virtue, nobility, beauty or positive worthiness[20] correspondingly is expanded and given room in Mill's system to have authority over areas of the art of living that Mill does not believe should be subject to coercion and punishment. Mill has a doctrine of Virtue that complements his theory of Morality. In 'Thornton on Labour and its Claims', first published in the *Fortnightly Review* in 1869, Mill's articulation could not be more explicit. He says

> Utilitarian morality fully recognizes the distinction between the province of positive duty and that of virtue, but maintains that the standard and rule of both is the general interest. From the utilitarian point of view, the distinction between them is the following: – There are many acts, and a still greater number of forbearances, the perpetual practice of which by all is so necessary to the general well-being, that people must be held to it compulsorily, either by law, or by social pressure. These acts and forbearances constitute duty. Outside these bounds there is the innumerable variety of modes in which the acts of human beings are either a cause, or a hindrance, of good to their fellow-creatures, but in regard to which it is, on the whole, for the general interest that they should be left free; being merely encouraged, by praise and honour, to the performance of such beneficial actions ... This larger sphere is that of Merit or Virtue.[21]

David Lyons' analysis of Mill's moral theory clarifies, in part, the upshot of this. Lyons says it is a mistake to claim that Mill's principle of utility in itself sets out moral requirements. On the contrary, 'Mill's principle of utility says nothing about right or wrong. It speaks of ends, and is not seen by Mill as requiring that acts maximize utility'.[22] The principle does not enjoin a moral requirement to maximize utility. Instead, it advocates limited moral obligations coupled with general approval of utility-promoting actions. Mill's model is grounded in coercive social rules, and sanctions include not only legal sanctions, but also social disapproval and the internal guilt pangs of conscience. Lyons claims that,

> To call an act wrong is to imply that guilt feelings, and perhaps other sanctions, would be warranted against it. But sanctions assume coercive rules. *To show an act wrong, therefore, is to show that a coercive rule against it would be justified.* The justification of a coercive social rule establishes a moral obligation, breach of which is wrong.[23]

Lyons accurately concludes that Mill's theory does not require, morally speaking, utility maximization. But his analysis of Mill's theory leaves out an important component. He argues that in Mill's theory, justice is a sector of morality and morality is a sector of expediency. That Lyons' explanation leaves something out is apparent from his further claim that 'Mill presents morality as the realm of right and wrong, duty and obligation. He thus ignores such things as supererogation, and his account is incomplete'.[24] But Lyons overlooks Mill's comment that his demarcation is of Morality from 'the remaining provinces of Expediency and Worthiness'.[25] Mill does not ignore supererogation; he assigns it to the separate, companion sphere of Worthiness or Virtue in the Art of Life.

How would the assessment and understanding of Mill's theory change if we were to begin where Mill in fact begins, with the foundational Art Of Life consisting of three complimentary spheres of Morality, Expediency (including self-interest) and Worthiness (including virtue and supererogation)? The focus would change, and the picture of Mill's vision and his understanding of the purpose and goals of utilitarianism would widen. The theory is complex and intricate, and while we might appreciate this complexity, the complications arising from this enriched structure would heighten the challenges of interpreting his utilitarianism. Persistent questions of interpretation regarding the proper relation of the domain of morality and the other departments would not be laid to rest, and indeed some might resurface with renewed perplexity. Philosophers have tended to focus their attention almost exclusively on the philosophical problems internal to the domain of morality. Their attention has been taken up with thorny questions internal to the structure of the moral domain and its relation to the principle of utility. For example the debates over act and rule utilitarianism predominate in the discussion in the literature. I do not underestimate at all the thorniness of these problems, but I do claim that the almost exclusive attention to them has distorted the dialogue and deflected attention away from the accurate picture of the architecture of Mill's theory, which is much richer. This enlarged view of Mill's utilitarianism as promoting the Art of Life has the virtue, I maintain, of capturing Mill's vision accurately. My focus here, then, deliberately is not on morality but is elsewhere, on the other neglected areas of the Art of Life. This wider interpretation would serve to relegate to the sidelines some critiques of Mill's moral philosophy premised on the erroneous claim that the principle of utility is a moral principle and thus that it enjoins more extensive moral demands than those Mill actually defends. In this light, many objections centering on the putative excessively demanding requirements of Mill's utilitarian morality are seen to be baseless. But undeniably this enlarged framework brings to the foreground a host of interpretive and philosophical questions about how this theory of life integrates, delineates and balances the reasonable requirements of morality with those of the other domains of the Art of Life to promote the good life.[26]

What are some of the consequences of yoking the principle of utility so tightly to the erroneous assumption that it enjoins a moral requirement to maximize or even to promote happiness, rather than the more modest (and accurate) interpretation that in many spheres it simply encourages us to make happiness the end, justification and controller of actions, rules of actions, characters, lives and the myriad objects of evaluation? One obvious consequence is the mistaken view that in Mill's theory there is a standing general moral requirement to promote happiness and minimize suffering. In other words, the suspect assumption is that we are 'on call' to maximize the good, and have to account for ourselves if we book off from moral duty. We adopt the role of the moralist by profession for which Mill faults Bentham and Comte. We venture far beyond Mill's actual enjoinder not to violate moral duties, which protect vital interests, including the principles of justice that protect rights. John Skorupski and Allen Fuchs both have recently examined Mill's theory through the lens of the divisions of the Art of Life, and, based on Mill's framework that the realm of morality is narrower than has been usually supposed. Fuchs argues, correctly I believe, that the moral duties in the narrower range are quite stringent, and he follows Lyons' analysis, also correctly I believe, of analyzing these moral obligations as coercive social rules.[27] But he concludes that 'when our moral obligations are satisfied, or when (as will usually be the case) they do not even apply to the question in hand, the other practices of the art of life such as The Expedient and the Noble may hold sway and directly lead us to the *summum bonum* of the greatest happiness'.[28] Skorupski also argues that Mill does not maintain that 'we have a standing moral duty to do that which is best for all'.[29]

A second result of too tightly identifying the principle of utility simply with the morality component is that there may be lingering temptations to employ coercion to produce utility even above and beyond the moral sphere.[30] Mill prizes individuality as a primary human excellence of self-development, but it is part of the domain of prudence and self-regarding action, beyond the reach of coercion. Coercing people to conform to other people's notions of desirable or virtuous forms of life scripts or character is ruled out of bounds in his schema as an exercise in despotism. The boundaries protecting liberty and individuality must be respected, because there will always be those tempted to think that if virtue is a good, then we need not be concerned if we use force to increase it. Such employment of coercion to ramp up value production is addressed in Mill's attack on these misguided 'moral police' who improperly attempt to induce conformism rather than individuality and in the process derail liberty and well-being.

Mill's anti-paternalism is very familiar. Properly situating Morality and Virtue within the Art of Life and correctly understanding their complementary efforts to produce well-being illustrate the deep roots of anti-paternalism in his philosophy. Mill's familiar defence of individuality in *On Liberty* is a prime example of his rejection of any action by 'the moral police' to force people to conform to life plans and character types that others around them find desirable and preferable. He incessantly defends liberty and individuality and attacks those who are misguided enough to resort to coercion in their attempt to enforce rather than encourage virtue. He highlights these arguments on this theme in different contexts, and they all aim at delineating the proper domain of morality and putting brakes on the potential of despots illicitly to extend morality beyond its appropriate sphere.

All of this is fully in line with his liberal philosophy of education. His educational agenda aims to habituate students in the liberal virtues, and these virtues centrally feature liberty and individuality which must be kept secure. However, the objection can be put to his theory that there are conflicts between individuality and training in virtue. I contend that this particular objection springs from misinterpreting his views about the relationship between virtue and morality. The objection claims that his perspective on liberal education leads to a kind of bias in favour of some character types that are supposedly seen as ideal. If this is so, the objection continues, it is difficult to bring into harmony certain of his cherished commitments. How can the purported ideal character types be brought into line with his commitment to individualism and autonomy? If Mill expects individuality to yield unanticipated, eccentric and even original life scripts and character types, this would raise difficulties for any educational agenda that aims for specific results from its programme. Mill undoubtedly favours some kinds of individuality and character, according to the objection, and would prefer, for example, that autonomous agents choose commitments in line with liberalism as a way of life and contra those built around ties with certain forms of illiberal or traditional communities bound by their religious or ethnic ways of life.[31]

I hope that my previous argument has illustrated that this particular objection does not have traction against Mill, since it is based upon a reading of his philosophy that he does not actually hold. Mill hopes that liberal education will cultivate certain quite abstract human capacities, not certain much more specific human character types. And it is these latter specific character types, the objection presumes, that Mill prefers. But Mill will not be drawn into this agenda of his opponents. He wants to promote individuality, not cookie-cutter human character types. His arguments for the value of individuality as a human excellence in *On Liberty* are his authoritative reflections on this. That is why he argues relentlessly in that essay that there are limits to 'the power which can be legitimately exercised by society over the individual'.[32] The liberty principle defines the boundaries of legitimate societal coercion over individuals. His philosophy permits coercion only in cases of conduct that violates other-regarding moral duties.

In this work he spurns the very idea that there are specific forms of character or lifestyle of concern to those who love liberty and value toleration as liberals. Mill's own professed analysis is deliberately abstract. His educational programme has as its purpose an education for freedom that furthers development and exercise of human virtues most favoured by liberals – rationality, emotional sensibility, autonomy, individuality, compassion and empathetic connections with others. The emphasis is always on the holistic balance among these excellences, and on the expectation of pluralism and diversity in their expressions in individual lives. If the educational programme of society is not education for freedom but education to conform to and fit the moulds that others favour, then individuality and autonomy are poisoned at the root. Liberals encourage diversity, self-authorship and fluid identity, while despots want to coerce others to conform to their preferred character forms. The other side of the coin of Mill's positive defence of individuality is his impassioned attack on the harms of despotism to well-being. Liberal self-development is his ideal, but he recognizes its fragility and the danger that it can be subjugated by despots and the 'moral police' under the guise of promoting virtue. In this manner, enemies of liberty would short-circuit liberal virtues. Mill counters the move to undermine individuality in the name of virtue when he argues that the aim of liberal education is 'to render people unlike one another'.[33]

Since coercion in Mill's system is legitimate only in the sphere of duty, perhaps critics could try to argue that the theoretical apparatus of duties to self or self-regarding duties could offer a pathway for finding a place for coercing people to be more virtuous. However, this won't work, since Mill breaks with other theories on the issue of self-regarding duty. Some other moral theories do work with the notion of duties to self. The legacy of Kant is apparent in the assumption that we do have duties to ourselves. In Kant's theory, there are imperfect duties 'to perfect ourselves morally (as well as to develop our own talents)'.[34] However,

Mill makes a point of denying the very notion of self-regarding duty. Since he rejects that it is meaningful to say that we can have duties to ourselves, Mill removes this pathway to the claim that we can be coerced for pursuing unpopular lifestyles or character traits. In *On Liberty* he distinguishes violations of moral duties from

> [T]he self-regarding faults ... which are not properly immoralities, and to whatever pitch they may be carried, do not constitute wickedness. They may be proofs of any amount of folly, or want of personal dignity and self-respect; but they are only a subject of moral reprobation when they involve a breach of duty to others ... What are called duties to ourselves are not socially obligatory, unless circumstances render them at the same time duties to others. The term duty to oneself, when it means anything more than prudence, means self-respect or self-development; and for none of these is any one accountable to his fellow creatures.[35]

It cannot be consistently maintained both that people have the right to liberty of self-development and that they can be coerced if they choose characters, connections or commitments that those around them, even close to them, think amount to folly. Mill regards these temptations to hold others to account for their personal choices as the misguided activities of the 'moral police'.

This illustrates one point of departure between Mill's complex variety of utilitarianism and the simple generic form of utilitarianism that often seems to be center stage in discussions. For example, Michael Slote says that utilitarianism is committed to self-other symmetry. 'In utilitarianism, if something is permissibly done or obligatory to do with respect to one individual, it is permissible or obligatory in regard to any other individual ... Therefore, if it is wrong for me in some way to neglect the good of another person, it is, according to utilitarianism, wrong for me to neglect myself in that way, and similarly with respect to hurting myself or hurting another '.[36] This is generic utilitarianism; it is not applicable to Mill's complex variant, as I have argued.

Mill's intentions are also clarified by the distinction he draws between self-regarding duties and self-regarding virtues. As I argue above, he repudiates self-regarding duties. However, he welcomes the notion of self-regarding virtues, and considers their tools of encouragement as important elements in promoting the development and exercise of the virtues while at the same time securing liberty. We are not entitled to coerce others to be more virtuous, but our encouragement of virtue is to be welcomed, as long as we follow the principles appropriate to that sphere. Self-regarding virtues belong to the domain of worthiness and nobility in the Art of Life. He says,

> Human beings owe to each other help to distinguish the better from the worse, and encouragement to choose the former and avoid the latter. They should be forever stimulating each other to increased exercise of their higher faculties ... But neither one person, nor any number of persons, is warranted

in saying to another human creature of ripe years, that he shall not do with his life for his own benefit what he chooses to do with it … In this department, therefore, of human affairs, Individuality has its proper field of action … Considerations to aid his judgment, exhortations to strengthen his will, may be offered to him … but he himself is the final judge. All errors which he is likely to commit against advice and warning, are far outweighed by the evil of allowing others to constrain him to what they deem his good.[37]

Thus engaging with others to encourage or honor them for conduct in the sphere of virtuous conduct is a significant form of social interaction, and much of human happiness is the beneficiary of these efforts. With coercion set aside, room is left to improve people's prospects for better lives if the game rules guiding the different departments of the Art of Life are respected. The sphere of virtue calls for persuasion, encouragement and mutual engagement and disallows resort to intolerance or force. Mill says,

I am the last person to undervalue the self-regarding virtues; they are only second in importance, if even second, to the social. It is equally the business of education to cultivate both. But even education works by conviction and persuasion as well as by compulsion, and it is by the former only that, when the period of education[38] is past, the self-regarding virtues should be inculcated.[39]

It is a question to be pondered why it so often happens that the tacitly assumed default position is one of moral requirement and coercion. Mill wisely avoids this stance. He recognizes that, in many cases, letting things be brings about more happiness by allowing room for spontaneity, which is a human trait he values very highly.

The territory of morality and duty within Mill's theory has been examined in minute detail. The territory of virtue, in contrast, is under explored. Kant's doctrine of virtue was largely ignored until recently. Bringing it to light has expanded and enriched his philosophy. Perhaps it is time to apply the same scrutiny to Mill's doctrine of virtue and examine it on its own terms and not simply as an afterthought appended to morality. Virtue's role in Mill's moral philosophy is multifarious. I have argued that virtue has pride-of-place in the sphere of Nobility or Worthiness. But virtue is also thoroughly embedded in the process of self-development that is at the heart of Mill's conception of happiness. Virtues are admirable character traits that are enduring sources of happiness. Virtuous capacities, such as compassion and rationality, when stabilized and habitual, function as reliable sources of happiness for self and others, including the whole of society. The exemplars of virtue that Mill relies upon to serve as models for others have reached a pinnacle of confirmed habitual character traits that experience shows are reliable sources of happiness. This is Mill's adamant conviction, fuelling his liberal philosophy of education.

Lawrence Blum draws a very fruitful distinction between noteworthy and ordinary virtue that is relevant to Mill's doctrine and helpful in beginning the project of sorting out these various roles. Blum says that one sense of virtue points to especially admirable features of character. 'It is especially admirable because it issues in actions, and expresses itself in emotional reactions, that go beyond what is normally expected of people and for which they are not thought to warrant special esteem'.[40] This is noteworthy virtue. But the notion of ordinary virtue refers to '*any* valuable trait of character—not only noteworthy ones but also ones issuing in actions and feelings which, while morally worthy, are simply what are to be expected of a normal moral agent'.[41] Ordinary virtue is not especially distinguished, but rather what we would normally expect. In such cases, virtue is good, but not notably so. According to this classification scheme, it seems that some kinds of virtues, for example courage, are usually or always noteworthy, while other kinds, for example honesty, are usually ordinary. However, this classification is not straightforward, for in some circumstances it may be noteworthy and take courage to be honest – examples of whistleblowers come to mind – while some examples of courage, like telling the truth to a friend, may be ordinary. Blum suggests that 'every virtue has both noteworthy and ordinary manifestations, depending on circumstances'.[42]

Mill's comments in 'Auguste Comte' focus on what Blum classifies as noteworthy virtues. Roughly they fall into the category of acts of supererogation, above and beyond what duty calls for.[43] This is perhaps why they merit a separate category in the Art of Life. Yet the placement of the Art of Life, in which all other arts are subordinate, seems to suggest that Mill maintains that *all* of these categories – Morality, Prudence or Self-Interest and Beauty or Nobility or Virtue – are to be thought of as usual or essential components of the art of life for normal human agents. So perhaps the lesson is that Mill expects acts beyond what duty calls for to be an essential component of every well-lived life. And this means that the domain of Nobility in the Art of Life includes much more than supererogation. Nobility includes actions that are not so much 'above and beyond' duty, but beside duty, a companion or corresponding element of a well-lived life. The spheres are not to be thought of as hierarchically arranged in all cases, but as interconnected domains that complement each other. Even if we don't expect people to exhibit noteworthy virtue each and every day, still a life lived without significant, even regular instances of notable virtue would be lacking. And the virtues central to the cultivation processes of self-development are treated as essential to normal moral agency. The development and exercise of these virtues beyond a minimum threshold are needed for all varieties and individual expressions of a well-lived life. They fall under Blum's classification of ordinary virtue.

Mill's childhood education laid the groundwork for his endorsement of a place of honour for virtue in the good life. He was steeped in the classics from a very early age and he easily acknowledged his indebtedness to the virtue tradition of moral philosophy. The imprint of virtue ethics is palpable in manifold forms in his ethics, and his version of utilitarianism is well equipped to meet Broadie's challenge to modern ethical theory to respect fully the significance of the *summum bonum*. Mill's distinctive doctrine of Virtue within the Art of Life is one prominent result.

Notes

1 See W. Donner, *The Liberal Self: John Stuart Mill's Moral and Political Philosophy*, Ithaca: Cornell University Press, 1991; and W. Donner, 'Mill's Utilitarianism', in: J. Skorupski (ed.), *The Cambridge Companion to Mill*, Cambridge: Cambridge University Press, 1998, pp. 255–92. Also W. Donner and R. Fumerton, *Mill*, Oxford: Wiley-Blackwell, 2009, chapters 2–8, pp. 15–143.
2 W. Donner, 'Mill's Theory of Value', in: H. West (ed.), *The Blackwell Guide to Mill's Utilitarianism*, Oxford: Blackwell, 2005, pp. 117–38.
3 See W. Donner, 'John Stuart Mill on Education and Democracy', in: N. Urbinati and A. Zakaras (eds), *J. S. Mill's Political Thought: A Bicentennial Reassessment*, Cambridge: Cambridge University Press, 2007, pp. 250–74.
4 J. S. Mill, *The Collected Works of John Stuart Mill*. All page references to Mill's writings are to *The Collected Works of John Stuart Mill*, J. M. Robson, General Editor, Toronto: University of Toronto Press, 1963–91, 33 volumes, VIII, p. 949. Hereafter *Collected Works* cited as: CW.
5 *CW*, X, p. 205.
6 S. Broadie 'On the Idea of the *Summum Bonum*', in: C. Gill (ed.), *Virtue, Norms, and Objectivity: Issues in Ancient and Modern Ethics*, Oxford: Oxford University Press, 2005, p. 43.
7 Ibid., 45.
8 *CW*, VIII, p. 943.
9 *CW*, VIII, p. 949.
10 *CW*, VIII, p. 951.
11 Ibid.
12 Ibid.
13 *CW*, X, p. 210.
14 *CW*, X, p. 247.
15 *CW*, X, p. 246.
16 *CW*, X, p. 336.
17 *CW*, X, pp. 337–38.
18 *CW*, X, p. 339.
19 *CW*, X, pp. 112–13.
20 Mill's choice of words varies in different writings. However, the underlying theme of this category is consistently concerned with merit beyond or outside of prescribed duty.
21 *CW*, V, pp. 650–51.
22 D. Lyons, *Rights, Welfare, and Mill's Moral Theory*, Oxford: Clarendon Press, 1994, p. 59–60.
23 Ibid., p. 55.
24 Ibid., p.49.
25 *CW*, X, p. 247.
26 For discussion of some of these questions and problems, see: D. Lyons, 'Mill's Theory of Morality' in: Lyons, *Rights, Welfare, and Mill's Moral Theory*, pp. 47–65; A. Fuchs, 'Mill's Theory of Morally Correct Action', in: West (ed.), *The Blackwell Guide to Mill's Utilitarianism*; C.L. Ten, *Mill on Liberty*, Oxford: Oxford University Press, 1980; and R. Crisp, *Mill on Utilitarianism*, London: Routledge, 1997, especially Chapter 5 'What Utilitarianism Is', pp. 95–133.
27 A. Fuchs, 'Mill's Theory of Morally Correct Action', p. 149.
28 Ibid., p. 156.
29 J. Skorupski, 'The Place of Utilitarianism in Mill's Philosophy', in: West (ed.), *The Blackwell Guide to Mill's Utilitarianism*, p. 58.
30 See W. Donner, 'John Stuart Mill on Education and Democracy'.

31 See W. Donner, 'Autonomy, Tradition, and the Enforcement of Morality', in: C. L. Ten (ed.), *Mill's On Liberty: A Critical Guide*, Cambridge: Cambridge University Press, 2008, pp. 138–64.
32 *CW*, XVIII, p. 217.
33 *CW*, XVIII, p. 274.
34 M. Slote, 'Virtue Ethics, Utilitarianism, and Symmetry', in: R. Crisp (ed.), *How Should One Live?*, Oxford: Oxford University Press, 2003, p. 109.
35 *CW*, XVIII, p. 279.
36 Slote, 'Virtue Ethics, Utilitarianism, and Symmetry', p. 100.
37 *CW*, XVIII, p. 277.
38 In this context Mill means childhood education.
39 *CW*, XVIII, p. 277.
40 L. Blum, 'Community and Virtue', in: Crisp (ed.), *How Should One Live?*, p. 235.
41 Ibid.
42 Ibid.
43 Although, as Blum argues, there is no *exact* correspondence between the ordinary/ noteworthy and the duty/supererogation classifications.

7 Justice as higher pleasure

Jonathan Riley

1. Introduction

John Stuart Mill argues in *Utilitarianism* that the higher pleasures include the pleasures of the moral sentiments: '[T]here is no known Epicurean theory of life which does not assign to the pleasures of the intellect, of the feelings and imagination, and of *the moral sentiments* a much higher value as pleasures than to those of mere sensation.'[1] The most important of the moral sentiments, he says, is the sentiment of justice: 'justice … [is] the chief part, and incomparably the most sacred and binding part, of all morality'.[2] The idea of justice 'implies something which it is not only right to do, and wrong not to do, but which some individual person can claim from us as his moral right'.[3] Any person's moral right is 'a valid claim on society to protect him in the possession of [something], either by the force of law, or by that of education and opinion'.[4] Protection is provided by enforcing other people's correlative moral obligations not to violate the person's right. Thus, the pleasure of the moral sentiment of justice is the pleasant feeling of living in a community in which certain vital personal concerns shared by all are rendered secure by being continuously recognized and enforced as rights.[5] This higher pleasure of security can only be experienced in common with other people who mutually cooperate in terms of social rules that distribute rights and correlative obligations. As I read him, Mill insists that this moral kind of pleasure trumps any other kind that conflicts with it, although aesthetic and spiritual pleasures that do not conflict with moral pleasure may be of the highest kind.

Mill makes clear in both *Utilitarianism* and *The Subjection of Women* that justice can be fully achieved if and only if society establishes and enforces a system of equal rights and duties which gives the most protection for the vital personal interests shared by all citizens. By implication, the moral pleasure of security inseparably associated with the sentiment of justice is a variable that can be *maximized* only under a *particular* social code of *equal* rights and duties *for all*. To experience the pleasure of security in this moral sense, an individual must be capable of imagining himself in other people's positions and inferring that, no matter which position he occupies, he receives the same protection for the vital personal concerns which he shares with everyone else, an inference that is warranted if equal rights and duties for all are recognized and enforced. His moral feeling of security is compromised when he knows either that some members of society are excluded from the system of equal rights, or that some people are able to escape due punishment even though they refuse to fulfil their duties to others. Even if equal rights and duties are distributed to everyone and there is full compliance with the rules, the moral pleasure of security varies in quantity across different possible social codes. The amount of it experienced by any individual capable of experiencing it depends upon the nature of the rights and duties distributed by the code. Roughly, the moral pleasure of security increases in intensity as more complete protection is provided for the vital personal concerns shared by all members of the community.

General security, as a component of general happiness, is nothing but the collection of individuals' moral feelings of security experienced under a social code that distributes equal rights and duties. It is maximized when each person's moral pleasure of security is maximized, that is, when certain vital personal concerns which everyone shares are given a maximal degree of protection by society. Society does this by establishing particular equal rights in its laws, customs and/ or shared dictates of conscience, and by suitably punishing any individuals who fail to perform their correlative duties, where punishment includes legal penalties, public stigma and/or feelings of guilt.

No doubt much more needs to be said to clarify this Millian theory of justice as higher pleasure and its crucial implications for his peculiar version of utilitarianism. Among other things, it will seem incredible to critics that *any* version of utilitarianism has the resources to identify the shared vital personal concerns that ought to be protected as equal rights for all in a 'society of equals'. How can a utilitarian like Mill even begin to determine the nature and relative weights of the rights that should be distributed to all so as to maximize general security? Should individuals possess rights to own the products of their labour and savings in some form of capitalistic market economy, for instance, leaving room for substantial inequality in the distribution of resources beyond some guarantee of subsistence for all? Or should they possess rights to participate in democratic decision-making processes within worker-owned cooperative enterprises in some form of decentralized socialistic economy, where distribution of market returns might be based on a principle of perfect equality or even a Marxist principle of 'from each according to his ability, to each according to his need?'

My present aim is to clarify the higher pleasure of security as Mill understands it, and thereby clarify how liberal justice retains its familiar importance within his unusual version of hedonistic utilitarianism. I shall proceed as follows. I shall begin by insisting that, for him, one pleasure is of a higher kind or quality than another if and only if the one is judged to be *infinitely* more valuable as pleasure than the other by most if not all people who are competently acquainted with both pleasures. According to his doctrine of higher pleasures, the pleasure of security inseparably associated with the moral sentiment of justice is infinitely more pleasant than any competing kinds of pleasure.

Given that a higher kind of pleasure is infinitely more valuable than a lower kind and that humans cannot actually experience a completed infinity of any kind of pleasure, the higher kind cannot be generated merely by increasing the quantity of the lower kind. No matter how large the finite mass of the lower pleasure is made, even a bit of the higher pleasure remains more valuable *as pleasure*. A discontinuity or gap in value always remains between higher pleasure and lower pleasure. Rather than being generated from lower pleasure alone, higher pleasure is generated, Mill suggests, by means of a 'quasi-chemical reaction' among multiple ingredients including lower pleasures. He views the moral sentiment of justice as such a quasi-chemical unity, and he offers a psychological analysis of its key ingredients. In the course of his analysis, he suggests why the kind of gratification inseparably associated with this complex moral sentiment is a pleasant feeling of such high quality or intrinsic value that it overrides any competing kinds of pleasure, irrespective of quantity.

Mill's analysis of the moral sentiment of justice requires a more detailed discussion than I can give here.[6] But his main conclusion is that the sentiment acquires its peculiar urgency from the 'animal feeling' of retaliation or vengeance which is one its ingredients, whereas what is moral in the sentiment is the intelligent subordination of the animal feeling to the 'social feeling' of being in unity with our fellows, where the idea of 'being in unity' is enlightened by reason to mean cooperating with others in terms of a social code of equal rights and duties designed to protect shared vital personal concerns. An individual in possession of this sentiment of justice has developed the power of will required to control his feeling of vengeance so that it is directed only against those who violate others' rights rather than against anyone who displeases or injures him personally. Such a fair-minded person does not desire to retaliate against anyone who beats him for a job in an open competition conducted without force or fraud, for example, or who chooses a self-regarding lifestyle of which he disapproves. Instead, his desire for punishment is reserved for those who violate the equal rights which society has decided to recognize and enforce as means of providing security for shared vital personal concerns. Retaliation or punishment includes self-inflicted feelings of guilt triggered by his own violations of others' rights.

Building on these points, I shall then outline how individuals with a sense of justice – that is, individuals who have developed the capacities required to form the moral sentiment of justice and to experience the higher pleasure of security associated with it – can in principle jointly determine the nature and relative weights of the particular equal rights that ought to be recognized and enforced within their society. It is important to see that, for Mill, any competent individual seeking justice is required by justice itself to participate in an impartial social decision procedure to select the social rules of justice which yield the greatest amount of security for the members of society. Infallible ideal observers are not available to perfectly perform this task. Rather, to complete the formation of his own moral sentiment, any fair-minded person must participate with his fellows in an impartial social choice process to choose the particular rules and rights that ought to be recognized and enforced by everyone in his society. Some such social choice process is *internal* to the moral sentiment of justice. Prior to the operation of the social decision process, individuals cannot know which particular rules and rights ought to be accepted by anyone seeking to cooperate fairly with others in the community.

Remarkably, Mill never depicts the required social choice process as a utilitarian aggregation procedure of the usual sort, whereby an optimal code of justice is selected that maximizes the sum total of happiness or security in some precise sense. Rather, he implies that competent judges must rely on majority voting if they fail to achieve a consensus. Majority rule is a purely ordinal decision process that attempts to generate an optimal social choice merely from individual preference orderings defined over some domain of feasible options. In this case, the options are distinct social codes that distribute distinct systems of equal rights. As is well known, however, majority rule is plagued by inconsistencies.[7] Nevertheless, the inconsistencies can be removed by giving an equal score or weight to every individual's preference ordering (or some portion of the ordering), as when society gives an equal vote to individuals for their top-ranked options and then adds up the votes to select an option with the greatest sum total of votes. Although any such majority voting process has certain minor disadvantages of its own, I shall suggest that it is what Mill has in mind.

Once these crucial aspects of his moral and political philosophy are clarified, the attainment of liberal justice understood in terms of security of equal rights can be seen to take absolute or lexical priority over all competing considerations within Mill's unusual version of utilitarianism. I shall conclude by emphasizing this and other important implications of my interpretation of his philosophy.

2. The doctrine of higher pleasures

2.1 Quantitative and qualitative superiority

Mill is a classical ethical hedonist. According to hedonism, pleasure (including absence of pain) is the sole ultimate end: all other values can be reduced to, and restated in terms of, pleasure, where mere absence of pain is deemed equal to a zero amount of pleasure. Given hedonism, one unit of pleasure is equal in intrinsic value to any other unit of pleasure of the same kind. Suppose for the sake of argument that pleasure is homogenous stuff, that is, there are not heterogeneous kinds of pleasure in the sense that some pleasures, or types of pleasure, are intrinsically more valuable than others. Call this the standard version of ethical hedonism. Now, since pleasure is homogeneous and it is the only basic value, standard ethical hedonism says that one unit of pleasure is *always* just as valuable as any other unit of it.

In the context of standard hedonism, for any two possible objects, actions or outcomes x and y, one pleasure $u(x)$ is more valuable than another $u(y)$ if and only if the one is larger in quantity than the other. Mill recognizes, of course, that 'one pleasure can be more valuable than another, merely as a pleasure' by 'being greater in amount'.[8] How can this 'question of quantity' of two pleasures of the same kind be decided? He tells us that the answer can only be supplied by 'the judgment of those who are qualified by knowledge of both, or, if they differ, that of the majority among them'.[9] The final 'tribunal' is the judgment of most human beings who have competently experienced both pleasures: 'What means are there of determining which is the acutest of two pains, or the intensest of two pleasurable sensations, except the general suffrage of those who are familiar with both?' If most report that a larger amount of pleasure is involved in the experience of $u(x)$ than is involved in the experience of $u(y)$, taking for granted that human nature is not capable of experiencing an infinity of pleasure, then $u(x)$ is more valuable than $u(y)$ to some finite degree because $u(x)$ is quantitatively superior to $u(y)$ to that finite degree.

But Mill moves beyond standard hedonism to defend a non-standard qualitative version of hedonism: 'It is quite compatible with the principle of utility to recognize the fact, that some *kinds* of pleasure are more desirable and valuable than others'.[10] He says that there is another way in which one pleasure $u(x)$ can be more valuable than another pleasure $u(y)$, namely, by being higher in kind or quality, where 'higher in quality' means that the one is 'placed so far above the other [by competent judges] that they prefer it, even though knowing it to be attended with a greater amount of discontent, and would not resign it *for any quantity of the other pleasure which their nature is capable of*.[11] Again, how can this question of quality of two pleasures be decided? According to Mill, the same tribunal must be employed as with the question of quantity, that is, the judgment of most people who have competently experienced both pleasures: 'When, therefore, those feelings and judgment declare the pleasures derived from the higher faculties to be preferable *in kind*, apart from the question of intensity, to those of which the animal nature, disjoined from the higher faculties, is susceptible, they are entitled on this subject to the same regard'.[12] If most people who are competently acquainted with both feel that they would not resign even a bit of $u(x)$ for any amount of $u(y)$ which they are capable of experiencing – again taking for granted that human beings are not capable of experiencing a completed infinity of any kind of pleasure, then $u(x)$ is more valuable than $u(y)$ because $u(x)$ is qualitatively superior to $u(y)$ regardless of the quantities of each pleasure involved. Given that a higher kind A of pleasure $u^A(x)$ always remains more valuable than a lower kind B of pleasure $u^B(y)$ no matter how large the finite amount of pleasure involved in $u^B(y)$ is assumed to become, $u^A(x)$ may be said to be *infinitely* more valuable as pleasure or utility than $u^B(y)$, although we must be careful about the idea of infinity which is at work (see Section II.2).

It is worth emphasis that a higher pleasure $u^A(x)$ is qualitatively superior, or superior in kind, to a lower pleasure $u^B(y)$ by virtue of the higher pleasure's intrinsic nature: the higher has 'intrinsic superiority' over the lower.[13] Mill stresses this point when he defends his view that mental pleasures are qualitatively superior to bodily pleasures. Bodily pleasures are purely somatic sensations – pangs, tickles, surges, rushes and so forth – that people can experience merely as a result of physical capacities which are possessed by other animals as well as humans. The relevant sensory capacities can in principle be 'disjoined' from a human being's distinctive intellectual, imaginative and moral capacities. Mill admits that 'utilitarian writers in general [following Bentham] have placed the superiority of mental over bodily pleasures chiefly in the greater permanency, safety, uncostliness, &c., of the former – that is, in their circumstantial advantages rather than in their intrinsic nature'.[14] Without denying that these writers 'have fully proved their case', however, he argues that utilitarians 'might have taken the other, and, as it may be called, higher ground, with entire consistency'. The 'other, and ... higher ground' is that which affirms that the mental pleasures, including those of the moral sentiments, are superior by virtue of their intrinsic nature. A higher kind of pleasure feels qualitatively superior to a lower kind because the higher's intrinsic nature gives it a superior quality apart from the question of quantity.

Qualitative or intrinsic superiority must not be conflated, then, with quantitative superiority. Qualitative superiority is an intrinsic superiority of one kind over another whereas quantitative superiority is a finite difference of degree within a given kind. Mill consistently emphasizes the point. In his notes to the 1869 edition of his father's *Analysis of the Phenomena of the Human Mind* [1829], for example, he remarks that a difference in degree is a difference of 'more or less', and that this is one particular way in which our feelings (including feelings of pleasure) can be unlike one another: '[T]here is a mode of likeness or unlikeness which we call Degree: some feelings *otherwise like* are unlike in degree, that is, one is unlike another in intensity, or one is unlike another in duration; in either case, one is distinguished as more, or greater, the other as less'.[15] This mode of likeness or unlikeness is predicated of any two feelings that are 'otherwise like' one another, that is, feelings of the same kind: 'We say there is *more* of something, when, to what there already was, there has been superadded other matter *of the same kind.* And when there is no actual superadding, but merely two independent masses *of the same substance,* we call that one the greater which produces the same impression on our senses which the other would produce if an addition were made to it. So with differences of intensity.'[16] Any difference of degree or quantity which we feel exists between two separate masses of the same kind of thing (including *pleasure*) is a relation present in the *feelings* themselves, as they are experienced by people competent to experience them: '[T]he fact of being more or less only means that we feel them as more or less ... [T]he difference ... is ... unsusceptible of further analysis'.[17]

An intrinsic difference is *not* 'the particular mode of likeness or unlikeness which we call Degree'. Any two feelings (including feelings of pleasure) may be unlike one another in kind, apart from any question of intensity or duration. We have different kinds of 'bodily' sensations, for example, which are produced in us by the interaction of our sense organs with external objects (including other bodies) that to us feel, say, red or green, soft or hard and pleasant or painful. These various kinds of 'bodily' feelings are all different in kind from 'mental' feelings, of which there are also various types, including ideas and emotions, memories and expectations, desires and volitions and so forth. Unlike the simple 'bodily' feelings, which are produced in our bodies independently of our higher faculties, the 'mental' feelings do depend on our faculties of intellect, imagination and sympathy which make use of 'bodily' sensations as well as other ingredients (such as 'animal' instincts) to produce the various kinds of 'mental' feelings. The higher faculties can infer coherent *ideas* of objects by attending to combinations of sensations of colour, touch and the like which have been experienced in conjunction, for example, and these faculties can also produce *desires* for objects by associating ideas of the object with an expectation of pleasure (including absence of pain). In addition to ideas and desires, the higher faculties generate many other sorts of mental feelings, some of which are apparently far more complex than others.

These myriad differences in kind of feeling are not differences of more or less. Rather, one kind of feeling has qualities or properties not shared by another kind. By identifying such properties, we can classify different kinds of feelings such as sensations of redness, sensations of greenness, ideas of red objects, ideas of green objects, memories of red ponies, fantasies of green unicorns, desires for blue women, aesthetic emotions of beauty and sublimity, moral sentiments of justice and charity and so forth. But different kinds of feeling do not always differ in terms of intrinsic value. Even though sensations of redness have a different quality than sensations of greenness, for instance, and both sensations feel unlike an idea of a red pony, these different kinds of feelings do not differ in terms of intrinsic value. Rather, different kinds of feelings have no intrinsic value unless they are associated with pleasure. As a hedonist, Mill holds that pleasure (including absence of pain) is the sole intrinsically desirable or valuable feeling. By implication, different kinds of intrinsically valuable feelings must be different kinds of pleasant feelings. In effect, the term 'pleasure' must denote a family of enjoyable feelings, some of which are felt to be intrinsically more valuable than others.

As already indicated, Mill insists that any mere 'bodily' sensation of pleasure is a feeling which is inferior in kind to any 'mental' feeling of pleasure associated with, say, the idea of this or that object or bundle of objects: the latter feeling of pleasure has a higher quality because its production involves the higher intellectual faculties. Indeed, some mental feelings of pleasure are higher in kind than others, a point to which I shall return in due course. As with differences of degree, however, any difference of kind or quality of pleasure is a relation present in *feelings* of pleasure as they are experienced by people competent to experience them. Mental feelings of pleasure simply feel like they are of a higher dimension entirely than mere 'animal' sensations of pleasure, independently of considerations of more or less. That pleasures are felt to be of different kinds or qualities is an ultimate fact of our feelings, 'unsusceptible of further analysis'.[18]

2.2 Qualitative superiority is infinite superiority

I have claimed that, for Mill, a higher pleasure $u^A(x)$ is *infinitely* more valuable as pleasure than a lower pleasure $u^B(y)$ because $u^A(x)$ remains more valuable than $u^B(y)$ no matter how large is the finite amount of pleasure involved in $u^B(y)$. But it is crucial to understand the idea of 'infinity' which is at work. Specifically, there is no suggestion that it is possible to experience an actual completed infinity. Rather, 'infinity' stands for a hypothetical process of unlimited expansion, an endless process that necessarily remains incomplete because any termination of it would imply that a finite limit has been reached. 'Infinite' does not denote an actual magnitude. It is not a real number or quantity. Thus, to say that a higher pleasure is infinitely more valuable than a lower means that the higher is more valuable than any quantity of the lower. No finite amount of the lower, however large, can ever be equal in value to even the smallest finite bit – or unit – of the higher.

That Mill understands infinity in this way must be gathered from remarks scattered across his writings. But some of his most helpful remarks occur when he comments on his father's psychological explanation of the feeling of infinity attached to space, an explanation that the son calls 'one of the most important thoughts in the whole [*Analysis*]'.[19] As the elder Mill explains:

> The idea of a portion more, adhering, by indissoluble association, to the idea of every increase, in any or in all directions, is the idea of 'infinitely extended', and the idea of 'infinitely extended', the connotation dropped, is the idea of Infinite Space ... one of the most complex ideas [of all] ... Extreme complexity, with great closeness of association, has this effect – that every particular part in the composition is overpowered by the multitude of all the other parts, and no one in particular stands marked from the rest; but all, together, assume the appearance of ONE.[20]

As finite portions of space are added together without limit, James suggests, they become inseparably associated into a single undifferentiated mass of unlimited extent which we call 'infinite space' The distinct portions become blended together so that space as a whole comes to seem larger than any finite magnitude.

In his comments, the younger Mill remarks that the idea of 'infinite space' does not depend on experience of an *actual infinity* of distinct portions of space. Rather, the idea emerges because we never experience an end to space:

> Every object is associated with some position: not always with the same position, but we have never perceived any object, and therefore never think of one, but in some position or other, relative to some other objects. As, from every position, Space extends in every direction (i.e., the unimpeded arm or body can move in any direction), and since we never were in any place which did not admit of motion in every direction from it, when such motion was not arrested by a resistance; every idea of position is irresistibly associated with extension beyond the position: and we can conceive no end to extension, because the place which we try to conceive as its end, raises irresistibly the idea of other places beyond it. This is one of the many so-called Necessities of Thought which are *necessities only in consequence of the inseparableness of an association*; but which, from unwillingness to admit this explanation, men mistake for original laws of the human mind, *and even regard them as the effect and proof of a corresponding necessary connexion between facts existing in Nature.*[21]

His view is that the idea of infinite space need not correspond to anything real in nature. The idea is manufactured by our imagination as a result of our inability to conceive any termination to space: 'As we have never had experience of any point of space without other points beyond it, nor of any point of time without others following it, the law of inseparable association makes it impossible for us to think of any point of space or time, however distant, without having the idea irresistibly realized in imagination, of other points still more remote'.[22] But our inability to conceive an ending to space or time does not imply that there is an actual infinity of points of space or time:

> Space or Time may, for aught we know, be inherently terminable, though in our present condition we are totally incapable of conceiving a termination to them. Could we arrive at the end of space, we should, no doubt, be apprised of it by some new and strange impression upon our senses, of which it is not at present in our power to form the faintest idea.[23]

Meanwhile, we cannot help but imagine that space is an unlimited whole because the idea of any finite portion of space, no matter how far away, is inseparably associated with another finite portion of space beyond it: 'the association is indissoluble, since every moment's experience is constantly renewing it'.[24]

Mill evidently agrees with Aristotle and many others that human beings have no coherent idea of a completed infinity. According to this Aristotelian tradition, humans cannot experience an actual infinite set of objects, or an actual infinite series of steps converging to some end-point, or an actual infinite extent of space or time. We cannot even conceive what any completed infinity would in fact look like. The term 'infinite' (like its counterpart 'infinitesimal') does not correspond to anything observable in nature: it is merely a convenient way of talking about a mathematical process (never completed even in theory let alone practice) in which either more and more units are added endlessly to some given quantity, or more and more bits of progressively smaller size (i.e., the size declines as units are added to the bit's divisor) are added endlessly to a given finite amount of something. Any such process is always incomplete: it never actually terminates. For that reason, any such process is never actually realized: it is always interrupted because we are incapable of actually completing it. Thus, the infinite must always remain merely *potential,* as Aristotle insisted.[25]

To claim that a higher pleasure is infinitely more valuable than a lower, then, is *not* to claim that a unit of higher pleasure is equivalent to a *completed* infinity of units of lower pleasure. If a unit of higher pleasure is ever said to be equivalent to an infinity of lower pleasure, this must be understood to mean that the higher unit equals *no finite number* of units of the lower, no matter how large. The term 'infinity' must be taken to refer merely to an incomplete never-ending process of expansion without limit.[26] Consistently with that usage of the term, a unit of higher pleasure is viewed as more valuable than any quantity of the lower pleasure, no matter how many units of lower pleasure are piled up together into a finite mass. In short, higher kinds of pleasant feelings are incommensurable with lower kinds: they cannot be reduced to a single scale of rational numbers. The different kinds are intrinsically different. Their intrinsic values or qualities are discontinuous. They must be kept separate from one another. Qualitatively superior pleasures must be

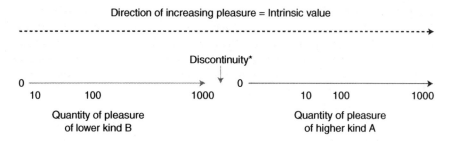

Figure 1

Note
*   The discontinuity of value is produced by the qualitative superiority (that is, infinite superiority) of the higher kind A of pleasure over the lower kind B. No finite quantity of a lower kind of pleasure, no matter how large, can ever equal in value even a bit of a higher kind of pleasure. Note that pleasure of kind B might be qualitatively superior to a third kind C of pleasure. In that case, pleasure of kind B would be a higher pleasure in relation to pleasure of kind C, and also a lower pleasure in relation to pleasure of kind A. Pleasure of kind A would be qualitatively superior to both kinds B and C of pleasures. The ranking of the different kinds or qualities of pleasure is transitive.

given absolute priority over qualitatively inferior ones in order to appreciate a fully competent person's idea of happiness and to calculate the general welfare. Figure 1 depicts how two different kinds of pleasures constitute a hierarchy in which the higher kind A is qualitatively or infinitely superior to the lower kind B, such that any quantity of the higher pleasure, however small, is more valuable than any quantity of the lower pleasure, however large.

2.3 The genesis of higher pleasures from lower

Remarkably, Mill's comments on his father's explanation of the idea of infinite space suggest that higher pleasure might conceivably be generated in a mechanical fashion solely from lower pleasure. We would not need to experience an actual infinity of lower pleasure for the idea of higher pleasure to emerge in our imagination. Rather, if every time we experienced some finite amount of pleasure we immediately experienced more of it in a continuous series with no perceived end-point, we might eventually imagine the whole series as one 'infinite pleasure' akin to 'infinite space'. This 'infinite pleasure' would be a unit of higher pleasure which is perceived as being larger than any of the particular pleasures or sums of pleasures making up the series to date. If we never experienced an end to the series, every particular pleasure in the composition would be overpowered by the multitude of all the other pleasures such that 'all, together, assume the appearance of ONE'.

If it were valid in the case of pleasure as it is in the case of space, this mechanical process of generating higher pleasure from lower would explain how a finite difference of degree within a kind of pleasure could in fact be *transformed* into an infinite difference of kind. Quantitative superiority would be transformed into qualitative superiority by an expansion of quantitative superiority which is perceived to have no end or limit. Adding together more and more units of pleasure of the same kind would eventually lead us to ignore the particular units and see them all united as 'one', that is, as a unit of some entirely new higher kind of pleasure. This higher pleasure would feel infinitely more valuable than the first kind of pleasure. A unit of the higher pleasure would feel larger than any finite amount of the lower kind. Qualitative superiority would be an unlimited difference of degree.

But this mechanical way of generating higher pleasure from lower, though conceivable, is incompatible with empirical observation. We observe that human beings do not experience amounts of pleasure as parts of an endless series of continual pleasures. Rather, humans experience an end to any particular pleasure or sum of pleasures. Given that we have no experience of pleasure (unlike space) as an interminable phenomenon, it is reasonable to suppose that human nature is capable only of registering limited – finite – amounts of any kind of pleasure. People eventually experience decreasing marginal pleasure from consuming an extra bottle of wine, for example, or from performing an additional act of sexual intercourse. The decrease will be sufficiently steep that a limit is imposed on the feasible pleasure from the wine or sex.

Nevertheless, even if it is not the way higher pleasures are actually generated from lower, the mechanical process remains useful as a thought experiment. It does show how higher pleasure might be generated from lower under certain conditions, to wit, if amounts of the lower were experienced in an endless series of continual pleasures. It is a conceivable way in which higher pleasure might come to be felt as infinitely more pleasant than lower pleasure, keeping in mind that 'infinitely more pleasant' does not imply that higher pleasure is an actual infinity of lower pleasure. Qualitative superiority is properly viewed as infinite superiority, where the infinite superiority of $u^A(x)$ to $u^B(y)$ means that even a bit of $u^A(x)$ is more valuable *as pleasure* than any finite amount of $u^B(y)$, no matter how large.

According to Mill, higher pleasure is generated from lower in a non-mechanical way, namely, what he calls a 'quasi-chemical method'. In his view, higher pleasure is produced by something akin to a chemical reaction among various ingredients including lower pleasures which are repeatedly experienced in combination. Thus, higher 'mental' pleasures are generated by the higher faculties from various ingredients which include the lower 'bodily' pleasures that arise from our animal nature alone. For example, certain intellectual pleasures are generated by combining various bodily sensations, including sensations of colour, sound, touch and so forth, *as well as inchoate sensations of pleasure*, into one coherent idea of a pleasing object or bundle of objects – more generally, an outcome – from which pleasure or enjoyment may be expected. The qualitative superiority of the intellectual pleasure in comparison to any mere bodily sensation of pleasure among its parts seems to be related to the 'extreme complexity' of the mental feeling. Every particular element in the composition is overpowered by the others, and no element in particular stands marked out from the rest; but all are united together into a mental feeling of pleasure inseparably associated with the idea of an outcome. Any mere bodily sensation of pleasure is overpowered as it is blended together with the other elements of the composition, and the new whole somehow imparts a higher quality – an infinitely more valuable dimension – to the mental feeling of pleasure. Why a higher quality attaches to the mental feeling of pleasure is 'unsusceptible of further analysis' – it simply feels infinitely more valuable than any bodily sensation of pleasure feels to people competently acquainted with both mental and bodily kinds.

Now I shall try to clarify the hierarchy of higher and lower pleasures by illustrating how it can make sense to claim that mental feelings of pleasure are infinitely more valuable than mere somatic sensations of pleasure *as pleasures*.

2.4 Making sense of the hierarchy of pleasures: An illustration

Assuming that a higher pleasure is infinitely more pleasant than a lower pleasure, there is never any need for an ethical hedonist to balance the positive value contribution of the higher pleasure against that of the lower to whole pleasure: any quantity of higher pleasure, no matter how small, always trumps any quantity of lower, no matter how large, in cases of conflict. A unit of higher pleasure is deemed to be infinitely 'larger' than a unit of lower, and this unlimited difference of degree is translated into an intrinsic difference, that is, a difference in kind or quality. There is no other way that a hedonist can consistently count one pleasure as qualitatively superior to another regardless of quantity. If pleasures do not differ in quality in this way, then the hedonist must always count equal quantities of pleasure as equal in intrinsic value.[27]

As indicated earlier in Figure 1, qualitative superiorities in the Millian sense give rise to a hierarchy of different kinds of pleasant feelings. Within this hierarchy, mental pleasures, which engage the intellectual faculties such that the feeling of pleasure is inseparably associated with a concept or idea of an outcome, are infinitely more pleasant than, and thus take absolute priority over, mere bodily sensations of pleasure, which do not engage the intellectual faculties and thus are mere tinglings, tickles, pangs and the like. Before exploring further aspects of a Millian hierarchy, in particular, the location near the top of it of the kind of pleasure associated with the moral sentiment of justice, I shall try to illustrate why it makes sense to say that mental pleasures are infinitely more valuable than simple somatic sensations of pleasure, given the Millian understanding of 'infinity'.

Suppose that the act of sexual intercourse results in certain bodily sensations of pleasure which human animals, like other animals, can experience independently of the higher faculties. To isolate these bodily feelings for analytical purposes, the sex must be seen as purely physical, disjoined from any coherent ideas, let alone aesthetic and moral ideas such as that of a loving relationship with another person. Indeed, a person could be having sex with an ape or a pig rather than another human: it does not matter for the experience of crude animal pleasure. Now, the question to pose is: Would any competent person give up the intellectual capacities required to enjoy even a bit of mental pleasure in order to experience any amount of bodily pleasure he is capable of experiencing from sex with an ape or a pig? Would he sacrifice even a unit of the mental pleasure that depends on his intellectual ability to form the idea of a loving relationship or even the idea of an exciting liaison with another human, for example, for any finite number of units of mere sensory pleasure he might be able to experience from thoughtlessly rubbing his genitals against another warm body?

This is the relevant question. Assuming that a competent person will never sacrifice his intellectual capacities, and thus will not exchange mental pleasure for any amount of mere sensory pleasure which his animal nature is capable of experiencing, it might be asked how a competent person will choose between, on the one hand, a bundle of five units of mental pleasure and a hundred thousand units of bodily pleasure, and, on the other, a different bundle of six units of mental pleasure and a thousand units of lower pleasure. The answer is clear, keeping in mind that distinct capacities are required to experience the two kinds of pleasures. As a rational hedonist, he will choose six rather than five units of mental pleasure, which can only be experienced by creatures with intellectual capacities; he would also choose a hundred thousand instead of a thousand units of mere sensory pleasure, if his sensory capacities could be 'disjoined' from his intellectual capacities; but he will not sacrifice any mental pleasure for any amount of mere sensory pleasure, because he refuses to give up his intellectual capacities to become a simple sensory machine that is incapable of forming ideas or of experiencing the mental enjoyments inseparably associated with them. Thus, the competent person will prefer the bundle with six units of mental pleasure. He will not give up even one unit of higher pleasure to gain ninety-nine thousand units of lower pleasure.

This Millian argument does not suppose that mental pleasure can be experienced independently of bodily pleasure. Although bodily pleasure can be conceived in isolation from mental pleasure, we cannot assume that mental pleasure is independent of bodily pleasure, as if a person who experiences the mental kind might do so without possessing a body or ever experiencing any simple sensations of pleasure. Sensory capacities as well as intellectual capacities are needed to experience mental pleasure. The mental pleasure inseparably associated with the idea of some object, for instance, cannot be conceived without reference to the simple sensory pleasures that accompany the properties of the object in our experience, such properties being the elements of the idea of the object as inferred by the mind. This is so, even if we are not observing the object but instead remembering it or imagining it.

Mill emphasizes that bodily sensations of pleasure are among the ingredients of the mental kind. Thus, the person who is capable of competently experiencing both kinds never faces a choice between bodily pleasures alone and mental pleasures devoid of all traces of bodily sensations. Rather, when choosing between any two mental pleasures, he is also choosing between the bodily pleasures that are among their respective ingredients. A mental pleasure $u(x)$ that is larger in quantity than another mental pleasure $u(y)$ might also be composed of a larger quantity of the lower bodily sensations of pleasure.[28] But this need not always be the case. The lower pleasure interacts with other ingredients in the production of the higher pleasure, and these other ingredients may include pleasures of various intellectual operations *per se*, such as the pleasure of forming an idea of an object or the pleasure of reasoning about the consequences of an action. Given that these pleasures of the mental operations are also intrinsically valuable, it is conceivable that smaller quantities of the lower kind of bodily pleasure might interact with them in such a way as to produce more of the higher kind of mental pleasure than is produced by larger quantities of bodily pleasure interacting with the mental ingredients, *ceteris paribus*. All of these component pleasures, including bodily pleasures and pleasures of the intellectual operations, are apparently submerged in the whole mental pleasure, no one in particular standing out from the rest among the various ingredients making up the composition.[29]

But perhaps somebody is prepared to say that he is willing to give up his mental capacities altogether, merely to enjoy large quantities of lower bodily pleasure. Yet we cannot believe that such a person is a competent judge of the kinds of pleasure which human nature is capable of experiencing.[30] People competently acquainted with both mental and bodily kinds of pleasure as properly defined do feel it beneath the dignity of a human being to ever sacrifice the higher kind to the lower in cases of conflict, where a choice must be made for one or the other kind *per se*.[31]

2.5 Moral and aesthetic kinds of pleasures

In addition to the distinction in kind between mental pleasures and mere bodily pleasures, Mill indicates that there is a hierarchy of different kinds of pleasures nested within the mental kind itself. In particular, certain pleasures of the aesthetic emotions and of the moral sentiments are higher in quality than not only animal pleasures of mere sensation but also mental pleasures associated with merely expedient ideas. Again, *these* higher mental pleasures are extremely complex in comparison even to the lower mental pleasures. Higher kinds of pleasant feelings such as those of the emotions of beauty or sublimity as well as those of the sentiment of justice are higher up in the hierarchy, he insists, and do not feel anything like the lower kinds of pleasant feelings – bodily and mental – that enter into their composition: 'When a complex feeling is generated out of elements very numerous and various, and in a corresponding degree indeterminate and vague, but so blended together by a close association, the effect of a long series of experiences, as to have become inseparable, the resulting feeling *always* seems not only very unlike any one of the elements composing it, but very unlike the sum of those elements'.[32] Higher pleasures are 'quasi-chemical' products that *always* feel different in kind than any lower pleasures or sum of lower pleasures among their ingredients.

Mill also explicitly connects the higher pleasures of beauty and sublimity as well as the higher pleasure of justice to the idea of infinity when explaining why people who are capable of experiencing them feel them to be qualitatively superior to lower (mental and bodily) pleasures. Speaking of the aesthetic pleasures, for example, he says that they are 'excited' by things 'which have a natural association with certain highly impressive and affecting ideas' such as 'the idea of infinity', and '[i]t is no mystery ... why anything which suggests vividly the idea of infinity, that is, of magnitude or power without limit, acquires an otherwise strange impressiveness to the feelings and imagination'.[33] Since 'our experience presents us with no example' of such limitless magnitude or power, the idea of infinity 'stimulates the active power of the imagination to rise above known reality, into a more attractive or a more majestic world'.[34] In contrast:

This does not happen with what we call our lower pleasures. To them there is a fixed limit at which they stop: or if, in any particular case, they do acquire, by association, a power of stirring up ideas greater than themselves, and stimulate the imagination to enlarge its conceptions to the dimensions of those ideas, we then feel that the lower pleasure has, exceptionally, risen into the realm of the aesthetic, and has superadded to itself an element of pleasure of a character and quality not belonging to its own nature.[35]

Because of their inseparable association with elevated ideas of the creative imagination including that of infinity itself, the pleasant aesthetic emotions apparently acquire a qualitative superiority such that they are felt to be infinitely or intrinsically more valuable – of a different dimension altogether – than lower mental pleasures (not to mention mere bodily pleasures).[36]

As for the moral sentiment of justice, Mill argues that an 'extraordinarily important and impressive kind of utility' is involved, namely, the pleasant feeling of 'security' of legitimate expectations which is made possible by social rules that distribute equal individual rights and correlative duties.[37] This pleasure of security is extremely complex. It includes the gratification taken by a just person at due punishment of those who grievously harm any other individual by violating his constituted equal rights. In addition to the rules that distribute rights, society must establish institutions that deliver this service of punishment on behalf of individuals. Social rules and institutions of justice include legal codes that distribute legal rights, and political institutions to enact, enforce, and try cases and controversies arising under the legal rules. They also include social customs that distribute customary rights enforced by public opinion. And they include shared dictates of conscience inculcated in children by a social system of moral education. The education system properly equips young people to understand the idea of justice as equal rights, encourages them to develop a desire to follow just laws and customs, teaches them to feel guilty (and thereby punish themselves) if they intentionally, knowingly, recklessly or negligently break the rules, and also encourages them to blame anyone else who does so.

Such rules and institutions continually impress on everyone the extreme importance of the idea of equal rights and duties. The 'numerous and various' ingredients of the complex feeling of security that gathers around the idea of equal rights become inseparably associated such that the feeling of security itself is felt to be a new kind of feeling, a 'quasi-chemical' unity in which the separate ingredients are no longer discernible. Mill suggests that most if not all who are competently acquainted with this feeling of security judge that it is infinitely superior to competing kinds of pleasures. As he puts it:

[S]ecurity ... cannot be had, unless the machinery for providing it is kept unintermittedly in play. Our notion, therefore, of the claim we have on our fellow-creatures to join in making safe for us the very groundwork of our existence, gathers feelings round it so much more intense than those concerned in any of the more common cases of utility, that the difference in degree (as is often the case in psychology) becomes a real difference in kind. The claim assumes that *character of absoluteness, that apparent infinity, and incommensurability with all other considerations*, which constitute the distinction between the feeling of right and wrong and that of ordinary expediency and inexpediency.[38]

Given that the feeling of security is infinitely more pleasant than any competing pleasures, an individual who is competently acquainted with the different kinds of pleasures infers that a social code of justice and equal rights, the only source of the higher pleasure of security, takes absolute priority over any competing considerations *for his own happiness*. Justice has this priority within the conception of happiness formed by any fully competent hedonist. For happiness thus understood, an individual's rights can never be legitimately overridden without his consent to promote other people's happiness because even a bit of the moral enjoyment of security – no matter who feels it – is intrinsically more valuable *as utility* than any finite amount of lower enjoyment – no matter how many people the lower enjoyment is distributed across in a finite population.

Of course, the moral pleasure of justice can also be classified as an aesthetic pleasure insofar as the members of society aim at an ideal of equal justice which is more complete and perfect than any observed social codes and practices of justice, and this imaginary ideal feels beautiful to the competent and fair-minded people who are inspired to pursue it.

2.6 A lexical metaranking

It emerges that, for any person with the capacities required to competently experience them, there are plural different kinds, or qualities, or dimensions of pleasant feeling which can be arranged into a hierarchy such that a higher kind is infinitely, or intrinsically, and thus always, more pleasant than any lower kind. The hierarchy is a ranking such that all pleasures of a higher kind A take absolute priority over all pleasures of a lower kind B. Such a ranking is sometimes referred to as a *lexical* ranking because it mirrors the way in which all the words beginning with the letter 'A' take absolute priority over all the words beginning with the letter 'B' in a dictionary. The lexical ranking of the different kinds or qualities of pleasures holds regardless of the quantities of the pleasures. Different quantities of any one kind of pleasant feeling can be ranked in terms of more or less without affecting the lexical ranking of the different kinds. Thus, strictly speaking, the lexical ranking is a lexical *metaranking*, or ranking or rankings: it ranks plural kinds of quantitative rankings, one quantitative ranking (or ranking in terms of more and less) for each kind or quality of pleasant feeling.[39]

The pleasant feeling of security inseparably associated with the moral sentiment of justice is near to the top of this lexical ranking of the different kinds of pleasant feeling because this moral pleasure of security is intrinsically more valuable than any competing kind of pleasure. Nevertheless, it may not be the highest kind of pleasure. Aesthetic and spiritual kinds of pleasant feelings which do not conflict with the feeling of security may be qualitatively superior to the pleasure of security itself.

3. Justice and utilitarianism

The moral sentiment of justice involves a willingness to comply with social rules that distribute equal rights and duties, and a willingness to limit and control one's desire for retaliation in accord with those social rules. A just person has developed the power of will to direct his desire for punishment so that he takes gratification only at retaliating against those who refuse to fulfil their duties, rather than against anyone who does whatever he find personally disagreeable. Even in an ideal society of equals whose highly competent members unanimously desire to do right, however, any individual must be able to identify the social rules of justice with which to comply. Until he knows which particular rules of many distinct possible rules he ought to accept, he cannot know the particular equal rights and duties which he and everyone else in his community ought to recognize as belonging to all members of the community.

But how should the relevant social rules and equal rights be identified? We could perhaps assume for analytical convenience that there is an infallible impartial observer who calculates and dictates the optimal security-maximizing rules so that just persons can then voluntarily comply with them. But any such observer is evidently fictitious. Given that an omniscient and omnipotent impartial observer is not available, competent and fair-minded people themselves must jointly determine the optimal code by participating in some form of social choice process. This is in effect what Mill tells us. Taking for granted that human beings are fallible, he indicates that the code should be determined in principle by those who are competently acquainted with the higher pleasure of security or, if they disagree, by a majority of these competent judges.[40] In other words, the optimal code should be chosen by a majority of those who understand the idea of justice as equal rights, who at least upon reflection would feel highly gratified by its implementation, and who have developed the intellectual and moral capacities required to frame, propose and comply with the social rules that distribute the particular equal rights and duties which provide the most security for vital personal concerns shared by the members of the community.

Suppose for ease of analysis that an optimal social code of justice is to be wholly enshrined as a legal code of statutory rules, in which case the social decision process may be viewed as a formal political process of enacting statutes. This is obviously a simplifying assumption. Perhaps judges rather than legislators should make some laws, for instance, although Mill is inclined to endorse as generally expedient the project of 'codification', that is, the project of reducing a society's valid rules of law, including definitions of legal terms, rules of evidence and of interpretation and so forth, to a body of statutes.[41] In any case, as he also argues, it is inexpedient to recognize and enforce some rules of justice as laws.[42] An optimal code of justice will therefore consist not only of laws but also of extra-legal social customs and shared dictates of conscience. The social decision process for selecting these various sorts of social rules is correspondingly complex. It is not merely a legislative process but also a process of custom-formation and of education to encourage the development of shared rules of conscience. But I shall largely ignore such complexities.

Keeping in mind the simplifying assumption, it is important to see that an individual can only complete the formation of his own moral sentiment of justice *after* the operation of a political process that selects a particular legal code for him to recognize and use to guide his conduct. The *individual's* own sentiment of justice depends upon a *social* decision which is, in effect, an *internal* component of the sentiment. As already indicated, Mill's prescribed utilitarian procedure for selecting an optimal code is majority voting based on free discussion and debate of proposals, taking for granted that voters are suitably competent judges to render a decision. He never claims that rich cardinal and interpersonally comparable utility information is available, as is required to run a traditional utilitarian calculus that adds up personal utilities to determine the sum total of utility. Rather, restricting attention to security as a higher kind of utility, he apparently assumes that an optimal code of equal rights is properly determined by the majority verdict of people who are competent to assess the means of providing security.

Once particular legal rules are selected by consensus or majority voting among people with the relevant capacities to judge, the rules can play their essential role within any individual's moral sentiment of justice. Now, people seeking justice can each form and act upon a moral sentiment that gives the same content to justice: they are able to mutually coordinate by complying with the same rules and respecting each other's equal rights. Moreover, there is no need to view an optimal code as a once-and-for-all-time social construction. Rather, the political process may be seen as a dynamic process that unfolds in a series of steps. Human beings cannot possibly select an entire optimal code all at once. Even competent fair-minded people remain fallible. The optimal code can be constructed over time in a gradual and piecemeal manner, as competent and just majorities acquire additional knowledge, learn how to correct for their mistakes and reform the code of equal rights to take account of changing circumstances. Indeed, an optimal code can never be known with certainty by fallible humans, it seems, even if continual improvements to the established code are made.

Let us focus for a moment on an ideal society of equals, in which everyone is a highly competent person who seeks to do right. In this ideal context, everyone should have an equal voice in the political process because all are competently acquainted with security as a higher kind of pleasure, and all seek to interact with their fellows by complying with the best code for promoting security. The utilitarian political process boils down to an egalitarian democracy in which there is no need for counter-majoritarian checks and balances. All voters and their representatives, although fallible, have the intellectual and moral capacities required to give a rough estimate of how much security is likely to be associated with any proposed code of equal rights and duties. Each forms a personal preference ranking that ranks alternative possible codes from best to worst in terms of the amounts of security reasonably to be expected from them. If these individuals disagree, then the majority's judgement is accepted by all as final. The only information that counts in the process is the purely ordinal information about security – as a higher kind of pleasure – revealed by the individual preference rankings.[43]

Each voter in this majoritarian political process may only be concerned to identify the rules and rights that will give himself the most security for his own vital interests. The individual need not consciously intend to promote any independent notion of collective security. Given that the political process only considers personal preferences defined over distinct proposed codes of equal rights and duties, however, voters are implicitly constrained to treat everyone as if they have similar vital personal concerns that ought to be protected from harm. Moreover, as a happy by-product of the political process, the code of equal rights and duties selected by the majority is highly likely to give each person the most security for his own vital concerns. Majority voting gives a maximum likelihood estimate of the genuine security-maximizing code, assuming that competent voters are more likely to be correct than incorrect in their personal estimates of how much security to expect from any possible code of equal rights, and that they form their estimates independently.[44] Even if an individual is personally convinced that the majority has made an incorrect decision, he is morally and legally obliged to accept the incorrect majority verdict as authoritative for guiding his conduct, at least until he can persuade a majority to alter the decision.[45]

An ideal society of just cooperators must not be confused, of course, with our present stage of social advancement. In our non-ideal civil societies, individuals do not always develop their intellectual capacities or acquire a suitably intense desire to do right. As a result, constitutional checks and balances are required to discourage majorities and their representatives from abusing political power and enacting terrible laws. Mill continues to endorse a form of constitutional democracy, with a distinctive system of counter-majoritarian checks that nevertheless does not permit any elite to enact laws opposed by most people, as a utilitarian political process for any non-ideal civil society.[46] Legal penalties are also required in this context to force recalcitrant individuals to comply with the more or less flawed social code of justice established by the majority. Moreover, to the extent that most people do develop a conscience, however weak, this may be due largely to the visible operation of external sanctions against wrongdoing. The individual is spurred to develop a wish to do right because he repeatedly sees that wrongdoers are imprisoned, fined and stigmatized for their violations of others' rights. He fears that others will inflict the same forms of punishment on him if he also does wrong and is detected. Similarly, a holder of political office may develop a desire to use his power to better secure by equal right the shared vital concerns of his constituents because he repeatedly observes that office-holders who abuse their power are thrown out of office or otherwise checked by other officials. This means that many people may fulfil their duties merely because they fear punishment by others for not doing so. But there is no need to insist that an individual's motivation for doing right must be a pure self-determined rational will. What matters is that the person fulfils his recognized duties to others, even if he does not spontaneously wish on his own to fulfil them.[47]

It emerges that, for Mill as interpreted, a rational hedonist is logically committed to a purely ordinal version of utilitarianism by virtue of the higher pleasure of the moral sentiment of justice. A rational individual seeking happiness necessarily endorses justice understood in terms of equal rights and duties because there is no higher competing kind of enjoyment than his feeling of security associated with this moral sentiment. And he necessarily endorses a purely ordinal utilitarian social choice process because the sentiment of justice itself inherently involves such a social choice process to impartially determine an optimal social code that distributes the particular equal rights and correlative obligations which most if not all competent people judge are best for protecting the vital personal interests shared by all members of the community. A purely ordinal utilitarian political decision process boils down to some form of constitutional democracy.

The political decision process is concerned solely with the establishment of an optimal legal code of equal rights and duties for all. The ultimate purpose of the process is to maximize security, and codes of equal rights and duties are the sole source of this higher kind of utility. Once a code is selected, individuals have capacious freedom to act in accord with their recognized rights and duties. There is no call for political procedures to determine compulsory social rules by aggregating over personal preference rankings defined over sources of any other kind of utility besides security. Rather, an individual is legitimately left alone if he complies with the established social code of justice.[48] People are free to choose among the various sources of any kind of utility except security. Each individual is permitted to direct his own life as he thinks best, without fear of punishment, provided he fulfils his recognized duties to others.

4. Conclusion

My main claim is that, for Mill, the pleasant feeling of security associated with the moral sentiment of justice is a higher kind of pleasure which is infinitely more valuable as pleasure than any competing kinds of pleasures. As a result, an optimal social code that distributes particular equal rights and correlative duties takes absolute priority over any competing considerations within his extraordinary hedonistic utilitarian doctrine. Rights can be limited only by other rights as part of a scheme of equal rights whose ultimate purpose is to maximize security.

The infinite superiority of the moral feeling of security over competing kinds of pleasures implies that there is no fundamental conflict between personal happiness and the general happiness as Mill conceives them. An individual maximizes his own happiness 'both in point of quality and quantity' only if he gives absolute priority to considerations of justice when they conflict with other considerations.[49] But justice consists in equal rights and duties, and requires him to participate in a purely ordinal utilitarian political process to determine an optimal social code that distributes the particular equal rights and duties that provide the most security for vital personal interests shared by all. Every individual seeking justice endorses the particular social code selected as best by the majority of his fellows. It follows that any fully competent individual's *moral* feeling of security is the same in content as every other's because they all endorse the same optimal code which is the source of the moral feeling. Given that every individual's moral sentiment is the same, we can say that general security – the general moral feeling of security shared by all – is maximized if and only if every individual's own moral feeling of security is maximized. No competing kinds of enjoyments should ever override this shared moral pleasure of security, according to judges competently acquainted with the different kinds of pleasures. Thus, any fully competent individual's maximization of his own happiness necessarily coheres with others' maximization of their personal happiness because they all derive the same moral pleasure of security from the same optimal social code of equal rights, and this moral pleasure is infinitely more valuable than any competing pleasures. Neither personal happiness nor general happiness can be promoted by violating recognized equal rights.

True, even a fair-minded individual may wish that the competent majority had selected some other possible social code of equal rights, which he personally prefers and may have proposed for consideration in the political decision process. Nevertheless, he chooses as best the social code selected by the majority of his fellows because justice demands that he do so: unless he endorses that particular code, he cannot complete the formation of his own moral sentiment of justice. Yet, keeping in mind that the political process of constructing an optimal social code is an ongoing process of indefinite duration, he retains a moral right to try to persuade the majority to reform the optimal social code in the direction he prefers. In the meantime, he endorses as optimal the particular social code selected by the majority of his fellows.

General security is maximized because each and every competent individual who seeks to maximize his own happiness in point of quality endorses the same social code of justice in terms of which everyone can mutually cooperate. Each individual endorses the majority's judgement that *this* particular social code and *these* particular equal rights and duties provide the most protection for the vital personal concerns shared by everyone in the community. An individual maximizes the quantity of his own moral pleasure only if he invariably complies with the rules of the optimal code. In other words, he maximizes the intensity of his pleasant feeling of security only if he always acts as permitted by his own constituted rights and as required by own constituted duties to others. This is necessary but not sufficient because he also wishes to see others invariably comply with the same optimal social rules, and he feels the moral pain of insecurity until those who break the rules are duly punished. He feels morally gratified when unjust people who violate others' recognized rights suffer due retaliation, although it is a separate issue how society may most expediently deliver this service in any given situation, whether by means of legal penalties, public stigma and/or guilty feelings.

We can say that each person's moral pleasure of security is maximally intense without implying that the pleasures are cardinally measurable or interpersonally comparable. Each person's quantity of moral pleasure is maximized in a purely ordinal sense. Each individual chooses as best the particular social code of equal rights selected by the majority of his fellows, and thereby reveals that he expects the greatest amount of the moral pleasure of security for each and every individual from their general compliance with that particular code. In effect, that optimal social code is the top-ranked option in every competent individual's moral kind of preference. The formation of any individual's moral preference must be completed by the political decision process from the set of personal preference orderings defined over the domain of possible codes of equal rights.

Which particular personal interests shared by all are regarded by competent majorities as so important that they ought to be protected by equal right? What do most of those who are competently acquainted with the moral pleasure of security say about the nature and relative weights of the particular equal rights which in their view are the means of providing the most security? Given that the construction of an optimal social code of justice remains a work-in-progress from our vantage point, it may be premature to draw too many firm conclusions about the particular rights which would be chosen to maximize security by the competent and fair-minded members of any ideal society of equals. Nevertheless, there seems to be widespread agreement even in our non-ideal societies that certain vital personal interests shared by all ought to be protected by equal rights of some sort. Human beings share some fairly obvious biological vulnerabilities, for instance. They need protection for their vital interests in life and health, in supporting themselves by the fruits of their own labour and saving if able-bodied, in basic support from society if disabled or involuntarily unemployed and so forth. Public officials also share vital interests in being able to perform the duties of their office without obstruction from other people. Rights to protect these various vital concerns must be distributed by an optimal social code in any social context, even if different societies craft somewhat different rights for the purpose and disagree over their relative weights. Cross-cultural variation in recognized rights, even very basic human rights let alone rights that are contingent on particular social conditions such as the state of economic development, is compatible with security-maximization.

Mill takes it for granted that all humans share certain vital personal concerns that need to be protected from harm.[50] But, with one exception, he does not try to specify the rights which competent and fair-minded majorities will choose to provide such protection in any society. He does not insist that rights to privately own the means of production must always be included in an optimal social code, for example, although he argues that some form of capitalism will remain more expedient than any form of socialism in every civil society for the foreseeable future.[51] As far as I am aware, the only specific right that he insists must invariably be included in the social code of justice of every civil society is the right to complete liberty of 'purely self-regarding' conduct, understood as conduct that does not directly harm others without their consent.[52] Otherwise, he seems to think that competent majorities require no guidance from him to work out which particular system of equal rights and duties will give the most protection to shared vital personal concerns in their society. The shared vital personal interest in self-regarding liberty is exceptional and tends to be overlooked by majorities because the individual may like to employ his liberty in ways that most people dislike even though it causes them no perceptible damage. But majorities can be counted on to do a reasonable job of identifying other shared vital personal interests, such as the interest in life and bodily integrity.[53] Unlike the vital interest in self-regarding liberty, which varies in content across individuals depending on what they wish to do in their self-regarding affairs, these other vital interests are similar in content for every member of society. Any person can perceive harms to the latter interests by focusing on his own concerns, and so the rights he proposes to protect his own interests are likely to meet with at least some approval from others whose own interests are similar in content. But coercive interference with another's self-regarding liberty may not appear harmful to those who dislike the directions in which the other pursues his liberty. Equal protection of individuals' conflicting self-regarding choices demands mutual toleration of the choices.

Before concluding, it is worth remarking that Mill seems to have had Kant's alternative transcendental idealist theory in mind when elaborating his hedonistic utilitarian theory of the peculiar importance of justice and equal rights. Indeed, when he speaks in *Utilitarianism* of 'that character of absoluteness, that apparent infinity, and incommensurability with all other considerations' that attaches to the moral feeling of security associated with a social code of justice, Mill may be deliberately echoing the language in the *Groundwork of the Metaphysics of Morals* where Kant says that morality has an 'inner worth, that is, dignity' which is 'infinitely above' and 'incomparable' with any kind of 'worth' that depends on desires and inclinations.[54] For Kant, the dignity of morality is apparently tied to an innate human capacity for rational autonomy, that is, the capacity to freely will and comply with reasonable universal laws independently of considerations of pleasure and desire. But Mill agrees with Hegel and many others that Kant's approach to morality is problematic.

As is well known, Kant sharply divides the human self into a lower empirical self motivated by self-love to fulfil its own natural desires and pleasures, and a higher rational self inspired by an autonomous rational will to identify and fulfil universal moral duties. Mill classifies Kant as an 'intuitive' moralist in the strong sense that, for Kant, universal moral rules are self-evident ('evident *a priori*') to any fully rational individual who understands the meaning of the terms of the first principle of rationality, namely, the Categorical Imperative, which, as stated by Mill, referring to Kant's *Metaphysics of Ethics*, says: '"So act, that the rule on which thou actest would admit of being adopted as a law by all rational beings".'[55] Thus, Kant apparently believes that the rights and duties which ought to be recognized by any member of society can be deduced by a fully rational individual from the Categorical Imperative, without reference to any social choice procedure that generates moral choices by aggregating over hedonistic personal preferences defined over distinct social rules and rights. Moreover, once he deduces his duties, the rational individual is necessarily inspired to fulfil them by his self-determining will that operates independently of his desires and pleasures.

But the project of deducing moral oughts merely from the Categorical Imperative cannot possibly succeed. John Dewey states the fatal objection: 'Kant's separation of the self as reason from the self as want or desire ... compels the moral motive to be purely formal, having no content except regard for law just as law'.[56] The Categorical Imperative is compatible with laws of any content, and thus is compatible with immoral laws. Mill makes the same objection: 'when he begins to deduce from this precept [the Categorical Imperative] any of the actual duties of morality, [Kant] fails, almost grotesquely, to show that there would be any contradiction, any logical (not to say physical) impossibility, in the adoption by all rational beings of the most outrageously immoral rules of conduct'.[57] Fair-minded people reject immoral rules, Mill implies, not because rational consistency necessarily commands them to do so, but because the universal adoption of such a rule would have such bad consequences for collective well-being. Virtually all humans have a vital interest in preserving their own life, for example. Fair-minded people want to provide security for the vital interest in life which is commonly shared. A majoritarian political process that generates a moral choice from their personal preferences defined over proposed social codes of equal rights, will result in an optimal social code that maximizes security by distributing equal rights such as the right not to be killed or assaulted without any justification, the right not to be attacked merely because of one's religion or ethnic background, and so forth.

Even though the Categorical Imperative is morally empty on its own, Mill suggests that it is an ingredient of the moral sentiment of justice and thus can be accommodated within utilitarianism as he understands it: 'To give any meaning to Kant's principle, the sense put upon it must be, that we ought to shape our conduct by a rule which all rational beings might adopt *with benefit to their collective interest*'.[58] Any individual who seeks justice must prescribe universal maxims that any person in similar circumstances might reasonably affirm for the purpose of promoting collective security. In other words, the individual must propose social rules that distribute equal rights and duties, and he must accept the majority's judgement as to which one of the proposals made by individuals ought to be implemented to provide the greatest amount of the moral pleasure of security for each and every members of his society.

Kant's ideas continue to be influential within moral and political philosophy.[59] But John Rawls, perhaps the most eminent modern admirer of Kant, has engineered a revolutionary move away from comprehensive Kantian doctrines of the good life by proposing what he calls a 'purely political' (as opposed to 'metaphysical') liberal democratic theory of justice.[60] In Rawls' theory, certain equal rights (among other elements of justice) take absolute priority for purely pragmatic 'public political' reasons over any person's conception of the good including happiness, and thereby constrain what can count as a 'fair' or 'reasonable' conception of a good life.[61] There is still something of the old Kantian dualism in Rawls' theory, insofar as rational and reasonable people are assumed to choose a particular 'public political' conception of justice, and to construct a social code that embodies the political conception, more or less independently of their personal pleasures and ideas of a good life. Yet the dualism takes a different form from Kant's because Rawls argues that the political conception of justice must itself be constructed from certain bedrock ideas and convictions that are latent in the public culture of an advanced democratic society, and these cultural elements are clearly the products of a complex dynamic social decision process that operates over individual preferences.

Nevertheless, Rawls' move away from Kantian idealism toward political liberalism is not a move to embrace Mill's utilitarianism as I have interpreted it. It is not entirely clear how Rawls interpreted Mill's philosophy. At times, he reads Mill as a traditional utilitarian, more specifically, as an 'average utilitarian' who seeks to maximize average personal utility rather than the sum total of utilities.[62] Yet he also recognizes that Mill's higher pleasures doctrine implies a lexical hierarchy of pleasures, and he clearly thinks that Mill's comprehensive liberal doctrine of a happy life is a 'reasonable' doctrine that comports with a 'public, political' conception of justice.[63] Perhaps he found it difficult to combine Mill's various commitments into a consistent whole. He may have concluded that, at best, Mill might be interpreted to hold a 'mixed conception' of justice in which a first principle of equal rights as well as a second principle of fair equality of opportunity both have lexical priority over a conventional non-pluralistic principle of utility. If so, however, Mill can no longer be seen as a pure utilitarian because 'the conception of utility ... has a subordinate place'.[64]

In my view, Mill consistently embeds absolute priority for liberal justice within his unusual version of utilitarianism. The moral pleasure of security provided by a social code of justice and equal rights is said to be infinitely more valuable than any competing kinds of enjoyments in any fully competent individual's conception of a happy life. Unlike Rawls, who asserts that justice takes absolute priority over happiness independently of the consequences in terms of happiness, Mill as interpreted is arguing that the kind of enjoyment associated with justice and equal rights has absolute priority over competing components *within* any fully competent person's conception of happiness. Any rational person who has developed the mental capacities required to appreciate and act upon a moral sentiment of justice, he argues, endorses the social code of equal rights and duties selected by the majority of his fellows, because of the utility consequences of the code. The moral pleasure of security which results from society's recognition and enforcement of equal rights for all is infinitely more valuable than any competing pleasures.

Despite the inordinate length of the present discussion, much more requires to be said to defend a moral and political philosophy of the sort I have attributed to Mill. Elsewhere, I have tried to address some of the various possible objections, without pretending to have disposed of all of them.[65] But it should already be obvious that my reading of Mill's liberal utilitarianism calls into question some familiar objections that are commonly held to be fatal to *every conceivable* version of utilitarianism. Rawls' objection that 'utilitarianism does not take seriously the distinction between persons' is misplaced in the context of Millian utilitarianism, for instance.[66] So is Nozick's similar objection that utilitarianism 'does not sufficiently respect and take account of the fact that [the individual] is a separate person, that his is the only life he has'.[67] The Millian doctrine is also immune to the related complaints that utilitarianism ignores the fair distribution of benefits between different persons and runs roughshod over considerations of personal integrity. Admittedly, such charges have serious bite against the usual versions of utilitarianism.[68] But they do not tell against Mill's doctrine, in which a social code that distributes equal rights and duties takes lexical priority over competing utility considerations. Since the moral pleasure of security afforded by the social code is infinitely more valuable than competing kinds of enjoyments, the individual's equal rights cannot legitimately be violated to provide any amount of lower pleasure to others, no matter how large the finite mass of that lower kind of enjoyment is estimated to be. Indeed, Mill insists that recognized equal rights in any civil society must include a strong right to freely pursue one's own self-regarding projects. Thus, the security afforded by equal rights to each separate person's vital interests extends to a vital interest in individuality or self-development. The aesthetic and spiritual pleasures made possible by one's right to pursue one's own development as one pleases may be of the highest kind, because they do not conflict with the moral pleasure of security.[69]

Any distinction between persons is ignored, of course, when it comes to equal rights *per se*: different individuals are treated as if they are the same person for the purpose of impartially distributing equal rights to all. But this is not a problem. Nobody seeking justice maintains that the vital interests of some should be protected by right whereas the same interests of others ought to be left unprotected.

Finally, the political decision process which is internal to the moral sentiment of justice gives separate individuals an opportunity to express and vote their diverse opinions about the rules of justice which their society ought to recognize and enforce. Thus, the Millian theory is immune from the complaint, pressed with reason by some critics even against Rawls himself, that undue reliance is placed on a single hyper-rational observer instead of separate bargainers in the original position under the veil of ignorance. The Millian theory makes no essential use of the device of the original position. Rather than assume that a fair-minded person is a rational agent who must imagine himself in a state of ignorance about his own personal circumstances as a way to blunt his bias towards his own narrow selfish concerns, a moral individual is assumed to be a highly developed rational *and emotional* agent who knows his own circumstances yet acts on the moral sentiment of justice because he feels and understands that the associated pleasure of security is infinitely more valuable than competing enjoyments are *for his own happiness*. Such individuals may have conflicting opinions about which rules of justice would be best for society to implement. They may continue to protest that a particular social code selected as best by the majority is not the code which they would have personally selected. Nevertheless, all are committed to accept the majority's code as optimal, to respect the particular equal rights distributed by it, and to guide their desires for punishment in accord with its rules. This is compatible with any individual working at the same time to try to persuade his fellows to reform the code.

Notes

1   J. S. Mill, 'Utilitarianism' [1861], in J.M. Robson, ed., *Collected Works of John Stuart Mill* [*CW*], 33 vols., London and Toronto: Routledge and University of Toronto Press, 1963–91, X, p. 211, emphasis added.
2   'Utilitarianism', p. 255.
3   'Utilitarianism', p. 247.
4   'Utilitarianism', p. 250. Elsewhere, Mill argues that a legal right is always viewed as a desirable thing for the individual who possesses it: the claim is established either for the individual's particular advantage (that is, it protects his own vital interests) or because it is needed for the individual's performance of his own legal duties such as the duties of political office. Mill's argument extends to the case of moral rights. This Millian conception of rights has considerable appeal. It covers the cases which are often used to object to a pure benefit theory of rights, according to which a right is always given for

the particular advantage of the possessor. These cases include fiduciary rights, rights of government officials and contractual rights of those who negotiate contracts that fulfil their moral obligations to third parties. Moreover, the Millian conception can admit that other instruments such as powers' may be attached to core claims, but it does not insist (as the competing choice or will theory of rights does insist) that powers are necessary components of genuine rights. See Mill, 'Austin on Jurisprudence', *CW*, xxi, pp. 178–81.

5 The term 'vital personal concerns' can be suitably extended to include a concern to fulfil one's own legal and moral duties to others.

6 See J. Riley, 'Mill's Analysis of the Moral Sentiment of Justice', to be published in a volume edited by L. Katz for Palgrave.

7 See, e.g., K. J. Arrow, *Social Choice and Individual Values*, 2nd ed. New Haven: Yale University Press, 1963.

8 'Utilitarianism', p 211.

9 'Utilitarianism', p. 213.

10 'Utilitarianism', p. 211, emphasis original.

11 'Utilitarianism', p. 211, emphasis added.

12 'Utilitarianism', p. 213, emphasis original.

13 'Utilitarianism', p. 212.

14 'Utilitarianism', p. 211.

15 J.S. Mill, 'James Mill's Analysis of the Phenomena of the Human Mind' [1869], *CW*, XXXI, p.189, emphasis added.

16 'James Mill's Analysis', pp. 190–91, emphasis added.

17 'James Mill's Analysis', p. 189.

18 Rem Edwards, in: *Pleasures and Pains: A Theory of Qualitative Hedonism*, Ithaca: Cornell University Press, 1979, describes bodily sensations of pleasure as 'localized' feelings that are felt in some part of the body, and contrasts them with mental feelings of pleasure that are felt to be 'nonlocalized' and to somehow transcend the body altogether. His defense of qualitative hedonism from criticisms commonly taken to be decisive deserves a more prominent place in the literature. But he is not committed to my reading of Mill's qualitative hedonism, for instance, he does not accept that a higher kind of pleasure is qualitatively superior to a lower kind if and only if the higher pleasure is infinitely more valuable than the lower (see Section II.2).

19 'James Mill's Analysis', p. 202.

20 'James Mill's Analysis', p. 202, capitals original.

21 'James Mill's Analysis', pp. 202–3, emphasis added.

22 J.S. Mill, 'Bain's Psychology' [1859], *CW*, XI, p. 346.

23 'Bain's Psychology', pp. 346–47.

24 'Bain's Psychology', p. 347.

25 See Aristotle's *Physics*, III, 4–8; VI, 9; and VIII, 8. For illuminating discussions of Aristotle's view, see J. Lear, 'Aristotelian Infinity', *Proceedings of the Aristotelian Society* 80 (1979–80): 187–210; J. Lear, *Aristotle: The Desire to Understand*, Cambridge: Cambridge University Press, 1988, pp. 65–95; and A.W. Moore, *The Infinite*, 2nd ed., London and New York: Routledge, 2001, pp.1–2, 34–44. As Moore says, 'the mathematically infinite and the potentially infinite were, for Aristotle, one and the same … What he abhorred was … the actual infinite – a kind of incoherent compromise between the metaphysical and the mathematical, whereby endlessness was supposed to be wholly and completely present all at once' (p.44). Those who take a view similar to Aristotle's include Hobbes, Galileo, Leibniz, Gauss, Cauchy and Hume, for instance, as well as De Morgan, Hilbert, Brouwer and Wittgenstein. Mill specifically mentions De Morgan as being the first to have 'thoroughly cleared up … the puzzle arising from the conception of different orders of differentials – quantities infinitely small, yet infinitely greater than other infinitely small quantities' ('Berkeley's Life and Writings'[1871], *CW*, xi, p.468). See, e.g., A. De Morgan, 'On Infinity; and on the Sign of Equality', *Transactions of the Cambridge Philosophical Society*, 11 (1871): 145–89.

26 When I say that a unit of higher pleasure is equal to an infinity of lower pleasures, I
    regard that usage as strictly analogous to the usage in the theory of the calculus which
    says that the sum of an infinite convergent series is equal to the limit of the series. In
    both cases, the usage is merely convenient. Strictly speaking, the sum of the infinite
    series never actually reaches the limit, just as a unit of the infinitely more valuable
    pleasure never actually equals a completed infinity of units of the lower pleasure (al-
    though it can be made to approach arbitrarily near to it). By the way, I do not mean
    to imply that Georg Cantor's theory of transfinite arithmetic is of no interest. But
    we must recognize that his idea of a hierarchy of infinite sets of different sizes is not
    based on observation of any actual infinity. Moreover, his theory remains controversial
    because it suggests that an infinite set can be limited in size and thus measurable, a
    suggestion that is at odds with the Aristotelian idea of infinity as an unlimited process
    (see previous note). Cantor himself might not be bothered by such empiricist qualms
    since, as a religious idealist, he seems to have been convinced that his ideal realm
    of actual infinities was in fact a divine realm of absolute perfection unrelated to the
    natural world of our experience. Yet the qualms suggest that the elements of Cantor's
    hierarchy are not really infinite sets. As Adrian Moore has pointed out, given Cantor's
    assumption that the collection of infinite sets in his hierarchy expands without limit
    because there is no ultimate set of all sets, the idea of infinity is perhaps properly
    confined to the collection of sets rather than to any member of the collection. Indeed,
    Moore makes a provocative but persuasive claim that Cantor's theory really just serves
    to 'corroborate the Aristotelian orthodoxy that "real" infinitude can never be actual'
    ('How to Catch a Tortoise', *London Review of Books* 25, no. 24 (2003)). For further
    discussion, see A. W. Moore, 'A Brief History of Infinity', *Scientific American* 272,
    no. 4 (1995): 112–16; Moore, *Points of View*, Oxford: Oxford University Press, 1997;
    and Moore, *The Infinite*, 2nd ed.
27 Gustav Arrhenius and Wlodek Rabinowicz have argued, in 'Millian Superiorities',
    Utilitas 17 (2005): 127–46, that Millian qualitative superiorities are possible without
    assuming that any pleasure is infinitely superior to another. But their analysis is fatally
    flawed in the context of ethical hedonism, where the assumption in question is neces-
    sary and sufficient for genuine qualitative superiorities in Mill's sense. Arrhenius and
    Rabinowicz confuse things by speaking of the 'decreasing marginal value' of extra
    units of pleasure of the same type. Since the value referred to in the phrase 'decreas-
    ing marginal value' must be some value other than pleasure itself, this is incompatible
    with hedonism. Under hedonism, pleasure is the sole ultimate value so that one unit of
    pleasure must have the same intrinsic value as any other unit of pleasure of the same
    kind. For further discussion, see Jonathan Riley, 'Millian Qualitative Superiorities and
    Utilitarianism, Parts 1 & 2', *Utilitas* 20 (2008): 257–78 & *Utilitas* 21 (2009): 127–43.
28 Strictly speaking, bodily sensations of pleasure are not defined over well-defined out-
    comes such as x and y. Thus, such lower pleasures cannot really be distinguished as
    $u(x)$ and $u(y)$. Rather, sensations of pleasure are inchoate. Although different quanti-
    ties of them can be experienced, we apparently associate these quantities with distinct
    objects only after experiencing mental pleasures associated with ideas of the objects.
    Different quantities of the bodily sensation of pleasure are among the ingredients of the
    different mental pleasures.
29 The quantity of the higher mental pleasure is not necessarily a positive linear function
    of the quantity of lower bodily pleasure entering into its composition. The amount of
    the higher might not even be an increasing function of the amount of the lower. The
    whole mental pleasure is composed of an indefinite multitude of ingredients, including
    bodily sensations of pleasure as well as pleasures of the intellectual operations *per se*.
    Too much bodily pleasure might impede the operations of the intellect.
30 Mill admits that some people are observed to sacrifice mental pleasure for mere sensory
    pleasure but he argues that these people do not really do so voluntarily. Even if they are
    competent, he insists, they feel ashamed of what they are doing, and regret their inability

to control their behaviour (*Utilitarianism*, pp. 211–13). It should be noted that even noble and virtuous people may enjoy mere sensory pleasure when they are temporarily incapable of choosing mental pleasures, for instance, when too tired to think.

31 Evidently, in many situations, the higher and lower pleasures can be experienced together in harmony, in which case there is no need to choose between them. Indeed, mental pleasures are constituted in part from bodily pleasures so that it must always be possible to experience any given mental pleasures in harmony with at least some bodily pleasures, namely, those found among the ingredients of the mental pleasure itself. This is an important point to which I shall return later in the text.

32 'James Mill's Analysis', p. 239, emphasis added.

33 'James Mill's Analysis', pp. 224, 226.

34 'James Mill's Analysis', p. 226. Other ideas can stimulate the imagination in this way, Mill says. He refers to Ruskin's list (which includes such ideas as 'unity', 'symmetry' and 'purity') for examples (pp. 224–26). See, also, Mill, 'Bain's Psychology', pp. 363–64.

35 'James Mill's Analysis', p. 226. Mill makes clear that lower pleasures here include not just animal pleasures but also 'common-place and everyday' mental pleasures. 'In a windy country', he says, 'a screen of trees so placed as to be a barrier against the prevailing winds, excites ideas of warmth, comfort and shelter, which belong to the "agreeable," as distinguished by Coleridge from the Beautiful; and these enter largely into the pleasurable feeling with which we contemplate the trees, without contributing to give them the peculiar character distinctive of aesthetic feelings. But besides these there are other elements, constituting the beauty, properly speaking, of the trees, which appeal to other, and what we are accustomed, not without meaning, to call higher, parts of our nature; which give a stronger stimulus and deeper delight to the imagination, because the ideas they call up [such as the idea of infinity] are such as in themselves act on the imagination with greater force' (p. 225).

36 Mill claims that 'among our various pleasures, the aesthetic are without doubt the most complex' ('James Mill's Analysis', p. 225). This suggests that the aesthetic pleasures are at the very top of the hierarchy, above even the moral kinds.

37 'Utilitarianism', pp. 250–51.

38 'Utilitarianism', p. 251, emphasis added.

39 As is well known, a lexical ranking cannot be represented by a real-valued utility function because of the discontinuities in the hierarchy. In the context of the Millian hierarchy, the infinite superiority of a higher kind of pleasure in relation to a lower implies that the value of the higher is discontinuous with that of the lower. For further discussion of lexical rankings, see P. Fishburn, 'Lexicographic Orders, Utilities and Decision Rules: A Survey', *Management Science* 20 (1974): 1442–71; and J.E. Martinez-Legaz, 'Lexicographic Utility and Orderings', in S. Barbera, P.J. Hammond and C. Seidl, eds., *Handbook of Utility Theory*, I, Dordrecht: Kluwer, 1998, pp. 345–69.

40 'Utilitarianism', pp. 211–13,

41 See, e.g., Mill, 'Austin on Jurisprudence', pp. 188–94.

42 See, e.g., Mill, *On Liberty*, pp. 224–25, 276; and 'Utilitarianism', pp. 245–46.

43 As is well known, Arrow's impossibility theorem shows that majority rule is subject to logical incoherence. See K.J. Arrow, *Social Choice and Individual Values*, 2nd ed. Majority preference inconsistencies can be removed by restricting any person's vote to his top-ranked feasible alternative, or by imposing a scoring rule such as the Borda method to count each person's entire preference ordering equally. Indeed, generalized scoring rules, which are less arbitrary than Borda, are available to implement what Mill calls 'Bentham's dictum "everybody to count for one, nobody for more than one"' ('Utilitarianism', p. 257). Using any scoring rule to defeat the possibility of majority cycles does, however, violate Arrow's condition of 'independence of irrelevant alternatives'. Moreover, this scoring approach also fails at times to select a Condorcet winner when such a winner exists. A Condorcet winner is a feasible alternative – in

this case, a code of equal rights and duties – that beats every other feasible alternative by majority vote in a series of pairwise contests. For further discussion of the scoring rule approach as a way of interpreting of what a utilitarian counting procedure looks like in the context of purely ordinal utility information, see Riley, 'Classical Ordinal Utilitarianism', unpublished working paper.

44 This is an application of the basic Condorcet jury theorem. See, more generally, H.P. Young, 'Condorcet's Theory of Voting', *American Political Science Review* 82 (1988): 1232–44.

45 For pertinent discussion of this point, see S.J. Shapiro, 'Authority', in J. Coleman and S. Shapiro, eds., *The Oxford Handbook of Jurisprudence and Philosophy of Law*, Oxford: Oxford University Press, 2002, pp. 382–439.

46 For an extended discussion of Mill's preferred form of constitutional democracy, see J. Riley, 'Mill's Neo-Athenian Model of Liberal Democracy', in N. Urbinati and A. Zakaras (eds), *J.S. Mill's Political Thought: A Bicentennial Reassessment*, Cambridge: Cambridge University Press, 2007, pp. 221–49.

47 See Mill, 'Utilitarianism', pp. 219–20.

48 Mill, *On Liberty*, p. 266. I am ignoring moral rules of charity and beneficence which (unlike rules of justice) distribute imperfect duties that do not correlate to rights. Rules of charity are not expediently made into laws enforced by the state, he makes clear. Rather, such rules ought to be established as social customs enforced by public stigma ('Utilitarianism', pp. 246–48).

49 'Utilitarianism', p. 214.

50 'Utilitarianism', p. 256.

51 J. Riley, 'J.S. Mill's Liberal Utilitarian Assessment of Capitalism Versus Socialism', *Utilitas* 8 (1996): 39–71.

52 For further discussion of Mill's doctrine of individual liberty, see J. Riley, *Mill: On Liberty*, London: Routledge, 1998; and Riley, *Mill's Radical Liberalism*, London: Routledge, 2010.

53 *On Liberty*, pp. 283–84.

54 I. Kant, *Groundwork of the Metaphysics of Morals* [1785], ed. & trans. M. Gregor, Cambridge: Cambridge University Press, 1995, pp. 42–43.

55 'Utilitarianism', p. 207.

56 J. Dewey, 'Green's Theory of the Moral Motive', in J. Boydston, ed., *John Dewey: The Early Works, 1882–1898*, vol. 3, Carbondale: Southern Illinois University Press, 1978, p. 159.

57 'Utilitarianism', p. 208.

58 'Utilitarianism', p. 249, emphasis original.

59 The failure of Kant's Categorical Imperative *per se* to deliver moral rules is beyond dispute. As A. Gibbard reiterates, 'the Categorical Imperative ... just tells us to be consistent in our rationales for action ... but ... consistency won't on its own carry us to morality' ('Morality as Consistency in Living: Korsgaard's Kantian Lectures', *Ethics* 110 (1999): 140–64, at p. 147). C. M. Korsgaard proposes to revive and complete the Kantian program by supplementing the Categorical Imperative with further considerations of rational consistency, but her critics are unconvinced. See Korsgaard *et al.*, *The Sources of Normativity*, ed., O. O'Neill, Cambridge: Cambridge University Press, 1996. Gibbard makes a powerful case that any such Kantian program (what he calls the program of 'moral logicism') cannot succeed: morality cannot be derived merely from considerations of rational consistency alone. Lear gives a helpful discussion of Hegel's critique of Kant, and proposes to go back to Aristotle's account of the moral sentiments to remedy the deficiencies of the Kantian approach (*Aristotle*, pp. 150–56).

60 J. Rawls, *A Theory of Justice* [1971], Cambridge, MA.: Harvard University Press, revised ed., 1999; J. Rawls, *Political Liberalism* [1993], New York: Columbia University Press, expanded ed., 2005; J. Rawls, *Justice as Fairness: A Restatement*, ed. E. Kelly, Cambridge, MA.: Harvard University Press, 2001.

61 In Rawls' theory, 'inalienable' rights specified by a first principle of equal basic liberties also have lexical priority over other rights marked out by a second principle of fair equality of opportunity. Moreover, basic political rights are afforded special treatment. But I ignore such complications here. Purely pragmatic public reason does not rely on any metaphysical claims of 'truth' whose justification is tied to a comprehensive doctrine of the good life.

62 Rawls, *Theory of Justice*, p. 140.

63 See, e.g., Rawls, *Theory of Justice*, pp. 37–38, note 23; and Rawls, *Political Liberalism*, pp. 37, 145, 211, note 42.

64 Rawls, *Theory of Justice*, p.278. The utility principle replaces the Rawlsian difference principle (or maximin principle) within such a 'mixed conception' of justice.

65 For further discussion, see, e.g., J. Riley, 'The Interpretation of Maximizing Utilitarianism', *Social Philosophy and Policy* 26 (2009): 286–325; Riley, 'Millian Qualitative Superiorities and Utilitarianism, Parts 1 & 2'; Riley, 'Optimal Moral Rules and Supererogatory Acts', in B. Eggleston *et al.*, eds., *John Stuart Mill and the Art of Life*, Oxford: Oxford University Press, 2009; and Riley, 'Mill's Extraordinary Utilitarian Moral Theory', *Politics, Philosophy and Economics* 9 (2010).

66 Rawls, *Theory of Justice*, p. 24.

67 R. Nozick, *Anarchy, State and Utopia*, New York: Basic Books, 1974, p. 33.

68 Powerful arguments against the usual versions of utilitarianism are provided by, among others, B. A. Williams, 'A Critique of Utilitarianism', in J.J.C. Smart and B. Williams, *Utilitarianism: For and Against*, Cambridge: Cambridge University Press, 1973, pp. 77–150; Williams, *Ethics and the Limits of Philosophy*, Cambridge, MA.: Harvard University Press, 1985; S. Scheffler, *The Rejection of Consequentialism* [1982], Oxford: Clarendon Press, rev. ed., 1994; Scheffler, *Human Morality*, Oxford: Oxford University Press, 1992; and Scheffler, *Boundaries and Allegiances*, Oxford: Oxford University Press, 2001. Like Rawls and Nozick, however, Williams and Scheffler do not consider the distinctive pluralistic structure of Mill's utilitarianism as I interpret it.

69 Lear (*Aristotle*, pp. 293–320) points out that Aristotle also associated the highest kind of pleasure with a self-regarding 'way of life', to wit, a life of contemplating the basic 'substances' or forms or essences that humans can in principle discover in nature (including human nature) on the basis of experience. Indeed, Aristotle appears to have been committed to a fundamental ontology, which Lear calls 'objective idealism', such that a human replicates the activity of a divine Mind and thereby becomes godlike when contemplating the forms. This is certainly a beautiful vision and, as Lear also emphasizes, it exerts a powerful pull on any individual with Aristotle's commitments to withdraw as much as possible from politics and society, leaving behind as second-best a 'merely human' life of moral virtue. Aristotle may well have justified an oligarchy as ideal so that an educated minority could have the leisure needed to live as far as possible the quasi-divine life of contemplation, with the majority consigned to a second-best ethical life in which, among other things, they supplied the material needs of the elite. Unlike Aristotle, Mill remained uncommitted to any fundamental ontology or theology. His agnosticism or skepticism in this regard permits him to defend as ideal a liberal democratic 'society of equals' in which all have an equal right to complete liberty of self-regarding conduct. This right of self-regarding liberty is consistent with equal protection of the vital interests of others. There is no conflict between a life of equal justice, in which each person respects the rights of others, and the purely self-regarding lifestyle that each individual freely chooses for himself.

8 Mill's feminism

Liberal, radical and queer

Martha Nussbaum

Mill's feminism is usually called 'liberal feminism.' Such a designation is in one sense obviously correct, since Mill was a liberal, and his feminism is part of his philosophical thought. 'Liberal feminism,' however, is usually taken to be a bland doctrine focused on sameness of treatment, with little potential for the radical critique of hierarchies of power or the social deformation of desire. In particular, it is often understood as a kind of formalism that mandates sameness of treatment no matter what the underlying realities are like and no matter where people are socially placed at the start. It is also taken to be a doctrine that focuses on public legal remedies, eschewing all interference with the so-called 'private sphere,' where desire and emotion are pervasively shaped. Feminists who read Mill as holding such a doctrine justly feel that his views are open to a number of strong objections; typically they hold that today's insights render liberal feminism inadequate as a guide to contemporary thought and practice.

Calling this characterization into question, I shall hold up the arguments of *The Subjection of Women*[1] (and of related texts in *On Liberty* and the *Autobiography*) against the major claims of four varieties of philosophical feminism that are influential today: liberal feminism, radical feminism, 'difference' feminism and 'queer' feminism. I shall argue that *Subjection*, while recognizably in the liberal tradition in its focus on human autonomy, liberty and self-expression, nonetheless anticipates the best insights of radical feminism, with its shrewd analysis of power structures in the family and in sexual relationships and its insightful account of the ways in which power deforms desire. Mill cannot be called a proponent of 'difference' feminism: indeed, he gives us some strong reasons not to buy into Carol Gilligan's programme of naturalizing gender differences. Nonetheless, by according great importance to the cultivation of emotion and imagination in all people, he affirms the most worthwhile insight of that deeply defective brand of feminism. Most surprisingly, Mill, who writes like a proper Victorian and in many ways was one, turns out to have significant affinities with the 'queer' feminism of followers of Michel Foucault. In his assault on the tyranny of convention and the ways in which social notions of normalcy inhibit the development of unusual ways of life, Mill anticipates some of Foucault's most valuable insights. Once again, as with Gilligan, he has the best insight without the worst excesses: he attacks deforming social customs without buying into Foucault's dismissal of all norms – including liberal norms – as inherently tyrannical.

I shall conclude, however, that Mill's 'queer' instincts should have been pushed much further. In particular, these aspects of *On Liberty* should have informed *The Subjection of Women* far more than they did. Because *Subjection* stops short of imagining radical alternatives to dominant social norms in the areas of social division of labour, sexuality and the shape of the family, it remains an excessively cautious work. It fails to call for 'experiments in living' precisely where the tyranny of convention is especially deforming. Nonetheless, it is a work that still offers a great deal to feminist thought. It can provide answers to some of the most powerful charges that feminists have made against liberalism.

1. Liberal feminism

Both friends and foes of Mill often impute to him a view, which they call 'liberal feminism,' or 'equity feminism,' that focuses on sameness of treatment under law. Typical is the friendly characterization offered by self-styled follower of Mill, Christina Hoff Sommers, in her book *Who Stole Feminism?*[2] For Sommers, the follower of Mill, the 'equity feminist,' holds that women should have full legal equality with men, but that once this battle is won, nothing further should be demanded. Sommers summarizes this view with a quote from Elizabeth Cady Stanton, who said in 1854, 'We ask no better laws than those you have made for yourselves. We need no other protection than that which your present laws secure to you.' This equity agenda, she says is by now 'a great American success story.'[3] Moreover, once women can record their preferences by voting, there should be an end to all critical scrutiny of women's preferences. Sommers explicitly imputes to Mill the view that 'any other attitude to … women is unacceptably patronizing and profoundly illiberal.'[4]

Such a view is open to some obvious objections, influentially developed by Catharine MacKinnon and other radical feminists, and by now widely accepted within feminist thought generally, and even within legal thought that is not particularly feminist. Sameness of treatment, the objection goes, is all very well when people begin in equal positions, but not when they begin from entrenched hierarchies of domination and subordination. Changing such hierarchies may, and usually does, require more than simply adopting race-neutral, class-neutral or gender-neutral laws. Typically, it requires specific attention to the dismantling of the hierarchy in question, often through affirmative measures. Even when laws treat people the same, one should not conclude that there is no injustice: for there may be a hierarchy in place, and sameness of treatment may perpetuate it.

To give one example of this point from recent American legal history, laws against interracial marriage treated blacks and whites the same: they said, whites can't marry blacks, and blacks can't marry whites. On this basis, when they were challenged for violating citizens' rights to the equal protection of the laws, some courts upheld them. The US Supreme Court, however, did not. In a landmark 1967 case called, remarkably, *Loving v. Virginia* (since the interracial couple in question really were named Mildred and Richard Loving), the Supreme Court said that the laws are obviously a way of upholding 'white supremacy,' and declared them unconstitutional on equal protection grounds. Earlier, in 1954, they handed down a similar judgment concerning the policy of 'separate but equal' schooling. The idea is, sameness is not sufficient for true equality, when it protects an invidious hierarchy. So that is a key objection to the sort of liberal feminism that Christina Sommers defends, which does insist that sameness of treatment is sufficient.

Such formalist views were actually rather common in the area of gender. One particularly odd case concerned the refusal of employers to give women pregnancy benefits. When women went to court complaining of sex-based discrimination, the employers responded, not so: for men and women are treated precisely the same. All 'non-pregnant persons' get health benefits, and no 'pregnant persons,' male or female, get them. The evident absurdity of this response didn't mean that it wasn't influential. Eventually, courts treated this case the way the race-based cases had been treated, saying that pregnancy imposes an unequal burden on working women, and so denial of those benefits is a way of perpetuating inequality.

A further point made against 'liberal feminism' concerns the nature of preference and desire. According to MacKinnon, Dworkin, and other radical critics, one way in which subordination becomes entrenched is by influence over the preferences and desires of the subordinated. But, as we've seen, 'equity feminism,' at least as Sommers reconstructs it, eschews all criticism of desire and preference. Such a limited view seems to be designed to perpetuate subordination.[5] So if Mill *qua* liberal necessarily has such a view, his thought might be quite a bad guide to contemporary argument and practice.

The formalist sameness view that both friend Sommers and critic MacKinnon impute to 'liberalism' has not been very influential in liberal philosophy. Indeed, most of the leading forms of contemporary philosophical liberalism are acutely aware both of the social deformation of preferences and of the need to take affirmative measures to redress historical inequalities. John Rawls's thought, one obvious and central example of contemporary liberal thought, uses a moral ideal of impartiality in a way that cuts far deeper than mere sameness of treatment, since the parties in the Original Position are ignorant of their race and sex: they must therefore design institutions that are fair to all sexes and races, not imposing systematic disadvantages on anyone on such a basis.[6] One might then wonder whether the position is a straw man. The fact that the clearest philosophical exponent of it that I can find, within feminism, is Christina Sommers does not exactly inspire confidence: although she is a reputable philosopher, the particular book in question is a facile work of journalism funded by right-wing foundations, with an obvious polemical purpose. Nonetheless, the 'equity feminist' view has actually been quite influential – if not in philosophy, still in liberal *legal* thought. I have said that the sameness model was influential in the decisions of courts, in the areas of both race and gender. It was also given a famous theoretical development in the writing of federal judge Herbert Wechsler, whose 'Toward Neutral Principles of Constitutional Law'[7] is one of the most influential law review articles ever published. Wechsler, criticizing the Supreme Court's decision in *Brown v. Board of Education*, which declared 'separate but equal' schools to be unconstitutional, insisted that judges must confine themselves to neutral principles that require sameness of treatment. Any further or deeper critique of the status quo is an illicit politicizing of the judicial process. Thus courts should not say, as they had in *Brown* and would again in *Loving*, that segregation reinforced 'White Supremacy'.[8] That is not the right sort of 'neutral' reason. If the principle is truly neutral, then that is the end of the constitutional question of equal protection of the laws. (In fact Wechsler thinks that in at least some cases enforced segregation is unconstitutional, but for different reasons: it violates the right to freedom of association. Here he finds a neutral reason that can take the place of what he regards as a flawed reason.) So this is the view to which Mill is being assimilated, and it is with this very powerful US paradigm in mind that MacKinnon and others are calling Mill's views outdated, while conservative Sommers praises them.

So far as I can see, however, Mill never endorses, or even comes close to endorsing, the key contentions of the legal-formalist view. Neither in *Subjection* nor anywhere else does he say that once laws are the same for both women and men, then all will be well. He does indeed think that women's suffrage is very important, and that in other ways the 'legal subordination of one sex to the other' (2) ought to be undone. As a Member of Parliament he made good on that view, introducing the first bill for women's suffrage. He also, however, attaches great importance to laws that will redress women's asymmetrical vulnerability in marriage, where he sees that sameness of treatment would not remove an underlying power imbalance. He argues vehemently, for example, for the criminalization of rape within marriage, which surely is not a crime that can be correctly characterized without acknowledging women's asymmetrical physical and economic vulnerability (32).

Moreover, as we shall see, Mill prominently recognizes the social deformation of desire and preference and wishes to change it: so his programme is not confined to the approved Sommers 'liberal' preference-based programme.

In my view, this entire line of critique goes wrong at the start by thinking of liberalism as a view that is in its nature and fundamental motivation insensitive to hierarchies of power. Both historically and in today's most influential versions, liberalism is all about undoing hierarchies of power founded on wealth, class, honour, race, and, by now, sex. It is, at its heart, anti-feudal and anti-monarchical.[9] The problem is not that liberalism itself is unable to acknowledge hierarchies, and to make proposals that will help us to undo them. The problem, instead, is the problem that Mill identifies right at the outset of *Subjection*: men who think they are liberals, and in some ways are so, refuse to carry their insights into the domain of gender. They are quick to see hierarchy in relationships based on class, caste, inherited wealth, even race, and to propose remedies for these traditional asymmetries. Gender, however, seems to them profoundly 'natural,' and they are often unable to see conventional male–female relationships as characterized by unreasonable hierarchies.

One part of traditional liberalism does indeed militate against serious or deep critique of women's inequality: this is the distinction between a 'public realm,' which is the realm of law and justice, and a 'private realm,' which the law must leave alone, and which is putatively run in accordance with different principles, love rather than justice, sentiment rather than law. The public/private distinction was not created by liberalism: we can find it in Aristotle, and we can also find it in traditional Indian thought.[10] Traditional liberalism, however, does indeed recognize such a distinction of realms, and even some contemporary liberals have upheld it.[11] John Rawls, while officially rejecting the public/private distinction and while stating that the family forms part of the 'basic structure' of society that is regulated by principles of justice, in some ways moves uncomfortably close to the older liberal view when he ultimately concludes that the family is a 'voluntary association' like a church or a university.[12]

If the family is off-limits to liberal justice, then it seems right to conclude that many of the most serious inequalities of women cannot be redressed. The education people receive in the family is crucial to their formation as citizens. Even as adults, women's persistent vulnerability to abuse, both physical and mental, surely undermines their attempts to achieve full equality in work and in the political realm. So here is an apt criticism that radical feminists have to make against many traditional liberals. One could hardly make this critique of Mill, however. Mill insists that it is both wrong and profoundly inconsistent to talk the language of liberty but to condemn women, in the family, to a lot that is 'worse than that of slaves in the law of many countries' (32). His critique of marital rape and domestic violence, in *Subjection*, is radical: it insists that what happens behind the doors of the family is political, is a matter of law, justice and equality. If there are realms of intimacy that law, for Mill, cannot or should not regulate – and I believe there clearly are, though this is not a topic that occupies his attention in *Subjection* – these are not the realms of concern to radical feminists, who themselves typically defend at least some protections for intimacy, as MacKinnon explicitly does.[13] Once one removes the public-private distinction, one still needs to protect freedom of association, especially intimate association; Mill and radical feminists have no deep disagreement here.

What does it mean, then, to call Mill's feminist thought liberal at all, if it does not simply mean to misread him? It means, I think, in the first instance that Mill carries the traditional liberal critique of feudal and monarchical hierarchies into the sphere of gender relations, asking for the full recognition of human rights and human dignity in these relations. He asks liberal thought to be thoroughgoing and consistent, where it has been half-hearted and inconsistent.

In connection with this demand, Mill places characteristic liberal emphasis on each individual person's right to self-expression and self-development, with education playing a key role in a decent society's attempt to promote these goods for its citizens. Above all, it means that Mill sees each person as an end in him or herself, not simply as a support for the ends of others, or as a continuer of a tradition or a family line. The idea that the individual, not the group, is the locus of moral worth, and that all individuals are of equal and independent worth, not simply deriving their worth from relationships to others, can be said to be liberalism's core normative insight. Mill's point is that traditional liberals have made good points against feudalism by emphasizing the entitlements of the individual and the equal worth of all individuals. In the bosom of the family, however, feudalism has continued to reign, since it is convenient to men to hold that women are not ends in themselves, but means to male comfort and reproduction. By asking the radical question, 'What would it be to treat *all* individuals as ends in themselves?', Mill reveals the radical potential inherent in liberalism.

2. Radical feminism

I turn now to the views of radical feminists Catharine MacKinnon and Andrea Dworkin, which are paradigmatic of what is standardly called 'radical feminism.' I've already indicated that this movement makes criticisms of standard liberalism that do not go through against Mill. I now want to argue that Mill's feminist thought, in its most central aspects, has close affinities with the central positive claims of radical feminist thought.

The central insight in radical feminism is an insight about power. Relations between men and women, as we now find them, are characterized by a systematic hierarchy of domination and subordination. Although this hierarchy is often rationalized by claiming that it has its roots in 'nature,' there is no basis for these claims. The appeal to 'nature' is just an illicit way to rationalize a hierarchy that is deeply habitual and conventional. Radical feminists typically lack interest in how this hierarchy arose. What concerns them is that it is there, it is perceived as natural, unchangeable and right, and it deforms everything. Power differences give rise to women's inequality in law, in society, and in personal relationships themselves.

Of course all of these inequalities, in turn, further reinforce the power differential. That is why MacKinnon is so focused on law – not because she thinks that women's inequality begins with law, but because she thinks that law is one thing we can change relatively straightforwardly that contributes to the maintenance of the baneful hierarchy. We may as well start where we can do some good. Radical feminists know, however, that the inequality lies very deep: so deep, in fact, that it has crept into women's very desires. Just as men have learned over time, and through the transmission of social norms, to eroticize domination, so women have learn to eroticize submission. They don't just pretend to find male domination sexy, they actually do find it sexy. So the business of changing things is a slow and complicated business. It is for this reason that pornography gradually became important to the thought of both MacKinnon and Dworkin: because they see it is one place where the eroticization of power is formed in youth, and they imagine that it is one place where the stranglehold of misogyny might possibly be broken by some kind of legal or political intervention.

Radical feminists are sometimes taken to hold that sexual intercourse itself is always, and inevitably, a form of domination. Some of Dworkin's more hyperbolic statements conduce to this reading, but I think that it is, in the end, a deep misreading.[14] What Dworkin really holds, I would argue, is that we cannot wave away the problem of male sexual violence by simply saying that it is the work of a few 'perverts', or people who are not sexually 'normal.' The problem is in the norms themselves, in the way in which they define male initiative and female compliance, the way in which a husband's 'rights' are understood to include inter-course on demand, and so forth. So it's the whole structure of conventional norms that needs to be reconceived, if sex is ever to express equality on a reliable basis.

In one way Mill makes an odd companion for the forthright sexual talk of MacKinnon and Dworkin, since he was a very reticent writer, in keeping with the manners of his time. Nonetheless, he anticipates their key insights in most respects. In the first chapter of *Subjection*, he makes it clear that he believes male–female relations to be hierarchical, a form of domination akin to feudalism. Both are 'forms of unjust power' and are 'arbitrary' (12). Like the radicals, he also targets the notion of 'nature,' saying, '[W]as there ever any domination which did not appear natural to those who possessed it? ... It hardly seemed less so to the class held in subjection ... The subjection of women to men being a universal custom, any departure from it quite naturally appears unnatural' (12–13). (Mill supports this contention with an account of how forms of feudal and racial domi-nation have been taken to be 'natural.') More generally, Mill is one of the great critics of the normative appeal to 'nature' in philosophy. Not only in *Subjection*, but also in the wonderful essay 'Nature,' he shows exactly what MacKinnon and Dworkin more briefly show, how nature serves as a screen behind which tradi-tional power interests protect themselves.

Because domination over women is useful to men, it isn't surprising that they cling to it. 'Did not the slaveowners of the Southern United States maintain the same doctrine, with all the fanaticism with which men cling to the theories that justify their passions and legitimate their personal interests?' (12) Precisely be-cause self-interest is so obviously present, however, we should not trust what these people say: we should scrutinize every claim about 'natural' sex differences with a relentless determination to follow the evidence and to weed out bias.

As for the passions and sentiments that shape the relationship between men and women, here Mill makes one of his boldest and most creative contributions. The domination of men over women, similar though it is to other forms of domi-nation in many respects, has, he argues, one important difference. In other areas, what the master needs is that the slave does his assigned job and doesn't rebel. The master doesn't care whether the slave likes the work. All that matters is that the work gets done, and the slave doesn't kill him or run away. The domination of men over women, however, concerns much more daily and intimate matters, connected in a very basic way with a man's self-esteem and self-conception. Men therefore need to feel that women like their role, and them:

> Men do not want solely the obedience of women, they want their sentiments. All men, except the most brutish, desire to have in the woman most nearly connected with them, not a forced slave but a willing one, not a slave merely, but a favourite. They have therefore put everything in practice to enslave their minds. The masters of all other slaves rely, for maintaining obedience, on fear: either fear of themselves, or religious fears. The masters of wom-en wanted more than simple obedience, and they turned the whole force of education to effect their purpose. All women are brought up from the very

earliest years in the belief that their ideal of character is the very opposite to that of men; not self-will, and government by self-control, but submission, and yielding to the control of others. (15–16)

Because women are brought up this way, and because, in their socially and legally powerless condition, they cannot obtain anything except by pleasing men, women think that being attractive to men is the main thing in life.

And, this great means of influence over the minds of women having been acquired, an instinct of selfishness made men avail themselves of it to the utmost as a means of holding women in subjection, by representing to them meekness, submissiveness, and resignation of all individual will into the hands of a man, as an essential part of sexual attractiveness. (16)

Mill's language is reticent, but he is talking about the same thing that MacKinnon and Dworkin are talking about: the eroticization of domination and subordination, the way in which images of the powerful dominating male and the yielding submissive woman structure not just social behavior but the inner life of fantasy and desire themselves. The enslavement of women's minds may begin with ideas of proper meekness and obedience; it goes yet deeper, however, by affecting what women sexually desire and what men find sexually pleasing.

Now of course Mill lacks a detailed psychology of the emotions and desires to back up these claims. What he does have, the associationism he appropriated from his father, is probably not adequate to the task.[15] The same critique can be made of the radical feminists: they have too little interest in developmental psychology and in the nature of emotion and desire. What both Mill and the feminists see clearly, however, is that sexual desire is not an altogether 'natural' immutable phenomenon. Mill does think that there is something that can be called the 'natural attraction between opposite sexes' (16); radical feminists are agnostic here. Nonetheless, they both agree that this attraction is strongly shaped by social norms and power interests, and that this shape serves the interests of men and disserves those of women.

Radical feminists carry this theme further than Mill did, into a detailed critique of pornography and other social institutions that are involved in the reproduction of this deformed sexuality. Andrea Dworkin's fiction powerfully shows, in very frank sexual terms, how fantasies of domination and subordination, deep in the mental lives of both men and women, conduce to the abuse of women. All this is beyond Mill's reach. Nonetheless, he has the key insight – an extraordinary fact in his time, although not without precedent in English literature. (Richardson's *Clarissa* has most of the materials for such an insight.) Who knows how he came up with his ideas. Perhaps it was through reading English novels and pondering the lessons they teach (*Clarissa* in particular) about the deformation of desire. Perhaps it was something closer to home – by noticing the difference between his meek, submissive, and (to him) profoundly unsatisfactory mother, who was a conventional good woman, and Harriet, who somehow escaped the net of the norms;

perhaps by noticing, thus, that his own desires were not those of a 'normal' man, insofar as they aimed at genuine equality and reciprocity.[16] We don't know what kinds of conversations about women Mill had with his male friends, but it is easy to imagine that Mill would have been revolted by some common ways of talking about women and would have noticed in himself a reluctance to join in. Whatever the origin of the insight may be, it is an astonishing one, and sufficient to make Mill the first great radical feminist in the Western philosophical tradition. (Plato has a claim, but he didn't see hierarchy in sexual desire itself.)

3. 'Difference' feminism

According to the influential 'difference' feminism of Carol Gilligan and Nel Noddings, women's thinking displays a focus on care, relationship and connection, whereas male thinking typically focuses on autonomy and tends to rely on universal moral rules. Gilligan never quite says that these differences are natural, but she suggests it; Noddings does seem to think that they are natural. Gilligan believes that a good person needs both forms of thinking, both the 'perspective of care' and the 'perspective of justice.' Noddings appears to think that caring is far more important than justice, and that we can dispense with the latter if we sufficiently cultivate the former.

There are so many problems with the thinking of this 'feminist' school that it is irritating even to try to analyze it. Nonetheless, given its widespread influence, my present argument cannot ignore it. One problem is surely that Gilligan's empirical work is very bad. She repeatedly mischaracterizes the data she has found: if one looks at the full questionnaires that people gave back to her, one finds that she has self-servingly extracted just those bits that support her antecedent thesis about gender difference and neglected bits where men talk about relationships and women appeal to universal moral principles.[17] Her data sample, moreover, is very narrow in both class and regional terms. Her interviewing technique, too, seems defective: she seems obtuse about children's desire to please adults and to 'show off.' Some of the answers she gets from children (boys especially) seem calculated to impress, rather than to reveal how these children really make ethical choices, and Gilligan has no critical worries on this score. Finally, the conceptual apparatus is so ill-conceived that it is hard to do useful work with it. Why should 'justice' be contrasted with 'care'? What is the definition of each? Isn't 'care' one part of what complete 'justice' would include? Isn't good 'care' care that is justly given, meaning given to all, not just to the people whom one happens to like? And wouldn't a universal principle be one good way of capturing that insight?

Noddings's work is normative and not empirical, so it does not have some of the defects of Gilligan's work. Like hers, however, it suffers from definitional unclarity and from an unwillingness to admit that care and justice substantially overlap.[18]

We can say right away that Mill, prudently and rightly, would have resisted a central contention of this tradition: that women's actual ethical reasoning gives reliable information about how women are. Most of the argument of *Subjection* is devoted to a devastating critique of all such claims, establishing that we know next to nothing about how women and men 'are,' so early do power interests enter the picture. To my students, who read Gilligan after reading both Rousseau and Mill, Gilligan looks like a naïve and starry-eyed reinvention of Book V of *Emile*, in ignorance of Mill's trenchant critique of all such naturalizing claims.

Empirical psychology today gives strong support to Mill: experiments done with babies who are first labeled male and then labeled female show that the very same infant will be talked to differently, played with differently and talked *about* differently, depending on whether the experimental subject thinks the baby is male or female. A 'male' baby is typically tossed in the air and played with robustly. The 'girl' is sheltered and held close. The 'boy' is called 'angry' when he cries; the very same cries coming from the little 'girl' are called fear. It is difficult to believe that such differential treatment does not influence development profoundly. That being the case, we ought to say that we are just where Mill believed we were in 1869: there may indeed be innate gender differences, but we know nothing reliable about them. Mill, then, would be correct in his agreement with the radical feminist critique of Gilligan. MacKinnon, speaking of Gilligan's notion of the 'different voice' of women, says, 'Take your foot off our throats, and then we will hear in what voice women speak.' Mill is more polite, but no less damning.

Concerning women's so-called instincts of love and care, Gilligan's central theme, Mill has an additional point to make: given women's powerlessness, they need to ingratiate themselves with men by paying attention to how they feel and by taking care of them. What else can they do? So, what Gilligan thinks of as admirable might just be a sign of subordination.

Here we can observe that the problem has only grown larger with time. Today, given the general aging of populations, there is much more care work to be done in most families: not just children, but also aging parents, and anyone who happens to have a temporary or lifelong disability. Our society still maintains the fiction that this care work will be done for free, by women, out of their instincts of love, and women are often forced to buy into that fiction. The alternative is to be stigmatized as a bad mother or a bad daughter. Even if women know clearly that they do not *want* to care for their aging parents – and so are not 'enslaved' in their minds – they may have no choice but to do this caring with a cheerful face, because it is socially impossible to do otherwise, and society has offered them no decent alternatives.

If emotions of love and caring are to be defended as morally valuable, they must, then, be scrutinized first for signs that they are simply the result of a traditional gendered division of emotional life, and also for signs that they are ways of exploiting women. They, or some forms of them, must be defended as valuable with an independent argument that shows what, and when, they contribute to human flourishing. In *Subjection*, Mill focuses on the critical, suggesting that it is only when men and women live on a basis of true social and legal equality that we can even begin to trust the sentiments they express as possibly non-deformed expressions of their personal choice. In the *Autobiography*, he makes headway on the constructive account. Showing how his own early life was set up for a crisis of depression because it lacked cultivation of sentiment, and by describing the contribution of poetry, and the cultivation of sentiment it provided, to forming a personality capable of flourishing, Mill makes at least the beginning of an argument that emotional development, of a sort that many men do not get, is a crucial element in human flourishing. It is just the beginning of an argument, because Mill's case may be idiosyncratic. Modern psychology, however, has once again given it strong support, suggesting that male development is often emotionally stunted and that the consequences of this emotional illiteracy are quite bad both for the women these men love and for the men themselves.[19]

So, Mill not only shows us how and why we might reject some of the weaker claims of the 'difference' feminists, he also picks out the pearl of insight in the mire, and really gets to work making the kind of argument that would go somewhere as a normative argument. It is because many people, male and female, feel intuitively that male development is lacking in something that women more often cultivate, and that this something is pivotal to human flourishing, that Gilligan's thought has attained the widespread influence it does not deserve. Mill is not a 'difference feminist.' He is something much better, a philosopher who knows how to think evaluatively about the contribution of emotions to life.

4. Queer feminism

The final group of thinkers I shall consider are more known for their thinking about sexual orientation than for feminist thought, but the same insights carry over, and there are many feminists who make use of them today. Michel Foucault, and thinkers about sexuality who develop his ideas further (for example Michael Warner and David Halperin), notice that in the sexual domain ideas of what is 'normal' typically have a repressive role. Just like the notion of 'nature,' the notion of the 'normal,' though it parades as a descriptive notion, involves an un-argued slide from the descriptive to the normative: because things usually are a certain way, therefore it's fitting and proper that they be that way. Of course no such conclusion follows. Bad knees, bad backs and bad judgment are all 'normal' in the statistical sense, and nobody would conclude that they are therefore the way things ought to be. In areas where power interests are at stake, however, people make such illicit conclusions all the time. Foucault shows how, time and time again, notions of the normal and the proper tyrannize over people, creating ortho-doxies and banishing people who live and think differently. In the sexual domain, the tyranny of the normal has been particularly harsh toward gays and lesbians, and that is a theme of a lot of this writing. But Foucault's thought extends much more widely, calling into question normative ideas of crime and innocence, of madness and sanity.

In the end, Foucault is so suspicious of all norms that he typically advocates only acts of resistance to break their grip. In the works for which he is most known, he refuses to offer any principled account of what should be resisted, or on what grounds. In his last works, however, most unpublished at the time of his death, he seemed to move in a more Millian direction, praising ancient Greek notions of self-cultivation and self-fashioning and condemning as repressive norms that prevent this sort of autonomous activity from taking place.

Mill is the last person whom one would associate with the street theater of Act Up or any other public manifestation of 'queer' radicalism. So far as I know, he never even followed in the footsteps of Bentham, who made fun of the legal and moral judgments against pederasty and the notions of the 'natural' and 'normal' that went with them. (In an essay on pederasty, Bentham commented, '[I]t is wonderful that nobody has ever yet fancied it to be sinful to scratch where it itches, and that it has never been determined that the only natural way of scratching is with such or such a finger and that it is unnatural to scratch with any other.') In *On Liberty*, where reference to same-sex relationships would have been apropos, Mill certainly does not talk about sexual experimentation, or different forms of sexual life. Nor does he call for the repeal of sodomy laws. I would conjecture that he probably found homosexual relations shocking and off-putting, and simply did not wish to talk about them, much though his argument tells in favour of their decriminalization.

Nonetheless, we may contemplate the general nature of Mill's argument and its implications. In *On Liberty*, he strongly condemns the tyranny of social norms over unusual individuals who wish to undertake 'experiments in living.' His hatred of the tyranny of the normal in England, and his preference for France, are all part of his very Foucauldian rejection of the tyranny of ideas of normality, and his support for spaces within which people may flourish in their own way. His 'harm' principle clearly entails that consensual sex acts between adults be legal, a fact that was not lost on Lord Devlin, when he took Mill as his arch-adversary in *The Enforcement of Morals*.

Mill does not articulate his critique of the 'normal' in its rather extreme Foucauldian form, in which all norms whatsoever are to be eschewed, even ethical norms, such as fairness, justice, friendship and love. Like Foucault, he recognizes that such words can often prove the masks of a desire for domination, but he nonetheless clings to some definite norms as good guideposts: ideas such as liberty, self-development and flourishing. So he is like Foucault in his more complex late period, with a dose of liberal autonomy thrown in. As with difference feminism, so here: Mill has the valuable insight without the regrettable excess.

What is deeply to be regretted, however, is that, close though Mill's affinities with 'queer' thought are in *On Liberty*, *The Subjection of Women* is far from being a 'queer' text, or even a text that uses the best insights of *On Liberty*. Despite the radicalism of the text in some domains, Mill never considers any alternatives to the current form of the family organization, monogamous and heterosexual. In *On Liberty* he mentions the unfair treatment of the Mormons, but, while he objects to that treatment, he also makes it clear that he finds polygamy personally abhorrent. Certainly *Subjection* nowhere gives it a second thought. Nor, as I have said, do homosexual relations come in for any rethinking, as they do for Bentham. Even the idea, fairly common at the time, that marriage might be informal, or communal, not contractual, does not surface. In short, none of the sexual 'experiments

in living' that were going on at the time, and that cherished classical texts prominently described, get a hearing at all: the text takes its aim to be simply the reform
of monogamous heterosexual marriage in the direction of greater emotional and
legal equality.

Notoriously, moreover, Mill's conservatism goes well beyond a focus on heterosexual marriage. It includes an unexamined assumption that in such marriages
the division of household and childcare labour will remain the conventional one.
Women will be able to move outside the home only if they are lucky enough to
have servants to share some of these duties. Harriet's own more radical ideas
about women's work opportunities, not uncommon in radical circles at this time,
are neglected. Once again: such obvious 'experiments in living' as asking men to
do some of the washing up and to change a baby's diaper are not even mentioned.

So: why is Mill, so 'queer' in some ways, not 'queer' enough? One could try
to say that *Subjection* is already such a shocking work, and Mill is already so
aware that he might not get a hearing (see pp. 1–3), that he avoids making it yet
more shocking by tying his critique to radical changes in the family. This may
be a sufficient explanation for the text's silences, and in that case they would be
merely pragmatic and superficial silences. I believe, however, that they may well
lie deeper. Despite his radicalism, Mill was in many ways a rather conservative
man. If he wanted something as radical as genuine emotional, spiritual and intellectual equality – and I think he sincerely did – he still liked the orderly forms
of Victorian life to be observed. So far as anyone knows, he did not sleep with
Harriet until after her husband's death. When the pair married, furthermore, and
his radical brother George protested this capitulation to convention, Harriet wrote
– presumably with her husband's knowledge – a letter so angry and so defensive
that it suggests that the couple were clinging, at some deep emotional level, to an
institution they had many reasons to reject:

> I do not answer your letter because you deserve it – that you certainly do not –
> but because tho' quite inexperienced in the best way of receiving or replying
> to an affront I think that in this as in all things, frankness and plain speaking
> are the best rule, as to me they are the most natural – also it is best that every
> one should speak for themselves. Your letters to me and Haji must be regard-
> ed as one, being on the same subject and sent together to us. In my opinion
> they show want of truth modesty and justice to say little of good breeding or
> good nature which you appear to regard as very unnecessary qualities.
> Want of justice is shown in suggesting that a person has probably acted
> without regard to their principles which principles you say you never [under-
> stood?]. Want of modesty in passing judgement on a person thus far unknown
> to you – want of everything like truth in professing as you do a liking [?] for
> a person who in the same note you avoid calling by their name using an un-
> friendly designation after having for years addressed them in to say the least
> a more friendly way. In fact want of truth is apparent in the whole, as your
> letters overflow with anger and animosity about a circumstance which in no
> way concerns you so far as anything you say shows and which if there was

any truth in your profession of regard should be a subject of satisfaction to you. As to want of the good breeding which is the result of good feeling that appears to be a family failing.

The only small satisfaction your letter can give is the observation that when people desert good feeling they are also deserted by good sense – your wish to make a quarrel [?] with your brother and myself because we have used a right which the whole world, of whatever shade of opinion, accords to us, is as absurd as unjust and wrong.[20]

To get this angry over the suggestion that perhaps they ought to have lived ex-perimentally rather than conventionally betrays, I suggest, a deep attachment to conventional respectability. If the couple had the courage to prefer love over pub-lic opinion, it was not because they were deaf to its voice.

What *Subjection* should have had, its modern feminist reader feels, is an insti-tutional chapter asking what sorts of new rules for marriage, and what alternative lifestyles, what 'experiments in living,' this argument concerning the hierarchy of the sexes might suggest. Once we recognize that sexual domination is artificial rather than 'natural,' and once we recognize that it has, on the whole, not worked out so very well, depriving society of women's talents, depriving children of para-digms of equality, and depriving men and women of a type of happiness that requires equality, – it seems that the next step would be to ask, 'What different ways of doing things might we try out?' Mill, sadly, fails to take this next step.

Modern feminists can justly feel, however, that the text itself leads up to that next step. Its feminist readers have understood the way in which it points beyond itself. Modern Millians, lacking Mill's particular rhetorical problems and/or his particular personal hang-ups, have built upon his insights to ask the questions he fails to ask, imagining different ways of dividing household labour, of arranging for the care of children and the elderly, of supporting the demands of same-sex couples for legal and emotional equality. And they have done so in part because of the ideas of *On Liberty*, ideas of individual self-expression and freedom that are deeply woven into the 'radical' and 'queer' feminist movements, much though they would hesitate to call themselves liberals.

Mill's feminist thought, then, is not that dreary pablum popularly known as 'liberal feminism.' It is radical thought, both then and now, and it has deep af-finities with the best in contemporary radical feminist thought. At the same time, it cultivates well an insight about the value of emotions that difference feminism cultivates poorly. And it hunts down pernicious social notions of the 'natural' and 'normal' with much greater philosophical depth and consistency than the often polemical works of queer theory. It does all this, moreover, while being recogniz-ably liberal, that is, built around ideas of personal autonomy, self-expression and individual worth.

Indeed, Mill's thought gives us ways of answering the most common charges made by feminists against liberal thought today. To the charge that liberalism is 'too individualistic,' Mill can reply that the most valuable insight in liberalism is that of the equal and separate worth of each and every person. Far from being 'too individualistic' in that normative sense, conventional liberalism has not been individualistic enough, since it has allowed men to treat women as reproducers and caregivers, rather than persons of equal worth in their own separate right. Such a liberalism can value care and community, but it will not value these ideas uncritically, since they have often been used to exploit women.

To the charge that liberalism accepts all preferences as given and hard-wired, offering no criticism of the social deformation of emotion and desire, Mill can reply that this may be true of many liberals, but it is not in the least true of him. Moreover, his critique of desire, far from being an 'illiberal' element in his thought (as Sommers suggests, though not about Mill), is actually essential to his liberal programme: for it's only when we see how people are enslaved that we can think how to set them free.

Finally, to the imagined Foucauldian charge that liberalism proposes definite norms to guide choice and is therefore bound to be tyrannical, Mill can reply that the defense of liberty requires some definite norms. If the only advice is 'resist authority,' we could as well use this to resist norms of equal respect and equal liberty as to resist norms of gender discrimination. So the protection of people from tyranny requires normative commitment, commitment embodied in a good legal regime – particularly when convention gives little protection. What else could possibly protect the weak against the powerful?

On balance, then, Mill's feminist thought, while incomplete in many ways, is still alive philosophically, and still provides valuable guidance. When we consider how much women's position in the world has changed in the 200 years since Mill's birth, we can see that many of these changes were directly urged by Mill's thought. Still other and very significant changes, which he does not directly recommend, are nonetheless strongly suggested by the underlying ideas that inhere in his arguments. These facts should show us how insightful, and how radical, a feminist Mill was.

Notes

1 All page references to *Subjection* (given in the text in parentheses) are to the edition: J.S. Mill, *The Subjection of Women*, edited and introduced by Susan Moller Okin, Indianapolis: Hackett, 1988.
2 C. H. Sommers, *Who Stole Feminism?: How Women Have Betrayed Women*, New York: Simon and Schuster, 1994.
3 Sommers, *Who Stole Feminism?*, p. 22. I examine Sommers's book in detail in: 'American Women: Preferences, Feminism, Democracy,' in: M. Nussbaum, *Sex and Social Justice*, Oxford and New York: Oxford University Press, 1999, pp. 130–53.
4 Sommers, *Who Stole Feminism?*, p. 260.
5 These criticisms are made against liberalism in general by Catharine MacKinnon throughout her work, and particularly in 'Difference and Domination', in: *Feminism Unmodified: Discourses on Life and Law*, Cambridge: MA.: Harvard University Press, 1987. MacKinnon's own treatment of Mill, in *Toward a Feminist Theory of the State*, Cambridge, MA.: Harvard University Press, 1989, is, however, far more nuanced.

6 I don't think Rawls goes quite far enough, however: see my *Women and Human Development: The Capabilities Approach*, Cambridge: Cambridge University Press, 2000, Chapter 4.

7 *Harvard Law Review*, 1958.

8 See *Loving v. Virginia*, 1967.

9 See my 'The Feminist Critique of Liberalism,' in: Nussbaum, *Sex and Social Justice*.

10 See my 'Sex Equality, Liberty, and Privacy: A Comparative Approach to the Feminist Critique,' in E. Sridharan, Z. Hasan and R. Sudarshan (eds), *India's Living Constitution: Ideas, Practices, Controversies*, New Delhi: Permanent Black, 2002, pp. 242–83 (from conference on 50th anniversary of the Indian Constitution). A shortened version was published under the title 'What's Privacy Got to Do With It? A Comparative Approach to the Feminist Critique,' in: S. A. Schwarzenbach and P. Smith (eds), *Women and the United States Constitution: History, Interpretation, Practice*, New York: Columbia University Press, 2003, pp. 153–75.

11 See the excellent treatment in Susan Moller Okin, *Justice, Gender, and the Family*, New York: Basic Books, 1989.

12 See details in Chapter 4 of: Nussbaum, *Women and Human Development*, pp. 241–97.

13 Catharine MacKinnon, Law-Philosophy Seminar, University of Chicago, 2003.

14 See my chapter on Dworkin in: Nussbaum, *Sex and Social Justice*.

15 See C. Vogler, *John Stuart Mill's Deliberative Landscape: An Essay in Moral Psychology*, London and New York: Routledge, 2001.

16 For a related discussion of Mill's *Autobiography*, see M. C. Nussbaum, 'Mill between Bentham and Aristotle,' *Daedalus*, 133 (Spring 2004), pp. 60–68.

17 See John M. Broughton, 'Women's Rationality and Men's Virtues: A Critique of Gender Dualism in Gilligan's Theory of Moral Development', in: M. J. Larrabee (ed.), *An Ethic of Care: Feminist and Interdisciplinary Perspectives*, London and New York: Routledge, 1992, pp. 112–42.

18 See my critique in 'The Feminist Critique of Liberalism,' in: Nussbaum, *Sex and Social Justice*.

19 See especially D. Kindlon and M. Thompson, *Raising Cain: Protecting the Emotional Life of Boys*, New York: Ballantine Books, 2000

20 Quoted in: F. A. Hayek, *John Stuart Mill and Harriet Taylor: Their Correspondence and Subsequent Marriage*, London: Routledge & Keegan Paul, 1951, pp. 176–77.

9   Liberalism as free thought

John Skorupski

Introduction

Some people, myself included, tend to think that John Stuart Mill is the greatest philosopher of liberalism. Others disagree; they may give that status to Locke, or to Kant. Or they may sensibly insist that no one thinker has that status.

One can ask who best serves as a talisman or exemplar of liberalism in terms of outlook and practice. In this regard Mill has a strong claim. If I ask myself what a truly liberal attitude on a substantive ethical or political question *should* be, I find that I'm interested in what the characteristically Millian outlook *would* be. That is not the same as asking what he, in his particular circumstances and with his particular character would have said; everyone is prone to excessive or inadequate confidence, to a response coming from resentment, prejudice or sheer aberration, and Mill is no exception. All the same, what Mill did or would have said often goes to the heart of a liberal sensibility and in that way it gives human substance, as against a theoretical standard, to what it is to feel and think liberally.

However, there is also the question of who most penetratingly reveals the philosophical groundings or conditions of liberalism. Mill may stand out as the most centred and generous liberal sensibility; yet there is more to philosophy than sensibility. If, for example, one prefers Locke to Mill as a philosopher of liberalism, it will be because one thinks that natural rights of person and property provide a better philosophical framework for liberal thinking than utility in the largest sense, 'grounded on the permanent interests of man as a progressive being.' If one prefers Kant, it will be because one thinks that autonomy of the will is the proper philosophical framework or rationale for liberalism. My own view is that all of these – Locke's natural rights, Kant's autonomy, Mill's utility in the largest sense – play a role in the moral infrastructure of liberal institutions.

There is, of course, no one thing that the word 'liberal' refers to. It can refer to a principled overall preference for free competition and equal opportunity. It can refer to a moral doctrine limiting the authority of state and society over individuals. More broadly, liberalism can be thought of as a vision of how to live, what the human good is, and how our mutual relations should be regulated – what John Rawls called 'comprehensive liberalism.' In all these ways Mill stands out as a defining, though controversial, liberal presence. However, what gives Mill's philosophy a special importance in the liberal tradition is his insight into the foundations of free thought, or so I shall contend.

It is fair to say that Mill's general philosophy is still insufficiently understood and appreciated, even though his overall standing as a thinker is high. That is changing, and it will go on changing, in part because of changes within philosophy itself, and, even more, because the history of philosophy is catching up with the nineteenth century, and beginning to throw into relief striking contrasts and affinities between what was thought then and what is thought now. This is valuable for philosophy in general, but in particular it is a necessary step to getting an informed sense of the philosophical background of Mill's ethics and politics, in the same way that revaluing Hegel's absolute idealism is a necessary step for getting a sense of his. The process has some way to go before we can really assess Mill as the philosopher of liberalism, and not just as a great liberal. We need to take on board, for example, Mill's place in late-nineteenth century discussions of reality, consciousness and self. We need to understand the force of his radical empiricism. We need to grasp his place in the history of naturalized epistemology, and then to think critically about this naturalistic stance.

It is this last topic, Mill's epistemology, that I want to consider here. In particular, I want to consider how and why he thought it important for his ethics and politics, as he clearly did. The answer, I shall suggest, is that for Mill, and the tradition of liberalism that he represents, liberalism is most fundamentally commitment to the practice of free thought. This idea is the deepest source of liberalism in European culture from at least the early modern period. Liberalism is free thought, and Kant and Mill – Rawls's two examples of comprehensive liberalism – are both liberals in this deepest way. For both of them, I believe, the ideal of free thought is the most fundamental liberal ideal.[1] Let us examine it a little further.

Free thought

Free thought is thought ruled by its own principles and by nothing else; in other words, by principles of thinking that it discovers, or makes explicit, by reflecting on its own activity. It acknowledges no external constraints placed on it by doctrines of faith, revelation or received authority: it scrutinizes such teachings in the light of its own principles. One can also say that it is thought ruled solely by natural reason, where 'natural reason' is just a name for all those principles that are internal to thinking and reflectively acknowledged by it as its own. The contrast is with *apologetic* thought, in the traditional and respectable sense of that word – thought which seeks to make intelligible, so far as possible, the ways of God to man, without claiming to know those ways by its own principles alone.

The apologetic tradition is fideistic. It holds that free thought alone cannot tell us what to believe: natural reason must be a servant of faith, or at best a co-sovereign with it. Free thought, in contrast, is the doctrine of what Jonathan Israel has called the 'radical enlightenment'.[2] From the fideistic standpoint, it can only seem to rest on hubristic philosophical fallacy. A contemporary of Mill's, Cardinal Newman, puts the point very clearly:

Liberty of thought is in itself a good; but it gives an opening to false liberty. Now by Liberalism I mean false liberty of thought, or the exercise of thought upon matters, in which, from the constitution of the human mind, thought cannot be brought to any successful issue, and therefore is out of place. Among such matters are first principles of whatever kind; and of these the most sacred and momentous are especially to be reckoned the truths of Revelation. Liberalism then is the mistake of subjecting to human judgment those revealed doctrines which are in their nature beyond and independent of it, and of claiming to determine on intrinsic grounds the truth and value of propositions which rest for their reception simply on the external authority of the Divine Word.

Among the doctrines of liberalism which he enumerates and condemns is the following (no 9):

There is a right of Private Judgment: that is, there is no existing authority on earth competent to interfere with the liberty of individuals in reasoning and judging for themselves about the Bible and its contents, as they severally please.[3]

Newman is talking about liberalism in theology. However, the standpoint from which he condemns liberalism is wider. It ramifies into politics, as some of the other doctrines he condemns make clear – and it is grounded on a general thesis in epistemology. First principles of whatever kind, Newman says, cannot be known solely by free exercise of human thought: human judgment cannot determine their truth and value on 'intrinsic grounds'.

That goes to the heart of the problem of freedom and authority in matters of belief. It also helps us to separate two questions. The first is the question of whether free thought can give knowledge of, or at any rate, as some might prefer to say, *rational assurance* regarding, first principles. This is the sceptical question that has famously dogged modern Western philosophy since a new kind of reliance on human reason emerged in the sixteenth and seventeenth centuries. From that time there have been attempts to respond to scepticism on behalf of free thought, and deployments of scepticism about free thought on behalf of apologetics and dogma.

The second, by no means unrelated, question is about how individualistic we should conceive free thought to be. Here Newman seems to slip in a false dichotomy. He writes as though the exhaustive choice is between 'private judgement' on the one hand and an 'existing authority on earth competent to interfere with the liberty of individuals in reasoning and judging for themselves' on the other. However, liberals as well can very easily make the same mistake. They must endorse the basic point that free thought involves insight by *individuals* – free acceptance of what individual people find credible, without the dogmatic dictate of any authority. But that should not prevent them from recognizing that free thought is essentially dialogical. Reasoning and judging for yourself does not entail that you reason and judge entirely by yourself. Seeing for yourself is one essential moment of free thinking, discussing freely with other reasoners and judgers is the other. Within this collective process there must be free recognition of intellectual authority in specialized discourses, as Mill liked to emphasize. But his conception of intellectual authority is that in a healthy culture it earns free recognition, not that it is 'competent to interfere with the liberty of individuals in reasoning and judging for themselves.' It seems to me that the balance involved in Mill's conception of freedom and authority in cognition – a detailed reckoning that he evolved over several decades – is one of his great strengths as a liberal philosopher. It underlies what he has to say about democracy, elites and liberty of discussion.

By the way, Mill took a serious interest in the Tractarians. In a letter to Gustave d'Eichtal of 27 December 1839 he notes that they 'reprobate the "right of private judgement"' (XIII 416)[4]. In a letter to Comte of 22 March 1842 he compares them to the school of De Maistre, in particular in their wish to set up a historical philosophy, and says that they maintain the principle of authority against that of the unlimited liberty of conscience (*CW*, XIII 507). And then in January 1843 he defends them in two long letters to the Morning Chronicle in January 1843 (*CW*, XXIV 811 – 22). The sympathy he shows in these two letters for thinkers he nonetheless describes as 'conscientious bigots' (*CW*, XXIV 812) is not surprising, given that he himself conceives of both ethical and scientific thought as inherently collective, historical and developmental processes. The big difference is that while Mill agrees that thought is all of those things, he also, and crucially, thinks that it is always fallible. There is no indubitable revelation, no infallible church authority, nor even (despite his positivist moments) any final terminus of certainty.

This fallibilism, as against scepticism, will lead us to the epistemology underlying Mill's rationale for liberty of discussion. But to return for the moment to free thought. There is still another crucial question about how we conceive it. Certainly it must be *unconstrained* by any allegedly authoritative source external to it. But does that mean that it must be radically *presuppositionless*? It is basic to Mill's stance in epistemology that he takes free thought to be unconstrained, but necessarily *not* presuppositionless. There are no constraints on free thought, but that does not mean that free thought can start from nowhere.

Yet the idea that free thought must be presuppositionless is highly plausible. If free thought rests on some assumption how can it be free? Must it not question that assumption? That has been an enormously influential modern conception of what it is to think really freely. Call it the Cartesian idea. Descartes allows all our opinions to come under question from the radical sceptic and then tries to find a refutation of the sceptic that relies on none of those opinions but only on itself – that is, on the mere fact of thinking. This presuppositionless conception immediately imposes an individualistic or egocentric framework on free thought, since now *I* can only start from *my* thinking. And one can say without exaggeration that this project, of defeating the sceptic on his own terms without any presupposition – together with its complete failure – is one of the main shapers of modernity; which means that it has made a big difference to the fortunes of liberalism.

A way of spelling this out further would be to tell the story of German philosophy from Kant to Nietzsche. Kant responds to Descartes' failure to ground free thought by a critique of free thought itself – the 'Critique of Pure Reason'. Truly free thought, he says, must investigate the conditions of its own possibility. It turns out however that those conditions in one important way reinforce the ego-centric and transcendental predicament: as *free* thinker and agent the self is not a part of nature, but in some sense 'constructs' it. The story continues with Hegel. To overcome the subject/object distinction, as Hegel claims to do, is a very radical escape from epistemological individualism. But there remains a deep and genuine difficulty about free thought, even if one escapes the egocentric predicament (or as one might say, the predicament of merely private judgement). The difficulty is to see how free thought can be both self-authorizing *and* truth-finding, in the way that liberalism as free thought assumes. Hegel's absolute idealism addresses this question also; he tries to show how free thought, *Geist*, itself literally generates everything: a kind of apotheosis of presuppositionless free thought. Nietzsche sees the failure of all these epistemological heroics and diagnoses a crisis of Western values; in particular, of the value the West places, allegedly through its Christian heritage, on objective truth. We must give up on truth and recognize that we impose our own 'values'. That Nietzschean idea, so liberating and counter-cultural in its early-modernist day, went on to become a popular dogma of our time. As a result, epistemology has entered politics in a big way, in that sceptical or subjectivist attitudes have become basic to our ethical and political outlook – the very outlook about which Nietzsche was so scathing – the outlook, one may say, of *ersatz* liberalism.

Mill belongs to an alternative tradition of free thought. According to this tra-dition, free thought does not start by refusing to make any assumptions at all, but instead maintains a continuing critical open-mindedness about everything we take ourselves to know, without any exemptions whatever. This tradition, like the Cartesian one, goes back to the seventeenth century, originating in the outlook of that time that Richard Popkin has called 'constructive scepticism.'[5] But one might equally call it a naturalist and fallibilist empiricism. Mill is a very important fig-ure in its development, in part because of the purely philosophical contribution he makes to it in his *System of Logic*, or System of Epistemology as it might better have been called, and in part because he sees the importance of this epistemologi-cal conception for free thinking in ethics and politics as well as in science.

Let me highlight the two features of Mill's epistemology that I have already referred to in contrasting his view with Newman's. We perhaps associate them now with later philosophical currents, such as pragmatism, or in another way, with some aspects of twentieth century 'continental' philosophy, including the critical Marxist tradition. It is time to appreciate how fully developed they are in Mill. These fea-tures are, on the one hand, opposition to epistemological individualism in favour of awareness of the historicity and sociality of human thinking, and on the other, rejec-tion of a priori intuition in favour of a radical fallibilism that tests ideas by practice.

Mill is unimpressed by what he calls 'the well-meant but impracticable pre-cept of Descartes' of 'setting out from the supposition that nothing had been already ascertained' (*CW*, VII 318–19). That way he thinks lies only nihilism, for nothing can come of nothing. Nor does he think that an a priori critique can show us that human beings as thinkers have some non-natural noumenal side. He takes thinking itself to be a natural process:

> Principles of Evidence and Theories of Method are not to be constructed *a priori*. The laws of our rational faculty, like those of every other natural agency, are only learnt by seeing the agent at work ... we should never have known by what process truth is to be ascertained, if we had not previously ascertained many truths ...
>
> (*CW*, VIII 833)

These are quotations from the *System of Logic*. Compare the familiar introductory remarks in *Utilitarianism*. 'Questions of ultimate ends,' he there says, 'are not amenable to direct proof,' or as he also puts it, 'to what is commonly understood by proof.' But nor does an ultimate question of this kind, he thinks, 'depend on blind impulse, or arbitrary choice.' It remains

> within the cognizance of the rational faculty; and neither does that faculty deal with it solely in the way of intuition. Considerations may be presented capable of determining the intellect either to give or withhold its assent ... U I 6, X 207–8.

The formulation here is slightly different from the one from the *System of Logic*: ultimate ends are said to be 'within the cognizance of' rather than determined by 'laws of' our rational faculty. And Mill says that the rational faculty does not deal with them *solely* in the way of intuition. But that word 'solely' is I think a merely tactical weakening: Mill's considered epistemology actually rejects 'intuition,' understood as a supposed receptive faculty, altogether. The way free thought establishes truths about what we should believe, about what is good, about how we should act – truths that are normative for out thinking, feeling and doing – is by careful scrutiny of how we actually reason and reflective analysis of which principles in this practice of reasoning turn out to be treated by us as normatively basic: 'seeing the agent at work'. This is what Mill refers to as 'evidence' for basic normative claims, whether in science or ethics: the 'evidence' for normative fundamentals consists in what emerges from careful critical sifting of how we actually think in theory and practice.

Seeing the agent at work thus means seeing the development of reason in history. Mill's treatment of scientific method in the *System of Logic* takes the form of a natural history of the 'inductive process'. The idea is to show how scientific method is internally vindicated by its actual success in establishing regularities, which can then give rise to more searching methods of investigation. 'We have no ulterior test to which we subject experience in general; but we make experience its own test.' (*CW*, VII 318–19.) This is an internal and holistic epistemology. It works from within our experience and convictions as a whole. It tries to understand those convictions within a historical and sociological framework. It calls for imaginative understanding of other people and other times. Pinning down the fundamental norms of our thinking requires careful psychological and historical inquiry into how people think, and also into how they think they should think – what kind of normative attitudes they display in their actions and their reflection. Free thinking is not thinking from within my 'ego-redoubt,' it is thinking from within the shared totality of thought. Fallibilism is inherent to this dialogical epistemology – we continually try to reduce the likelihood of error but we can never guarantee to eliminate it completely, or to ringfence any element in our fabric of belief as incorrigible. Mill's conception of free thought incorporates the nineteenth century's sense of its historical and social nature, but still remains firmly planted in the tradition of Popkin's constructive scepticism, and Israel's radical enlightenment – and it gives no house room to the dubious baggage of Comtean or Hegelian social metaphysics.

Mill thinks it gives him critical leverage on political arguments. He's an epistemologist, but unlike many pure epistemologists he's also interested in the politics of epistemology. Here, to illustrate, is a well-known passage from his *Autobiography* in which he himself explains what he wanted to achieve by means of his radically empiricist account of mathematics in the *System of Logic*:

> The notion that truths external to the human mind may be known by intuition or consciousness, independently of observation and experience, is, I am persuaded, in these times, the great intellectual support of false doctrines and bad institutions. By the aid of this theory, every inveterate belief and every intense feeling, of which the origin is not remembered, is enabled to dispense with the obligation of justifying itself by reason, and is erected into its own all-sufficient voucher and justification. There never was such an instrument devised for consecrating all deep-seated prejudices. And the chief strength of this false philosophy in morals, politics, and religion, lies in the appeal which it is accustomed to make to the evidence of mathematics and of the cognate branches of physical science. To expel it from these, is to drive it from its stronghold ...
>
> (*Autobiography* I 233–35)

To this fiery utterance a critic might well reply that the existence of a priori intuition is one thing, its misuse in morals and politics is another. It is worth considering this reply at two levels, first the epistemological and then the political.

First, then, Mill thinks there can be no such thing as a non-natural receptive faculty of 'intuition.' He holds that basic normative claims are adequately grounded on our natural dispositions – the only task of epistemology being to make these explicit and refine them by critical scrutiny. Since that is what he thinks, it's not surprising that he looks suspiciously at the politics of an epistemology which posits a mysterious receptive faculty that can somehow give us a special kind of certainty not available to mere human experience and discussion. From his standpoint the idea that there is such a source of knowledge, a source that exists independently of collective human practice, inquiry and reflection, is just as objectionable as Newman's reliance on 'the external authority of the Divine Word.' The objection in either case is the same: it is to the idea that there could be an infallible epistemic hotline that trumps merely human experience and discussion. None of this of course implies that his own favoured starting points, say of utilitarianism in ethics or inductivism in epistemology, are defensible in the way he wants to defend them, by an appeal to natural dispositions. It is perfectly possible to agree with his epistemological framework, and then to argue within it that critical scrutiny of our dispositions points to other starting points, with less radical implications. He, of course, would disagree.

But doesn't free thought, however self-critical, internally self-vindicating and social it may be, need some a priori normative framework to be objective at all? And doesn't that call for a metaphysical account of a priori knowledge? This is indeed a forceful question, which Mill never addresses head on, as it must in the end be addressed. I will come back to it, but first I want to complete the picture by tracing how Mill's epistemology shapes his view of free discussion.

Liberty of discussion as a condition of rational assurance

Whereas the Liberty Principle is founded on the importance of giving individuality its legitimate scope, the deepest justification for the Principle of Liberty of Discussion is the epistemological importance of completely free dialogue. Of course much more is involved in working out defensible principles of free speech then such a general point can supply, and in fact Mill contributes little to the working out of such principles. But he does contribute significantly to something else. People have always puzzled about why speech acts should have a degree or kind of protection that differs from that afforded to actions in general. Mill's discussion of the issue makes the social importance of free dialogue, rather than the liberty of individuals within their private sphere, the key consideration.

As is well-known, his argument has three parts, focusing first on the possibility that the suppressed opinion is true, second, on arguments which remain even if that possibility is discounted, and finally, on the typical case in which received and unorthodox opinions share the truth between them. Mill's dialogical epistemology is evident throughout. But I particularly want to consider something he says in the first part. Here he starts from a 'common argument':

> the opinion which it is attempted to suppress by authority may possibly be true. Those who desire to suppress it, of course deny its truth; but they are not infallible ... To refuse a hearing to an opinion, because they are sure that it is false, is to assume that *their* certainty is the same thing as *absolute* certainty. Its condemnation may be allowed to rest on this common argument, not the worse for being common.
>
> (*CW*, XVIII 229)

That last sentence is a good example of the kind of populist eloquence that Mill occasionally liked to indulge in, sometimes to his cost. For to the common argument there is an obvious objection. *Any* action a person takes is based on his beliefs. What he believes he acts on; it does not follow that he takes himself to be infallible in believing it. To suppress a proposition because one believes it to be false is no more than a special case: the censor acts on his sincere belief that the proposition is false – he does not thereby take himself to be infallible.

On this occasion, however, Mill goes straight on to state and reply to this obvious objection. As he states it:

> If we were never to act on our opinions, because those opinions may be wrong, we should leave all our interests uncared for, and all our duties unperformed. An objection which applies to all conduct, can be no valid objection to any conduct in particular. It is the duty of governments, and of individuals, to form the truest opinions they can; to form them carefully, and never impose them upon others unless they are quite sure of being right. But when they are sure (such reasoners may say), it is not conscientiousness but cowardice to shrink from acting on their opinions ... There is no such thing as absolute certainty, but there is assurance sufficient for the purposes of human life. We may, and must, assume our opinion to be true for the guidance of our own conduct, and it is assuming no more when we forbid bad men to pervert society by the propagation of opinions which we regard as false and pernicious.
>
> (*CW*, XVIII 230–31)

He then gives an interesting reply:

> I answer, that it is assuming very much more. There is the greatest difference between presuming an opinion to be true, because, with every opportunity for contesting it, it has not been refuted, and assuming its truth for the purpose of not permitting its refutation. Complete liberty of contradicting and disproving our opinion, is the very condition which justifies us in assuming its truth for purposes of action; and on no other terms can a being with human faculties have any rational assurance of being right.
>
> (*CW*, XVIII 231)

That reply comes straight from his underlying epistemology. It is indeed true that a censor, like anyone else who acts, requires no more than 'assurance sufficient for the purposes of human life'. But fallibilism has an important consequence with regard to the conditions necessary for that assurance. I am warranted in my assurance only if I am warranted in holding that *no available and relevant evidence or argument has been ignored.* If I had, after all, a way of getting unmediated, infallible access to the truth, then I could justifiably discount apparent counter-evidence or argument in advance, sight unseen. But for Mill, no such access is available to 'a being with human faculties'.

This is the key point. The evidence and argument available to me at a given time may warrant any degree of rational assurance, however high – but it is always compatible with the possibility that my information and reflection may be enlarged, by future evidence or argument, into a new state in which I am no longer so justified. Warrant is a relation between a belief and a domain of evidence and argument. If the domain is expanded, the relation may no longer hold. The point applies to arithmetic and geometry as much as to anything else. Thus if we wilfully block new evidence or argument our warrant lapses:

> The beliefs which we have most warrant for, have no safeguard to rest on, but a standing invitation to the whole world to prove them unfounded. If the challenge is not accepted, or is accepted and the attempt fails, we are far enough from certainty still; but we have done the best that the existing state of human reason admits of; we have neglected nothing that could give the truth a chance of reaching us: if the lists are kept open, we may hope that if there be a better truth, it will be found when the human mind is capable of receiving it; and in the meantime we may rely on having attained such approach to truth as is possible in our own day. This is the amount of certainty attainable by a fallible being, and this the sole way of attaining it.
>
> (*CW*, XVIII 232)[6]

Now of course this is not Mill's only argument for liberty of discussion. C. L. Ten has usefully distinguished what he calls the 'Assumption of Infallibility Argument', and the 'Avoidance of Mistake Argument.'[7] The argument I've just been considering is the first. But while fallibilism precludes 'absolute' certainty, it is still compatible in principle with any degree of practical assurance in our existing beliefs. So if certain beliefs have repeatedly been tested against apparent counter-evidence, and have repeatedly won through, then the probability that they will win through against future apparent counter-evidence rises, and the practical urgency of examining apparent counter-evidence diminishes. On the other hand, if the record shows a history of thought in which confidently held – and in particular socially entrenched and protected – beliefs are repeatedly displaced or corrected by new evidence and further discussion, then the practical importance of re-examining them whenever they meet an apparent challenge increases. This is the 'Avoidance of Mistake Argument'.

I have focused on the Assumption of Infallibility argument because of its connection with Mill's general epistemology: the way he treats free dialogue as a precondition of collective rationality. Society cannot have rational assurance in its beliefs if information and argument does not circulate freely. That point establishes a philosophical support for liberty of discussion, in the purely epistemological thesis that rationally warranted thought must be free. But Mill is quite right to lay main emphasis, as he does, on the Avoidance of Mistake argument. There is obvious point in stressing that the record shows many entrenched beliefs to have been catastrophically wrong; whatever the cost of re-scrutinizing received beliefs may be, the cost of suppressing or ignoring further discussion is also great. And of course he goes on to other arguments, which turn more on his liberal ideal of what a developed human being should be like – a rational being whose convictions are not 'dead dogma' but 'living truth.' (*CW*, XVIII 243). Cut off from its rational context, he thinks, meaning is 'lost, or enfeebled, and deprived of its vital effect on the character and conduct' (*CW*, XVIII 258); 'the words which convey it cease to suggest ideas, or suggest only a small portion of those they were originally employed to communicate' (*CW*, XVIII 247).

But has Mill secured the objectivity of free thought?

But, finally, let us get back to the question whether Mill's epistemology really secures the objectivity of free thought. Free thought may encourage rationality in the negative sense of freedom from prejudice and one-sidedness – but how does it achieve positive rationality, in the sense of objective warrant? The fundamental problem about free thought, I noted above, is to see how it can be both self-authorizing and yet also truth-finding.

Let us go back to Nietzsche. He sees that if free thought cannot provide normative authority, neither can fideistic apologetics, or appeal to a platonic realm of Reason; he sees German idealism's failure to deal with the resulting problem. He concludes that free thought (which he sees as itself a historical thing, a product of the Christian value placed on truthfulness and conscience) is the final step to nihilism. He is the first, he thinks, to have seen where European culture is heading and that new values must be created in response, not through the pretence of objectivity, or appeal to a religious or metaphysical 'Beyond', but through an affirmation of the will. In other words, the denial of objectivity becomes in Nietzsche's hands a basic existential issue. And this has become, with the time lags by which culture sometimes follows philosophy, hugely influential.

If one is dazzled by it, it comes as a surprise and an anti-climax to find that Mill simply sees no 'problem' of objectivity. He is firmly established in the tradition that takes free thought to be unconstrained rather than presuppositionless. Instead of grappling heroically with scepticism, he mildly emphasizes fallibilism: taking it for granted that the methods of thinking from within – critical reflection on our inherited convictions, free discussion, the appeal to reflectively endorsed dispositions – are available and satisfactory. To use a well-established metaphor, he sees free thought as a ship on an open ocean. Any part can come to need repair, but we always have to rely on other parts to make the repair. So there is no crisis of scepticism, but there is an important task of improving and refining our methods in science and ethics.

Suppose we agree with Mill's confidence that free thought delivers objectivity. Then we might wonder why that kind of confidence collapses so spectacularly in the twentieth century, at least in politics and the humanities.

The collapse is manifest in a wide range of symptoms. Existentialism is one of them: it is the attempt to extract a super-value, an inspiring self-image, out of the very assertion of nihilism about values. In Nietzsche's version it is the glamorous dream of remaking a new aristocratic ethics after Christianity. Drabber, but far wider-spread as a symptom, is the assertion of purely 'means-end' conceptions of rationality, with more-or-less obviously fallacious attempts to base ethical and political principles on that. Nihilism has an exhilarating romantic variant and a plodding or aggressive philistine variant; either way it is irreconcilable with the humanistic content of classical liberalism.

So what causes it? Important as philosophy may be, it would be foolish to think that the sole causes are mistakes in philosophy. No doubt there are many answers. There is the ebbing of religious faith, the pressure on the normative exercised by the dominance of science and consequent scientistic models of objectivity (which are not the fault of science, of course). And further, might not part of the answer be that questioning of objectivity is itself a characteristic effect of democracy? Objectivism, especially in ethics and the arts, is felt as elitism. And a typical response to elitism about such values is a sense of humiliation and an angry assertion of equal worth. Nietzsche would have recognized that, though he would have hated its upshot: that his own view, popularized, becomes a characteristic form of democratic self-delusion and a refuge for popular mediocrity.

Whatever we think about these speculations, the purely philosophical question of how to vindicate the objectivity of free thought remains. Mill never tries to justify his approach against the heroic presuppositionless tradition. Is this wise avoidance of an ultimately pointless question, or unacceptable evasion of a fundamental question? To say that thinking from within is the method we actually use in our best philosophizing, and the only method we could use, still does not answer the Kantian question which asks what *right* we have to use it. How, to repeat again, can free thought be both self-authorizing *and* truth-finding? Mill's reply would be that free thought has the only vindication it can have: its own success in practice, as shown by its history. On its own record it does not lead to disaster but to the growth of knowledge and to an outlook that is humanistic and liberal.

But because the sceptical fall-out from the other, presuppositionless, tradition has become so culturally influential, it is now an important question not just for pure epistemology, but for aesthetics, ethics and politics, whether Mill's confidence in the process of fallible dialogue is legitimate. A strange alliance of religious apologists and post-modern nihilists disagrees. Do they not need to be confronted directly? Isn't ignoring them and just getting on with it a bit smug? Alas – this question can be put briefly but can be discussed only at subtle length. For my part I really do not think the issue can be avoided. Those of us who follow Mill in his conception of free thought need some meta-normative account of how free thought achieves objectivity without revelation or intuitionistic metaphysics – a defence of free thought from within free thought, as one might say. This is not a type of inquiry that suited Mill. He is patient in understanding other people's substantive outlooks, and vigorous and impressive in setting out his view of the substantive norms of theoretical and practical reasoning. But he clearly has no patience for elusive meta-discussions: they hardly feature in the whole of his philosophical writing. So in this respect we have to go beyond Mill if we want to defend Mill – and in doing so, to defend the properly liberal conception of free thought.

Notes

1 Thus Kant:
   'Reason must subject itself to critique in all its undertakings, and cannot restrict the freedom of critique through any prohibition without damaging itself and drawing upon itself a disadvantageous suspicion. Now there is nothing so important because of its utility, nothing so holy, that it may be exempted from this searching review and inspection, which knows no respect for persons. The very existence of reason depends upon this freedom, which has no dictatorial authority, but whose claim is never anything

more than the agreement of free citizens, each of whom must be able to express his reservations, indeed even his *veto*, without holding back.' Kant, *Critique of Pure Reason*, A739/B767 (translation by Paul Guyer and Allen Wood in: The Cambridge Edition of the Works of Immanuel Kant).

Kant and Mill both provide epistemological foundations for this idea. Each solution has its problems, though for what it is worth Mill is closer to prevailing current assumptions.

2　J. Israel, *Radical Enlightenment*, Oxford: Oxford University Press, 2001.

3　J.H. Newman, *Apologia Pro Vita Sua*, Oxford: Clarendon Press, 1967 (1865), Note A, 'Liberalism', pp. 255–56, 261.

4　J. S. Mill, *Autobiography*, in: John Stuart Mill, *The Collected Works of John Stuart Mill*, 33 vols, general editor F. E. L. Priestley and subsequently J. M. Robson, Toronto and London: The University of Toronto Press, 1963–91, hereafter referred to as: *CW*, Vol. I [*Autobiography and Literary Essays*], p. 87.

5　R.H. Popkin, *The History of Scepticism from Erasmus to Descartes*, New York: Harper and Row, 1968.

6　'In matters of evidence, as in all other human things, we neither require, nor can attain, the absolute. We must hold even our strongest convictions with an opening left in our minds for the reception of facts which contradict them; and only when we have taken this precaution, have we earned the right to act upon our convictions with complete confidence when no such contradiction appears' [VII 574] Cp: 'Why is it, then, that there is on the whole a preponderance among mankind of rational opinions and rational conduct? If there really is this preponderance—which there must be, unless human affairs are, and have always been, in an almost desperate state—it is owing to a quality of the human mind, the source of everything respectable in man, either as an intellectual or as a moral being, namely, that his errors are corrigible. He is capable of rectifying his mistakes by discussion and experience. Not by experience alone. There must be discussion, to show how experience is to be interpreted. Wrong opinions and practices gradually yield to fact and argument: but facts and arguments, to produce any effect on the mind, must be brought before it. Very few facts are able to tell their own story, without comments to bring out their meaning. The whole strength and value, then, of human judgment, depending on the one property, that it can be set right when it is wrong, reliance can be placed on it only when the means of setting it right are kept constantly at hand. In the case of any person whose judgment is really deserving of confidence, how has it become so? Because he has kept his mind open to criticism of his opinions and conduct. Because it has been his practice to listen to all that could be said against him; to profit by as much of it as was just, and expound to himself, and upon occasion to others, the fallacy of what was fallacious. Because he has felt, that the only way in which a human being can make some approach to knowing the whole of a subject, is by hearing what can be said about it by persons of every variety of opinion, and studying all modes in which it can be looked at by every character of mind. No wise man ever acquired his wisdom in any mode but this; nor is it in the nature of human intellect to become wise in any other manner. The steady habit of correcting and completing his own opinion by collating it with those of others, so far from causing doubt and hesitation in carrying it into practice, is the only stable foundation for a just reliance on it: for, being cognizant of all that can, at least obviously, be said against him, and having taken up his position against all gainsayers knowing that he has sought for objections and difficulties, instead of avoiding them, and has shut out no light which can be thrown upon the subject from any quarter—he has a right to think his judgment better than that of any person, or any multitude, who have not gone through a similar process.' Mill, *On Liberty*, ch. 2, *CW*, XVIII, pp. 231–32.

7　C. L. Ten, *Mill on Liberty*, Oxford: Oxford University Press, 1980, p. 125.

10 Mill's relevance today

A personal view

Peter Singer

1. Introduction

From the time I first read him, as an undergraduate, I have always felt a strong affinity to John Stuart Mill, both to his values, and to his clear, no-nonsense style of writing. But it was not until much later in life, when Roger Crisp, in his contribution to Dale Jamieson's volume *Singer and His Critics*, compared some of my views with those of Mill, that I began to think more explictly about the parallels. (Needless to say, I am not comparing the significance of my own philosophical contributions to those of one of the great founding fathers of the utilitarian tradition.)

Most obviously, we are both utilitarian philosophers. We both write for a broad audience, rather than only for professional philosophers, and to that end we strive to write clearly and without jargon. We have both written books seeking some form of equality for a group that has historically been denied the moral status to which we think it is entitled: in Mill's case, women, in mine, animals. These books have played a role in stimulating the development of a popular movement aimed at achieving the changes suggested – although, just as Mill died before women achieved full equality, so I am sure that I will not live to see the day when the interests of nonhuman animals are given equal consideration with the similar interests of humans. In order to advance our reforming agendas, on these and other issues, we both stood for our national parliaments. At electoral politics, neither of us was an outstanding success, although Mill did at least get elected one more time than I did.

As for religion, like Mill, I can say that I am 'one who has, not thrown off belief, but never had it.'[1] – although this is not as rare today as it was in Mill's time, at least not in England, where Mill grew up, nor in Australia, where I did. For me, as for Mill, the main reason I cannot believe in the kind of monotheism that is at the core of Christianity, Judaism and Islam is the existence of evil. I find it preposterous – indeed, monstrous – to believe that an all-powerful, all-knowing God could have created a world in which totally innocent people, including children – not to mention animals – die slowly and painfully in droughts, floods and other natural calamities. Like Mill, I am revolted at the spectacle of what he called 'a jesuitical defence of moral enormities.'[2] To those who say, as many still do, that we mere humans cannot understand God's infinite goodness, I would also repeat Mill's words: 'I will call no being good, who is not what I mean when I apply that epithet to my fellow-creatures; and if such a being can sentence me to hell for not so calling him, to hell I will go.'[3]

There are, of course, many differences between us. Perhaps the most notable, intellectually, is that Mill made major contributions to logic, metaphysics and philosophy of science. I can only stand in awe of the wide range of thought that he mastered. It is not surprising, therefore, that different people should prize different aspects of his work. What follows is very much a personal perspective, a statement of what I keep going back to Mill for.

2. Utilitarianism

Mill defined utilitarianism as:

> The creed which accepts as the foundation of morals, Utility, or the Greatest Happiness Principle, holds that actions are right in proportion as they tend to promote happiness, wrong as they tend to produce the reverse of happiness.[4]

I am a utilitarian, but a preference utilitarian, rather than a hedonistic utilitarianism. Thus, if I were to use Mill's definition, I would modify it to say that actions are right in proportion as they tend to promote the satisfaction of preferences, and wrong as they tend to thwart or frustrate the satisfaction of preferences.

Admittedly, there is some question as to whether Mill really takes a distinct view. It seems obvious that some people desire things like knowledge, virtue, glory, supporting one's family and friends, power, artistic achievement and so on, for their own sake, and not, or not only, as a means to happiness. Since Mill concedes that 'the sole evidence it is possible to produce that anything is desirable is that people actually do desire it,'[5] this creates a problem for him. He attempts to solve it by arguing that whatever we desire for its own sake 'is desired as itself a part of happiness.'[6] But this claim seems either false or vacuous, depending on how we define happiness. When, for example, Mill acknowledges that some people desire to be virtuous, but says that they desire it as part of their happiness, he is either saying something false, or he is stretching the ordinary meaning of happiness so that whatever anyone wants for its own sake is, by definition, part of their happiness. Preference utilitarians have no need for dubious empirical claims or stipulative definition. The preference utilitarian does not tell people what they ought to desire for its own sake, nor try to squash their disparate desires into a single mould. *Whatever* people desire really is desirable, other things being equal, simply because it is desired. Preference utilitarianism is, to that extent, less paternalistic and authoritarian in its fundamental conception of the good than the hedonistic version that Mill professes.

The difficulty of pinning down exactly what Mill means, plus a general suspicion that he is trying too hard to accommodate utilitarianism to the accepted opinions of his day is, unfortunately, a pervasive problem in Mill's *Utilitarianism*, not limited to his account of happiness. His notorious distinction between the quantity and quality of pleasures, and his unconvincing arguments for preferring the 'higher' pleasures is another example. But the work also has other weaknesses. His attempt to offer some kind of 'proof' of utilitarianism is, viewed kindly, very poorly expressed and, less charitably put, exhibits evident fallacies. It is for such reasons that, despite my evident broad sympathy with his approach to ethics, this is not among those of his works that I value most highly. If *Utilitarianism* has become the most widely read of the classic utilitarian tracts, it may be because, when it comes to readable prose, neither *Introduction to the Principles of Morals and Legislation* nor *The Methods of Ethics* offered much competition. In every respect other than brevity and elegance of expression, Henry Sidgwick's is the superior work. When I want to know how a great utilitarian thinker handled a particular objection, it is to Sidgwick, not Mill, that I turn.

3. On liberty

The work of Mill's that I do find myself always coming back to is *On Liberty*, both for its arguments for freedom of expression and opinion, and for its defence of personal liberty in matters that do not cause harm to others. I shall discuss these issues separately.

3.1 Freedom of thought and expression

There is nothing like being silenced to make one feel vividly the importance of freedom of expression. In 1989, and for several years thereafter, announcements of lectures that I was scheduled to give in Germany, Austria and the German-speaking part of Switzerland led to protests and threats of violence that caused the complete cancellation of two conferences – including Austria's celebrated Wittgenstein Symposium – and the withdrawal, at late notice, of several invitations to speak at universities and conferences. In Zurich, I had to stop lecturing after I was physically attacked on the stage and had my glasses smashed.[7] In the United States, after I was appointed to Princeton University, both I and the university's president received death threats, and Steve Forbes, a university trustee and then a candidate for the Republican presidential nomination, vowed to withhold all further donations to the university as long as I was on the faculty.

These protests were against my views on euthanasia for disabled infants. I will not discuss the merits of these views here. Indeed, many of my German opponents never sought to attack the substance of my position. Rather they held that, irrespective of the merits of the arguments, it is impermissible to question the inviolability of human life in general or the right to life of disabled people in particular.[8] The objection to my views urged by these German opponents of freedom of speech is exactly that discussed by Mill when he writes, in *On Liberty,* of those who would deny the right to challenge a belief, not because they are certain the belief is true, but because the belief is 'indispensable to well-being' and 'none but bad men would desire to weaken these salutary beliefs.' To this Mill's response seems to me devastating:

> This mode of thinking makes the justification of restraints on discussion not a question of the truth of doctrines, but of their usefulness; and flatters itself by that means to escape the responsibility of claiming to be an infallible judge of opinions. But those who thus satisfy themselves, do not perceive that the assumption of infallibility is merely shifted from one point to another. The usefulness of an opinion is itself a matter of opinion: as disputable, as open to discussion and requiring discussion as much, as the opinion itself.[9]

That was the approach that I took on the one occasion during those years when a fruitful discussion did take place in Germany between me and those who had sought to silence me (at the University of Saarbrücken, under the auspices of Professor Georg Meggle). Since the protestors blew whistles and made too much noise for me to be able to speak, Meggle invited one of them up on the stage to state why I should not be allowed to speak. That revealed some basic misconceptions about my views – including the belief that I was politically on the right – but also included the claim that Germany's past shows the danger of regarding some human lives as more valuable or 'worthy of life' than others. After the spokesperson for the protestors had been heard, Meggle said that, in fairness, I should be allowed to respond, not to discuss the sanctity of human life, but rather to discuss the claim that there must be no discussion of the sanctity of human life. That led, inevitably, to a discussion of my claim that no reflective society can avoid raising the issues that my opponents thought should not be raised. Since few people think that medical technology should always be used to preserve human life to the maximum extent possible, it is necessary to ask on what, if the patient is incapable of expressing a view, decisions to discontinue treatment are to be based, if not on a judgment about the nature of the life that the patient can be expected to live?

On one point here my experience does not entirely support what Mill writes. He asserts: 'And it will not do to say that the heretic may be allowed to maintain the utility or harmlessness of his opinion, though forbidden to maintain its truth. The truth of an opinion is part of its utility.' That is no doubt correct, if we are concerned with opinions about something that can be true or false. But, arguably, that is not the case with moral opinions. My German opponents seemed divided on this question. Some of them were conservative Christians, who thought that the sanctity of human life is God's law and hence a moral truth that I was denying. To this group Mill's point would apply. Others, however, were from the left, and regarded morality and politics as simply a power struggle. They saw themselves as on the side of the oppressed, whereas my views were part of a capitalist-fascist attempt to eliminate all who are not productive workers. It was precisely because they saw ethics as relative to economic interests that they rejected the idea of debate and discussion as a way of reaching truth.

So when Mill goes on to say: 'If we would know whether or not it is desirable that a proposition should be believed, is it possible to exclude the consideration of whether or not it is true?' at least some left-wing German opponents of free speech would have said yes, it is possible to exclude that, and their position refutes Mill's assertion that 'you do not find [those who defend received opinions] handling the question of utility as if it could be completely abstracted from that of truth: on the contrary, it is, above all, because their doctrine is 'the truth,' that the knowledge or the belief of it is held to be so indispensable.' The left-wing German opponents of my right to speak represent a different kind of challenge to free speech, one that sees it all as mere camouflage for the real issues of power and dominance that lie beneath its surface. This approach was not entirely unknown when Mill wrote *On Liberty* – it is outlined in *The Communist Manifesto* and can be traced back to Thrasymachus, in Plato's *Republic* – but it has become far more popular since, especially among postmodernists. It is alien to Mill's philosophical outlook, however, and so requires a separate refutation. That refutation should start from the fact that those who take this view are forced to recognize that their own moral and political claims – including the claim that a given view should not be heard – are equally lacking in objectivity. Those who oppose freedom of expression without assuming that reason plays a role in ethical argument face the problem of undermining their own ethical stance, for they thereby admit it to be no more true, and no better justified, in terms of reason and argument, than the view they would suppress.

Mill divides his discussion of freedom of expression into two parts, the first based on the supposition that the views held by those who wish to suppress dissent may be false, and the second based on the assumption that those views are true. My discussion so far has fitted into the first of these two parts, for I do believe that the conventional doctrine of the sanctity of human life is false. Now I shall move to a distinct controversy about someone who is saying things that are palpably false. Even here, as Mill argues, it is important to defend their right to free speech. I refer to David Irving, who is currently in an Austrian prison for saying that the Holocaust never happened.[10]

Here it is relevant to turn to Mill's argument that if a view is not 'fully, frequently, and fearlessly discussed,' it will become 'a dead dogma, not a living truth' and say that the best way to persuade anyone who is still sceptical about the enormity of the Nazi atrocities is to confront them with the evidence. It is hard to see how imprisoning someone who denies the existence of the Holocaust is going to persuade anyone that the Holocaust happened – just the contrary, in fact, they are likely to think that if the government locks such people up, they must be onto something that the government wants to keep secret.

A more immediate reason for defending Irving's right to free speech relates to the recent controversy over the Danish cartoons depicting Mohammed in an unflattering light. For all the reasons Mill gives in defence of freedom of expression, we should be free to deny the existence of God, and to criticize the teachings of Jesus, Moses, Mohammed and Buddha, as reported in texts that millions of people regard as sacred. The fact that an expression of opinion causes offence is not an adequate ground for suppressing it. As Mill wrote:

> … if the test be offence to those whose opinion is attacked, I think experience testifies that this offence is given whenever the attack is telling and

powerful, and that every opponent who pushes them hard, and whom they find it difficult to answer, appears to them, if he shows any strong feeling on the subject, an intemperate opponent.

Without the freedom to criticize religion, progress will always be running up against a roadblock. Nor should we say that calmly stated objections to religious belief are permitted, but ridicule is not, for ridicule may be the most effective weapon against a false but influential belief. Noting that those critical of prevailing opinion generally need to be much more moderate in their language, simply to get a hearing, than those who defend orthodoxy, Mill went so far as to say that 'if it were necessary to choose, there would be much more need to discourage offensive attacks on infidelity, than on religion.' That may no longer be the case in countries that are far less religious than the Britain of Mill's day, but it is still true in the United States, where many people seem to believe that an atheist who lives ethically must have failed to understand the logical implications of denying the existence of God.

We should, therefore, defend the right of newspapers to publish cartoons depicting Jesus, Moses, Brahma, Buddha or Mohammed in a manner that will offend at least some Christians, Jews, Hindus, Buddhists or Moslems. (To defend the right of a newspaper to publish something is not to say that it was wise to publish it. With the benefit of hindsight, given the number of innocent lives lost in the ensuing riots, publication may have been the wrong thing to do – but that is a separate issue.) The problem with the conviction of David Irving is that as long as he remains in prison, and the laws that put him there remain in force, Moslems have some grounds for believing that the failure of European governments to take steps against the newspapers that published the cartoons indicates their hostility to, and bias against, Islam. Only when Irving has been freed will it be possible for Europeans to turn to the Islamic protesters and say: 'We apply the principle of freedom of expression even-handedly, whether it offends Moslems, Christians, Jews, or anyone else.'

Does the defence of freedom of speech also require that we oppose laws against inciting racial hatred? Certainly such laws should not prevent discussion of the possibility of different races or ethnic groups having distinct characteristics, or of these characteristics being judged favourably or unfavourably. But here too we can again agree with Mill that 'even opinions lose their immunity, when the circumstances in which they are expressed are such as to constitute their expression a positive instigation to some mischievous act.' That sentence immediately precedes his oft-quoted distinction between publishing in a newspaper one's opinion that corn dealers are starvers of the poor, and saying the same to an excited mob in front of a corn-dealer's house.[11] Admittedly, this example is not easy to translate into a modern context, in which electronic media provide an immediacy that newspapers do not have. Everything will depend on the circumstances, and on the extent to which the climate that prevails is one in which the remarks are likely to be understood as an incitement to violence. It is for the courts to determine when that is the case.

3.2 Freedom of the individual

Mill's arguments in *On Liberty* about the limits of authority over the individual have been important to me in several areas, but for brevity I will here focus only on one of them, and that is the issue of voluntary euthanasia and assisted suicide. (Henceforth, for brevity, I shall speak of 'voluntary euthanasia' as including assisted suicide, except where there is reason to distinguish the two.) There are, of course, straightforward utilitarian arguments for legalising these practices. Despite good palliative care, some terminally ill people experience considerable suffering, and if they do not wish to endure it to the very end, then both hedonistic and preference utilitarians will agree that, other things being equal, there is greater utility in granting their request than in denying it. There is one utilitarian objection: that legalising voluntary euthanasia will be a step down a slippery slope to all kinds of killings that are involuntary and clearly wrong. But now that we have more than two decades of experience with the open practice of voluntary euthanasia in the Netherlands, without any evidence of a progression down a slippery slope, we can set that objection aside.[12] Since many people are not utilitarians, however, and a considerable number believe that voluntary euthanasia is morally wrong, it is – at least – a good political strategy to be able to bolster the direct utilitarian case for legalising the practice with Mill's argument about the limits of proper state authority over the individual.

Mill sums up his position in these famous sentences:

> ... the only purpose for which power can be rightfully exercised over any member of a civilised community, against his will, is to prevent harm to others. His own good, either physical or moral, is not sufficient warrant ... Over himself, over his own body and mind, the individual is sovereign.

In support of this view, Mill argued that 'each is the best judge and guardian of his own interests.' So, he said, if you see people about to cross a bridge you know to be unsafe, you may forcibly stop them in order to inform them of the risk that the bridge may collapse under them, but if they decide to continue, you must stand aside and let them cross, for only they know the importance to them of crossing, and only they know how to balance that against the possible loss of their lives. The example presupposes, of course, that we are dealing with beings who are capable of taking in information, reflecting and choosing.

It is easy to agree with Mill that the person whose life it is, should normally be the one to decide if that life is worth continuing. If a person with unimpaired capacities comes to the considered judgment that his or her future is so clouded that it would be better to die than to continue to live, the usual reason against killing – that it deprives the one killed of the goods that life will bring – is turned into its opposite, a reason for acceding to that person's request.

This would seem to be an argument that those who defend freedom would accept. Yet curiously, often they do not. Here, for example, is a statement that at first glance looks very much as if it comes from someone who shares Mill's outlook on individual liberty:

> My philosophy trusts individuals to make the right decisions for their families and communities ... I believe government should be limited and efficient, that it should do a few things and do them well ...[13]

The author of these words is George W. Bush (or at least, they were published in a book with his name on it). In respect of Oregon's popularly supported law allowing physician-assisted suicide, Bush had a chance to act on his trust in individuals to make the right decisions and set limits to the reach of the federal government. Instead, his attorneys-general fought a long and ultimately futile legal battle to stop Oregon physicians prescribing drugs, in accordance with the law, to assist terminally-ill patients to die. Like many other conservatives, it seems that Bush's support for individual freedom is not based on principle, but rather on opposition to specific government actions, such as taxation, or environmental protection.

But I need to put myself to the same test: as a utilitarian, can I support Mill's principle that power can be rightfully exercised over individuals only to prevent them harming others? Or is my use of his principle *merely* strategic, an invocation of something that I do not really believe?

I have to admit that there are some measures that violate Mill's principle, and yet have my support. The compulsory wearing of seatbelts is an issue I have followed closely, perhaps because I come from Victoria, Australia, which in 1970 had the distinction of becoming the first jurisdiction in the world to require the use of seatbelts in cars. By 1973, all other Australian states and territories had passed similar laws. Prior to this legislation there had been an attempt to educate the public about the benefit of wearing seat belts, and some people wore them voluntarily, but many did not. The new legislation made a difference. Deaths on the road, which had been rising steadily up to that date, began to fall, and have, by and large, continued to fall ever since. By 1999 Australian road fatalities were less than half the 1970 figure, a saving of more than 2,000 lives per year. When expressed in proportion to the number of registered vehicles, the fall was even more dramatic, to less than a fifth of what they were in 1970.[14] (Compulsory wearing of seat belts is only one factor in this decline, of course, but it is a significant one.) It is hard for a utilitarian to deny that the benefits of saving so many lives and preventing so many serious injuries outweigh the minor restriction on individual liberty that the law involves.

Some argue that requiring people to wear seat belts does 'prevent harm to others' because accidental deaths and injuries impose costs on the community as a whole. But that does not seem to be the primary reason for supporting the law. If a billionaire libertarian seeking repeal of the law offered to pay, after the repeal, for all costs the community would bear because of the deaths and injuries of passengers not wearing seat belts, I would still not favour repeal. The problem is, it seems, that in some circumstances it is simply not true that individuals are the best judges and guardians of their own interests. Particularly when dealing with small risks of great harms, it seems that most of us do quite poorly in judging and guarding our own interests.[15]

Does this mean that I reject Mill's principle? Since H.L.A. Hart's partial defence of Mill in his *Law, Liberty and Morality,* it has been common to distinguish between legal moralism and legal paternalism. Where Mill says that the good of the individual, 'either physical or moral' is not sufficient warrant for state interference, Hart says that that the individual's physical good *is* sufficient warrant. Thus the law may require the individual to wear a seatbelt when in a moving car, or a helmet when driving a motorcycle or even when riding an ordinary bicycle. But it may not, on this view, say that homosexuality is immoral, and require people to restrict their sexual relationships to members of the opposite sex.

The problem with this approach is that it is not easy to see why legal paternalism is OK, but legal moralism is wrong. The distinction is often defended with the claim that the state should be neutral between competing moral ideals, but is such neutrality really possible? If I were a proponent of legal moralism, I would say that it is, after all, a moral judgment – if a widely shared one – that it is better not to be killed or injured in a car crash, and it is another moral judgment – not quite so widely shared – that it is better to die than to live a week or two when in pain or discomfort from a terminal illness. What tenable definition of morality would exclude such judgments, while including others that prefer some forms of sexual activity to others?

Here utilitarians may find themselves in an odd situation. If they attempt to argue that the state may prohibit conduct that harms the agent, but should permit other conduct that, while immoral, does not harm anyone else, they can then be challenged to say in what, on their view, this last cateogry consists. If the act does not harm the agent, and does not harm anyone other than the agent, what can be immoral about it? Only, it would seem, that it does not produce as much good as some other act that the agent might perform – but no one is suggesting that the law should require each of us to do as much good as we possibly can, so this response will not do.

When utilitarians say that the state should permit conduct that, while immoral, does not harm the agent or anyone else, what they really mean is: 'The state should permit conduct that most citizens consider immoral, but does not harm anyone else.' But it is not clear why the state should take this view. If most citizens were right, and there really were acts that are immoral, even though they do not harm anyone else, why should they not be prohibited? The real problem is that in the situation we are considering, some citizens believe that certain acts – homosexuality, prostitution, suicide, or whatever it may be – are immoral when they really are not immoral at all. The utilitarian's strongest argument is that the moral views that condemn such acts are mistaken. If that argument fails to persuade, then objecting to legal moralism may be another way of reaching a desirable goal, but it ventures over more dubious philosophical ground.

4. Some brief remarks on other works

Apart from *On Liberty,* I shall mention four other works, or parts of works, by Mill that I particularly admire: *The Subjection of Women, On Nature,* a brief passage in his *Whewell on Moral Philosophy,* and *A Few Words on Non-Intervention.*

4.1 The Subjection of Women

Mill's *The Subjection of Women* is a wonderful work to which I cannot possibly do justice in a short space of time. It is uncompromising in its demands: Mill argues for 'a principle of perfect equality,' between men and women. It is a model of how to argue against a more or less universal social prejudice. Consider, for instance, this passage from the opening chapter, in which Mill discusses the difficulty of success in the project in which he is about to embark. (I like to think of it in regard not only to efforts to change the status of women, but also to efforts to change the status of animals):

> The difficulty is that which exists in all cases in which there is a mass of feeling to be contended against. So long as opinion is strongly rooted in the feelings, it gains rather than loses in stability by having a preponderating weight of argument against it. For if it were accepted as a result of argument, the refutation of the argument might shake the solidity of the conviction; but when it rests solely on feeling, the worse it fares in argumentative contest, the more persuaded adherents are that their feeling must have some deeper ground, which the arguments do not reach; and while the feeling remains, it is always throwing up fresh intrenchments of argument to repair any breach made in the old. And there are so many causes tending to make the feelings connected with this subject the most intense and most deeply-rooted of those which gather round and protect old institutions and custom, that we need not wonder to find them as yet less undermined and loosened than any of the rest by the progress of the great modern spiritual and social transition; nor suppose that the barbarisms to which men cling longest must be less barbarisms than those which they earlier shake off.[16]

4.2 On Nature

When Mill begins his essay *On Nature* by noting the influence on our thinking and feelings wielded by words like 'nature' and 'natural,' he could have been writing for the twentieth or twenty-first century as much as the nineteenth. In discussions of issues like *in vitro* fertilization, euthanasia, genetic enhancement and cloning, no objection is more common than that some new or proposed technique or procedure is 'unnatural.' After dealing with such arguments over the years, I am convinced that Mill is absolutely correct when he writes that these words have become 'one of the most copious sources of false taste, false philosophy, false morality, and even bad law.'

The argument of the essay is brilliantly simple. The word 'nature' either means everything that exists in the universe, including human beings and all that they create, or it means the world as it would be, apart from human beings and what humans bring about. In the first sense, nothing that humans do can be 'unnatural.' In the second sense, the claim that something humans do is 'unnatural' is no objection at all, for everything that we do is an interference with nature, and obviously much of that interference is highly desirable.

Mill concludes his essay with the comment that, far from seeking to follow nature, we should be 'perpetually striving to amend, the course of nature – and bringing that part of it over which we can exercise control more nearly into conformity with a high standard of justice and goodness.' Some of my friends in the environmental movement might consider that suggestion an instance of the overweening human arrogance that has led us to do so much damage to the ecosystems on which all life depends. But that was not Mill's attitude. In his *Principles of Political Economy* he shows a fine appreciation of the importance of leaving some parts of the world unaffected by human activity:

> A world from which solitude is extirpated is a very poor ideal. Solitude, in the sense of being often alone, is essential to any depth of meditation or of character; and solitude in the presence of natural beauty and grandeur, is the cradle of thoughts and aspirations which are not only good for the individual, but which society could ill do without. Nor is there much satisfaction in contemplating the world with nothing left to the spontaneous activity of nature; with every rood of land brought into cultivation, which is capable of growing food for human beings; every flowery waste or natural pasture ploughed up, all quadrupeds or birds which are not domesticated for man's use exterminated as his rivals for food, every hedgerow or superfluous tree rooted out, and scarcely a place left where a wild shrub or flower could grow without being eradicated as a weed in the name of improved agriculture. If the earth must lose that great portion of its pleasantness which it owes to things that the unlimited increase of wealth and population would extirpate from it, for the mere purpose of enabling it to support a larger, but not a better or a happier population, I sincerely hope, for the sake of posterity, that they will be content to be stationary, long before necessity compels them to it.[17]

4.3 On Animals

In his refutation of William Whewell, Mill has a few paragraphs that have an obvious resonance for me. Since these paragraphs are buried in what is now a little-read work, let me read some passages and summarize others.

> Dr Whewell puts the last hand to his supposed refutation of Bentham's principle, by what he thinks a crushing *reductio ad absurdum*. The reader might make a hundred guesses before discovering what this is. We have not yet got over our astonishment, not at Bentham, but at Dr Whewell. See, he says, to what consequences your greatest-happiness principle leads! Bentham says that it is as much a moral duty to regard the pleasures and pains of other animals as those of human beings …[18]

Mill then quotes Whewell's objection to Bentham, which includes the following:

> We are bound to men by the universal tie of humanity, of human brother-
> hood. We have no such tie to animals ... It is ... to most persons not a
> tolerable doctrine, that we may sacrifice the happiness of men provided we
> can in that way produce an overplus of pleasure to cats, dogs, and hogs.

It is fascinating to me that Whewell's line of argument is one I still commonly
encounter, in discussions about ethics and animals. Mill's crushing response is
part of a line of utilitarian arguments on behalf of animals which begins with
Bentham's parallel, in a footnote in the *Introduction to the Principles of Morals
and Legislation*, between the treatment of animals and the treatment of black
slaves, and continues in my own work. Mill's response, written in 1852, prior to
the American Civil War, is as follows:

> It is 'to most persons' in the Slave States of America not a tolerable doctrine
> that we may sacrifice any portion of the happiness of white men for the sake
> of a greater amount of happiness to black men. It would have been intoler-
> able five centuries ago 'to most persons' among the feudal nobility, to hear it
> asserted that the greatest pleasure or pain of a hundred serfs ought not to give
> way to the smallest of a nobleman. According to the standard of Dr Whewell
> the slavemasters and the nobles were right. They too felt themselves 'bound'
> by a 'tie of brotherhood' to the white men and to the nobility, and felt no such
> tie to the negroes and serfs.

After this, Mill closes the discussion with a statement that deserves our close
attention:

> We are perfectly willing to stake the whole question on this one issue. Granted
> that any practice causes more pain to animals than it gives pleasure to man;
> is that practice moral or immoral? And if, exactly in proportion as human be-
> ings raise their heads out of the slough of selfishness, they do not with one
> voice answer 'immoral,' let the morality of the principle of utility be for ever
> condemned.

Note exactly what Mill is saying here. It would have been remarkable enough if
he had merely said that he is ready to stake the entire case for utilitarianism on the
contention that it is immoral gratuitously to cause pain to animals. But he goes
much further than that. He is willing to stake the case on the immorality of any
practice that causes *more* pain to animals than it brings pleasure to man. In other
words, he assumes that the pains of animals count *equally* with the pleasures of
humans. Mill allows no discounting at all for the fact that the pleasures are for humans, and the pains for animals. He is, in essence, proposing what I thought was
a radical suggestion when I put it forward in *Animal Liberation,* 123 years later:
the principle of equal consideration for animals. We can have no doubt where

Mill would have stood on today's most important animal issue, factory farming, which causes such immense suffering for tens of billions of animals around the world, while bringing, at best, very slight benefit for human beings and arguably, considering its environmental costs, considerable harm.

4.4 A few words on non-intervention

I mention this brief essay, first published in 1859, because of its contemporary relevance. Mill begins by saying that few questions are more in need of attention from philosophers than the issue of when a state that is not itself under attack may go to war. He sought a 'definite and rational test' of when countries are justified in intervening, and when they are justified in refraining from intervention. That he sees the latter as also requiring justification is, of course, significant. It indicates that he considers some cases of what we now call 'humanitarian intervention' justified. He also, however, thought that it was dubious to intervene in order to bring democracy to a country that is not democratically governed. The exception would be if the government was receiving foreign assistance in suppressing an internal movement for democracy. Then he thought it was justifiable to intervene on the side of democracy in order to redress the balance. Creating democracy when there was no internal movement strong enough to bring it about, in the absence of outside support, Mill thought unlikely to be successful.

Notes

1 Mill, *CW*, I, p. 45.
2 *CW*, X, p. 456.
3 *CW*, IX, p. 103.
4 Mill, *Utilitarianism*, Chapter 2.
5 *Utilitarianism*, Chapter 4.
6 *Utilitarianism*, Chapter 4; see also Mill, *A System of Logic*, *CW*, VIII, p. 952, where Mill says that happiness is what 'human beings with highly developed faculties can care to have.' (I owe this reference to John Skorupski, *Why Read Mill Today?* (London: Routledge, 2006, p. 21).
7 For details, see P. Singer, 'On Being Silenced in Germany', *The New York Review of Books*, August 15, 1991; reprinted in P. Singer, *Practical Ethics*, 2nd edition, Cambridge: Cambridge University Press, 1993, appendix, and: P. Singer, *Writings on an Ethical Life*, New York: Ecco, 2000, pp. 303–18.
8 See, for example, F. Christoph, '(K)ein Diskurs über "lebensunwertes Leben"', *Der Spiegel*, No. 23/1989 (June 5, 1989); O. Tolmein, *Geschätztes Leben*, Hamburg: Konkret Literatur Verlag, 1990; T. Bastian (ed.), *Denken, Schreiben, Töten*, Stuttgart: Hirzel, 1990; F. Christoph, *Tödlicher Zeitgeist*, Cologne: Kiepenheuer und Witsch, 1990.
9 Mill, *On Liberty*, Chapter 2.
10 Should any readers think that what follows stems from insufficient empathy with those whose families suffered in the Holocaust, I would urge them to glance at: P. Singer, *Pushing Time Away: My Grandfather and the Tragedy of Jewish Vienna*, New York: Ecco, 2003.

11 Mill, *On Liberty,* Chapter 3.
12 See P. Singer, 'Voluntary Euthanasia: A Utilitarian Perspective', *Bioethics*, Vol. 17, Nos 5–6 (2003), pp. 526–41.
13 G. W. Bush, *A Charge to Keep*, New York: Morrow, 1999, p.235.
14 Australian Bureau of Statistics, *2001 Yearbook Australia,* Commonwealth of Australia, Canberra, 2001, pp. 854–57.
15 See, for example, D. Kahneman and A. Tversky, 'Prospect theory: An analysis of decisions under risk', *Econometrica*, 47 (1979), pp. 276–87.
16 Mill, *The Subjection of Women,* Chapter 1.
17 *Principles of Political Economy,* Book IV, Ch. 6, Paragraph 8.
18 *CW*, X, pp.185–87.

Index

age of transition: authority in 19, 21,
  24–7; French Revolution 1830 27–30;
  industrialization in 22–3; youth over
  age 11, 26, 32
*Analysis of the Phenomena of the Human
  Mind* (James Mill): explaining infinity
  106; Mill's notes to 1869 edition 104;
  without reference to Bentham's work
  on logic 69
animals 63–4, 169–70
anti-paternalism 92
apologetic thought 147
Aristotle 74, 75, 77, 79, 107, 134
Art of Life 12–13, 85, 86, 87, 91, 92, 95, 96
'Assumption of Infallibility Argument'
  (J.S. Mill) 155
Athenaeum 75, 76
Attwood, T. 22
'Auguste Comte and Positivism' (J.S.
  Mill) 63–4, 87–8, 96
Austin, J. 21, 24–5
authority: in age of transition 19, 21, 24–7;
  Austin's theory of 21, 24–5; intellectual
  149; and natural state 24, 26; of state over
  individual 3, 165; views on governing
  classes 24, 25; youth over age 11, 26, 32
Autobiography (G. Bentham) 69, 74
Autobiography (J.S. Mill) 9, 20; allusion to
  Mill's mental breakdown 73; educa-
  tion of fear 43; emotional sentiment,
  importance of cultivating 139–40;
  meeting George Bentham 70; politics
  of epistemology 152; reforming Mill's
  own character 11, 40, 42–5
'Avoidance of Mistake Argument' (J.S.
  Mill) 155

Bain, A, 35, 39
Barry, B. 6

Baynes, T.S. 75, 76, 78
beauty: as a higher pleasure 105, 112;
  natural 57, 59, 61, 62, 169
Bentham, G.: botanist 71, 74; classification systems 71, 72, 73, 74; critique of
  Whately's *Elements of Logic* 72, 73;
  on Bowring 82n; parallel work with
  Mill 70, 71–2; and quantification of
  the predicate doctrine controversy 75,
  76; relationship with Mill 69–70, 73;
  translation of *Chrestomathia* 70, 71
Bentham, J. 4, 43; Mill reducing accomplishments of 68; Mill's criticism of
  treatment of morality 88–9; on homo-
  sexual relations 141; relationship with
  James Mill 67–9; views on animals
  169–70
'Bentham' (J.S. Mill) 68, 88–9
Birmingham Political Union 22
birth control 2, 59
Blum, L. 95–6
Boole, G. 67, 74
botany: George Bentham's work on 71,
  74; Mill's interest in 57–8, 62, 63, 70
Bowring, J. 74, 82n
British Empire 8–9
British Idealists 4
Broadie, S. 85
Brown v. Board of Education (1954)
  132–3
Bush, G.W. 166

Carlile, R. 64
Carlyle, T. 62; letters from Mill to 27,
  30–1, 63
Carrel, A. 30–2
Categorical Imperative 121–2
character formation: civic 48–50; conditions favourable to strong 51–2;

deformation and re-formation of female characters 11, 46–8; James Mill and Robert Owen on 36–8; Mill refutes Owen's view of 40–1; reforming Mill's own character 11, 40, 42–5; *see also* ethology

childhood of Mill 42–3

Chrestomathia (J. Bentham) 12, 69; G. Bentham's translation of 70, 71; 'Geometry and Algebra' 79

Christianity: and discussion in *Utilitarianism* on morality 63; and environmentalism 65; Mill's essays on religion and 63–4; of Wordsworth 62

'Claims of Labour' (J.S. Mill) 57

Clarissa (Richardson) 137

coercion 92, 93, 94

'Coleridge' (J.S. Mill) 68

Coleridge, S.T. 20, 45, 62

Collini, S. 6

colonization 60

commons preservation 57, 62, 63

Commons Preservation Society 57, 62

comprehensive liberalism 146

Comte, A.: letter from Mill to 149; Mill's criticism of 63–4, 65, 87–8

Considerations on Representative Government (J.S. Mill): civic characters 48–50; on nationalism 10; problem of the state 3; scholarship on 7

constitutional democracy 117, 118

'constructive scepticism' 150, 152

Contemporary Review 75

cosmopolitanism 10

Cowling, M. 3, 6

Danish cartoons 164

De Morgan 74–5, 79; Mill's criticism of 77

d'Eichtal, G., letters from Mill to 21, 27, 149

democracy: conformitarian tendencies 52; creating strong characters for 51–2

democratic radicalism 11, 20–1

Descartes, R. 149

despotism 48–9, 93

Devlin, P. 3, 6, 141

Dewey, J. 121

'difference' feminism 14, 138–40

Dworkin, A. 135, 137

eclecticism 19, 20, 21

economic reform 22

economics, rise of modern 4

economy, state of British 60; *see also* political economy

'Education' (James Mill) 37, 69

education of Mill 42–3

education, philosophy of 84, 92–3

egalitarian democracy 116–17

Elementary Lessons in Logic (Jevons) 76

Elements of Logic (Whately) 72, 73, 74

environmentalism: botany as a foundation for Mill's 57–8, 62, 63, 70; and Christianity 65; commons preservation 57, 62, 63; economic version of Mill's 11–12, 59–61, 62–3; influence of Wordsworth on Mill's 11, 45, 58, 61–2; links with feminism 59; and natural beauty 57, 59, 61, 62, 169; and neo-Malthusianism 11, 58, 59; and peasant proprietorship 58, 59; railways 62–3; relevance today of Mill's 168–9; and religion of humanity 11, 62, 63–4, 65

epistemology 147, 148, 149, 150–3; shaping Mill's view of free discussion 153–5

'Essay on Nomenclature and Classification' (G.Bentham) 71

An essay on the New Analytic of Logical Forms (Baynes) 75

ethical theory 3, 4

ethology 11, 35, 38–42; applied in *Autobiography* 40, 42–5; challenging scholarly consensus on 35–6; in *Considerations on Representative Government* 48–50; in *On Liberty* 51–2; outline in *A System of Logic* 35, 39–42, 44, 45; in *Subjection of Women* 46–8

Examination of the Philosophy of Sir William Hamilton (J.S. Mill) 64, 76

Examiner 21, 27, 28

Existentialism 156

Expediency 87, 90, 91

fallibilism 149, 152, 154, 155, 156

feminism 143–4; 'difference' 14, 138–40; links with environmentalism 59; *see also* liberal feminism; queer feminism; radical feminism

'A Few Words on Non-Intervention' (J.S. Mill) 9, 10

Filipiuk, M. 74

foreign intervention 9

Fortnightly Review 90

Foucault, M. 14, 140–1

Fox, C. 43, 56n

free speech 149, 153–5; criticising religion 164; defending holocaust deniers' right to 163, 164; inviting racial hatred 164; *On Liberty* 161–4; relevance of Mill today regarding 161–4
free thought 147–53; and belief 148; Cartesian idea of 149; as a condition of rational assurance 153–5; 'constructive scepticism' 150, 152; fallibilism 149, 152, 156; individualism 148–9; and intellectual authority 149; and 'intuition' 152; Mill's epistemological framework 150–3; Newman's view 147–8; objectivity of 156–7; as pre-suppositionless 149–50, 156; problem of being both self-authorizing and truth-finding 150, 156, 157; relevance today of Mill's 161–4; and scepticism 148, 156
freedom of the individual 165–7; legal moralism vs. legal paternalism 167; voluntary euthanasia 165; wearing of seatbelts 166, 167
French Revolution 1830 9–10, 22, 27–30; Carrel's position on 30–2; Mill on 21
Fuchs, A. 91–2

Gilligan, C. 138, 140
Gladstone, W. 39
Graham, G.J. 43
Green, T.H. 4
Groundwork of the Metaphysics of Morals (Kant) 121

Habermas, J. 52
Hamburger, J. 3, 27
Hamilton, Sir W. 74–5, 76–7; Mill's critique of 64, 78
happiness: general security and 100, 114, 118–19, 123; promoting 51, 84, 86, 91, 160; as ultimate principle of Teleology 86; virtuous conduct for 95
Hart, H.L.A. 2, 5–6
Hayek, F. 5
Hayward, A. 2
hedonism 102
hedonistic utilitarians 13, 14, 100, 102–3, 105, 110, 114, 165; compared with preference utilitarians 160–1
Hegel, G.W.F. 121, 150
higher pleasures, doctrine of 102–14; genesis of higher pleasures from lower 101, 108–10; hierarchy of mental over bodily

pleasures 103–4, 105, 108, 109–12; hierarchy within mental pleasures 112–14; lexical metaranking 114; moral and aesthetic pleasures 112–14; moral sentiments 99; pleasure of security 99–100, 113–14, 116–17, 118–19; qualitative superiority is infinite superiority 13, 100–1, 105–8, 109, 112–13; quantitative and qualitative superiority 102–5; 'quasi-chemical method' 101, 109, 112
Himmelfarb, G. 6
Holyoake, G.J. 64
homosexuality 6, 140–1
human flourishing 139–40

imperialism 8–9
'individualism' 50; epistemological 150
individuality 2, 92–3, 134, 148–9
Industrial Revolution 23
'infinite' 105–6
infinity, understanding of 105–7
intellectual authority 149
international relations 7–11; canonisation of Mill in 7; relevance of Mill's views today 171
Introduction to the Principles of Morals and Legislation (J. Bentham) 170
'intuitionism' 39
Ireland 21, 23, 58
Irving, D. 163, 164
Israel, J. 147

Jevons, W.S. 4, 74, 76
Just and Unjust Wars (Walzer) 9
justice: accommodating the Categorical Imperative 122; constitutional democracy 117; egalitarian democracy 116–17; equal rights and duties 13, 99, 100, 101, 113, 115, 116–17, 118, 120; as a higher pleasure 99–102; legal penalties 117, 119; optimal social code 115–16, 119, 120, 123, 124; and the pleasure of security 99–100, 113–14, 116–17, 118–19, 123; Rawls' theory of 122; right to liberty of 'purely self-regarding' conduct 120; social choice process 101–2, 115, 118; and utilitarianism 99, 115–18, 123

Kant, I.: Categorical Imperative 121–2; doctrine of virtue 95; free thought 146, 147, 149–50; imperfect duties 93; morality 121–2

land tenure 58, 59
Law, Liberty and Morality (Hart) 166
legal moralism 167
legal paternalism 167
'liberal', defining 146–7
liberal feminism 13; answering criticisms
  of liberalism 14, 143–4; distinction between public and private realm 133–4;
  influential in legal thought 132; Mill's
  lack of endorsement for 133, 134–5;
  nature of preference and desire 132,
  133, 144; sameness of treatment 131–2
liberal moralism 5
'liberalism' 8
Locke, J. 39, 41, 146
logic: G. Bentham and Mill's parallel
  work on 70, 71–2; Mill's apparent
  rejection of modern studies 12, 67, 70,
  79; Mill's declaration of faith 72–3;
  Mill's position on the quantification
  of the predicate 76–9; quantification
  of the predicate controversy 74–6; and
  reasons for Mill's mental crisis 73–4;
  syllogistic 77–8, 78–9
London Debating Society 19, 20, 21, 73
Loving v. Virginia (1967) 131–2, 133
Lyons, D. 6, 90, 92

MacKinnon, C. 134, 135
majority rule 102
Malthus, T.R. 58, 62
marriage: Harriet Mill's letter to George
  Mill on 142–3; interracial 131; Mill's
  conservatism on 142; a partnership of
  equals 48; polygamy 141; rape and
  violence within 133, 134
Marshall, A. 4
The Mathematical Analysis of Logic
  (Boole) 67, 74
mental breakdown 43–5, 73–4
Metaphysics of Ethics (Kant) 121
Mill, G. (brother of J.S. Mill) 142
Mill, H. (wife of J.S. Mill) 43, 64, 137,
  142; letter to George Mill 142–3
Mill, J. (father of J.S. Mill): attitude
  to Mill's friends 54–5n; belief in
  Philosophical Necessity 44; as compared
  to Carrel 31; education of J.S. Mill
  42–3; letters from J.S. Mill 28, 29; on
  character formation 37–8; relationship
  with Jeremy Bentham 67–9; review
  of Owen's *A New View of Society* 37;
  views on representative democracy 20

Moore, G.E. 4
moral sentiments 99
morality: as a category of the Art of Life
  12, 85, 86, 87, 91, 92, 96; comparing
  Christian and utilitarian 63; Kant's
  121–2; Mill's criticism of Bentham
  88–9; Mill's criticism of Comte 87–8
morality, theory of 84–92; as distinct from
  Virtue 12, 84–5, 86–7, 89–90; morally
  wrong acts 89; results of misunderstanding of 90–2
Morley, J. 64
Morning Chronicle 149
Murray, G. 7

nationalism 10–11
natural state of society 24, 26
naturalism 4
'Nature' (J.S. Mill) 64–5, 136; relevance
  today 168–9
neo-Malthusianism 11, 58, 59
New Liberalism 4–5
A New View of Society (Owen) 37
Newman, Cardinal 147–8, 152
newspaper journalism 27
Nietzsche, F. 150, 156, 157
nihilism 150, 156
Nobility 12, 85, 89, 94, 95, 96
Noddings, N. 138
non-intervention 9, 10, 171; relevance
  today of Mill's views 171
'Notes on the Newspapers' (J.S. Mill) 27
Nozick, R. 123

obituaries 2, 38
On Liberty (J.S. Mill) 38, 51; defence
  of individuality 2, 92–3; formation
  of strong individual characters 11,
  51–2; freedom of the individual 165–7;
  freedom of thought and expression
  161–4; neglect of same-sex relationships 141; on Mormons and polygamy
  141; 'queer' thought in 131, 141, 143;
  relevance today 14–15, 161–7; scholarship 7; self-regarding faults 94; tyranny
  of convention 141
*Outline of a New System of Logic with a
  Critical Examination of Dr. Whately's
  'Elements of Logic'* (J. Bentham) 69,
  74, 75, 76; Mill declines to review 74,
  81–2n; Mill's neglect of 12, 69, 74, 79
Owen, R. on character formation 36–8,
  40–1

Parliamentary History and Review 20
paternalism 92; legal 167
patriotism 10
peasant proprietorship 58, 59
Peel, Sir Robert 21
Philosophical Necessity 40, 44
physician-assisted suicide 166
political ambition, Mill's personal 11, 26, 32
political economy: and colonization 60; effects of technological change 59–61; and environmental concerns 11–12, 59–61, 62–3; and law of diminishing returns 59, 60; and peasant proprietorship 58, 59; and the stationary state 60–1
political liberalism: 1873 to present 2–6; Mill's marginalization after his death 2–5, 6; and resurgence of interest in Mill 5–6
political philosophy 4–5
Poor Law Amendment Act 1834 62
Popkin, R. 150, 152
Popper, K. 5
population growth 23–4, 59, 60, 61
post-colonialism 8
preference utilitarians compared to hedonist utilitarians 160–1, 165
Principia Ethica (Moore) 4
Principles of Political Economy (J.S. Mill) 11, 58, 59, 169
'Prisons and Prison Discipline' (James Mill) 37

quantification of the predicate: controversy 74–6; Mill's position on 76–9
queer feminism 14, 140–4; anticipation by Mill 14, 131, 141; attitudes to homosexuality 141; and 'experiments in living' 141–2, 143; and *On Liberty* 131, 141, 143; and the tyranny of convention 14, 140, 141

'radical enlightenment' 147, 152
radical feminism 135–8; anticipation by Mill 13–14, 136–8; eroticism of domination and submission 135, 136–7; hierarchy in sexual desire 137; norm of male domination 135–6; and pornography 135, 137; power relations between men and women 135–6
railways 62–3
Rationale of Judicial Evidence (J. Bentham) 72

Rawls, J. 6, 52, 123, 132, 134, 146; interpreting Mill's philosophy 122–3
religion: comparison of Mill and Singer's views on 159–60; freedom to criticise 164; Mill's essays on 63–4
religion of humanity 11, 62, 63–4, 65
'Remarks on Bentham's Philosophy' (J.S. Mill) 68
Report on Homosexual Offenses and Prostitution 6
representative democracy 20
representative government 48–50
Richardson, S. 137
rights, equal: to establish and maintain justice 13, 99, 100, 101, 113, 115, 116–17, 118, 120; in Rawls' theory of justice 122; reliance on competent majorities to select 120; right to liberty of 'purely self-regarding' conduct 13, 120–1, 123–4
Roebuck, J.A. 43, 54–5n
Ruskin, J. 59, 65
Ryan, A. 6

Saint-Simonians 21, 22
seatbelt wearing 166, 167
security, pleasure of 99–100, 113–14, 116–17, 118–19
self-regarding conduct, right to 13, 120–1, 123–4
self-regarding duties 93–4
self-regarding virtues 94–5
Sidgwick, H. 3, 161
Skorupski, J. 91, 92
Slote, M. 94
social change 1750-1831 23–4
social choice process 101–2, 115, 118
social sciences, professionalisation of 4
Society of Students of Mental Philosophy 72
Sommers, C.H. 130, 132, 133
Spencer, H. 4, 75–6
The Spirit of the Age (J.S. Mill) 21–7; authority in age of transition 19, 21, 24–7; economic context 22; industrialization 22–3; Mill's political ambition revealed 11, 26, 32; 'moral and social revolution' 26; political context 21; and population growth 23–4; Protestant Reformation 22; views on governing classes 24, 25; youth over age 11, 26, 32
Stanton, E.C. 130
state, the: concept of 3, 5; limiting authority over 3, 165

Stephen, J.F. 2

Sterling, J. 27, 44; Mill's letter to 73

Subjection of Women (J.S. Mill): anticipating radical feminism 13–14, 136–8; deformation and re-formation of female characters 11, 46–8; justice through equal rights and duties 99–100; knowledge of who men and women 'are' 138–9; legal reform of women's position 133; marital rape and domestic violence 133, 134; marriage contract of equals 48; men's corrupted characters through sexual inequality 47–8; men's need to feel women like their role 136–7; relevance today 168; sexual desire hierarchy 137; sexual inequality 46, 133, 134, 136; status of women 46; stopping short of radical alternatives 131, 141–2, 143; women's desire to please men 137

summum bonum 85, 92, 96

A System of Logic (J.S. Mill) 38, 67; Art of Life 12, 85, 86, 87, 91, 92, 95, 96; development of free thought 150–3; footnote on Hamilton/De Morgan controversy 76; outlines of ethology 35, 39–42, 44, 45; principle of utility 86; scientific method in 151; structure of moral philosophy 85–6

Teleology, principle of 86

Ten, C.L. 6, 155

'Theism' (J.S. Mill) 64

theology, liberalism of 148

A Theory of Justice (J. Rawls) 6

'Thornton on Labour and its Claims' (J.S. Mill) 89–90

Three Essays on Religion (J.S. Mill) 63, 64

The Times 2

Tocqueville 52

'Toward Neutral Principles of Constitutional Law' (H. Wechsler) 132

Tractarians 149

utilitarianism: act and rule 91; comparing preference and hedonistic 160–1, 165; following Mill's death 4; hedonistic 13, 14, 100, 102–3, 105, 110, 114; and

justice 99, 115–18, 123; Mill answering critics of 63, 123; problem of politics 3; as a theory of life 87; Wordsworth's criticism of 62

Utilitarianism (J.S. Mill): 'competent judges' of 84; discussion of Christianity 63; feeling of security 121; importance of *summum bonum* 85; introductory remarks 151; moral sentiments 99; theory of morality 86, 87, 89

utility, principle of 14, 86, 90, 103; erroneous claims regarding 91–2

value theory 84

'Vindication of the French Revolution of February 1848' (J.S. Mill) 9–10

Virtue, doctrine of: coercion in 92, 93, 94; conflict between individuality and training for 92–3; different kinds of virtue 13, 92–3, 95; as distinct from Morality 12, 84–5, 86–7, 89–90; noteworthy and ordinary virtue 95, 96; self-regarding virtues 94–5; supererogation assigned to 90; underexplored in Mill 95

virtue ethics 12–13, 84, 96

voluntary euthanasia 165

Wakefield, E.G. 60

walking tours 58

Walzer, M. 7, 9

Wellington, Duke of 21

Wechsler, H. 132

Westminster Review 20, 74, 82n

Whately, R. 69, 72, 73, 74, 79, 81n

'Whewell on Moral Philosophy' (J.S. Mill) 15, 169–70

Whewell, W. 39, 169–70

Wight, M. 7

women's suffrage 133

Wordsworth: Christian beliefs 62; influence on Mill 11, 45, 58, 61–2; meeting with Mill 58, 62; opposition to railway extension 62

Worthiness 87, 89, 90, 91, 94, 95

Wrigley, E.A. 60

Zimmern, A. 8